ARCHITECTURE
an art for all men

Taliesin West, near Phoenix, Arizona:
main entrance. Frank Lloyd Wright, architect

TALBOT HAMLIN

ARCHITECTURE
an art for all men

Architecture is an art for all men to learn
because all men are concerned with it—*Ruskin*

GREENWOOD PRESS, PUBLISHERS
WESTPORT, CONNECTICUT

Library of Congress Cataloging in Publication Data

Hamlin, Talbot Faulkner, 1889-1956.
    Architecture, an art for all men.

    Reprint of the ed. published by Columbia University
Press, New York, which was a revision of the author's
The enjoyment of architecture.
    Bibliography: p.
    Includes index.
    1. Architecture. I. Title.
NA2550.H3 1975   720'.1   75-3798
ISBN 0-8371-8079-1

TO THE MATE OF THE
AQUARELLE

FOREWORD

THIRTY YEARS have passed since my *Enjoyment of Architecture* was first published. These three decades have seen a revolutionary change in the architecture of the whole world. The old eclecticism which then still reigned over large areas has faded into impotence, though here and there it continues to lead a strange half life in real-estate speculative building and in the minds of sentimental government or ecclesiastical authorities. The economic conditions which fed it and the ideals of culture in which it flourished have passed away, as industrialism has fired questions in our faces and new complexities have forced us to attempt a severer and a more disciplined thinking. Architectural movements which thirty years ago were merely little pinpricks in an almost universal complacency have grown into well-nigh universal acceptance; no longer revolutionary, the basic principles which lie behind what is generally termed "modern architecture" have established their validity. Now, most of us realize that our era is in every way a different age from that which existed before the First World War; it demands, and will inevitably achieve, a new kind of architecture as its expression.

The Enjoyment of Architecture, whatever its merits or faults when it was written, expressed that older age and not the present; it could no longer serve the purpose which engendered its writing. That purpose, as the title implies, was to open to readers the rich stores of feeling and understanding that a sympathetic appreciation of the building art might bring. It was a book on architecture in general and not on any one particular phase or style. Since its appearance there has been no other work in the United States of similar scope, and the increasing amount of architectural writing that has been published has been devoted to works on various phases of architectural history, to propaganda books on behalf of "modern architecture" (the necessary tools of a revolutionary struggle), and to books on special aspects of architecture such as housing, city planning, or home building. Yet the need for the more general type of approach still seems real. Architecture still remains *terra incognita* to large sections even of the more sensitive among the population; in our cluttered and stimulus-jaded existence the majority rush in and out of buildings and hurry past them without a thought as to their quality or any aesthetic emotion whatsoever, so that even the most thoughtful, the most creative of our architects are forced to work in a kind of intellectual vacuum, shut in and hampered by the wall of popular ignorance. It is only this nearly universal apathy—an apathy nourished by ignorance and insensibility—which permits our cities to grow into incoherent ugliness and spawns sordid and stupid real-estate subdivisions all over the countryside.

It thus seemed a propitious time to undertake a complete rewriting of *The Enjoyment of Architecture*, with the double aim of preserving its original character as an elementary guide to the understanding and appreciation of architecture as a whole and of making it an introduction to the architecture of today. We live in a world in which, despite wars and change, the past has left us a priceless heritage of buildings, and it would be as stupid to limit one's architectural appreciation to the buildings of the last few decades as it would to limit one's musical knowledge to the works of Stravinsky or Hindemith. *Architecture—an art for all men* is the result. So complete were the changes that were found necessary—changes frequently of basic attitude—and so large the amount of new material, both in text and illustration, that a new title to indicate the new approach seemed desirable. Understanding and appreciating architecture is no longer a mere matter of "enjoyment"; it is a matter so deeply implicated in the tissue of our living that it should be as much a part of our lives as is a basic understanding of politics or economics.

The major part of the work of this rewriting was performed during sabbatical leave from my regular work at Columbia and carried on during a protracted cruise on a small motor cabin boat, the *Aquarelle*. As the pressures of my customary work receded, as cities were dropped behind, as we passed through bay and sound, river and canal and marsh cut, with level horizons, with the challenges of wind and storm and the necessities of ordinary living—architecture seemed to take its rightful place in life with greater and greater per-

sistence. Its essential nobility of purpose and its enormous potentialities for the life of the future appeared with increased clarity, and
the pressing urgencies of its tasks today showed themselves in truer
and sounder proportion. This temporary separation from a too close
attention to buildings, instead of diminishing the importance of the
art of building, seemed to place architecture in a higher and stronger
position. It is my hope that something of this new and strengthened
sense of the high place architecture has held and must continue to
hold in the life of the world has entered into the new work.

My indebtedness for assistance in the preparation of this book is
wide. First of all, I owe more than I can say to the continual inspiring
and perspicacious assistance of my wife, Jessica Hamlin, as editor, as
preserver of standards, as long-suffering secretary. Next I must
express my gratitude to the staff of the Columbia University Press
for their co-operation in suggesting the continued need for this
work and in giving it physical and concrete reality. The staffs of the
Avery and Ware libraries have been continuously helpful in searching for and lending illustrative material.

I also wish to thank Dean Leopold Arnaud of the School of Architecture of Columbia University for encouragement and for reading
the manuscript; Mrs. Elizabeth Mock and the staff of the architectural department of the Museum of Modern Art for help and suggestions in connection with illustrations and for the loan of many
photographs; Mr. F. L. S. Mayer for photographs of the Nebraska
State Capitol; Mrs. James Ford and the Architectural Book Publishing Company for permission to use illustrations from Ford and
Ford's *The Modern House in America* and the same authors' *Design
of Modern Interiors*; G. P. Putnam's Sons for permission to repro-
duce figures 1, 22, and 28 from the author's *Architecture through
the Ages*; the New York *Daily News* for the photograph of the Daily
News Building; Bonwit Teller, Inc., for the photograph of the Bonwit Teller store; and the Austin Company for the photograph of the
Vickers plant in Detroit. The complete credits for the illustrations
are given in the list of illustrations.

T. F. H.

Columbia University, June, 1946

CONTENTS

LIST OF
FIGURES

LIST OF
PLATES

ARCHITECTURE
an art for all men

1

THE APPEAL OF
ARCHITECTURE

THE DAYS are swiftly passing when, to the normal American, art was valued as something distinctly secondary to the practical matters of life. We have grown into the precious heritage of appreciation, and music and painting and sculpture and literature bring us a real joy. But there is one enormous source of artistic pleasure of which too few are as yet aware; there is one art whose works confront us wherever man lives, which all too many of us daily pass blindly by. That source is to be found in the buildings all around us; that art is the art of architecture.

This blindness is the more strange since new avenues of pleasure are constantly opening to one who has even a slight measure of appreciation of architecture. To him a city is no grey prison, shutting him in from God and nature; it is rather a great book on which is written large the history of the aspiration, the struggles, the social ideals, and the constant striving for beauty of all mankind. To him a building may no longer be merely stone and brick and iron and wood; it may become vital with beauty, a symphony thrilling in its complex rhythms of window and door and column, enriching all who are willing to look at it appreciatively with its message of peace or struggle.

Architecture is of all the arts the one most continually before our eyes. To hear music at its best we must go to concerts or operas of one kind or another, or at least turn on the radio; to enjoy literature we must read, and read extensively; our best painting and sculpture are segregated in museums and galleries to which we must make our pilgrimages; but architecture is constantly beside us. We live in houses and our houses may be works of architecture. We work in office buildings or stores or factories, and they may be works of architecture. Nine-tenths of our lives are spent among buildings, yet how many of us feel a distinct warmth of pleasure as we pass a beautiful building? How many of us give one hour's thought a month to the beauty or ugliness, the structural perfection, the architectural value, of the buildings surrounding us? Wherever there is the slightest attempt to make a building beautiful, there is the touch of architecture, and if we pass by with this touch unnoticed, we are by just so much depriving ourselves of a possible element of richness in our lives.

Architecture, then, is an art, and any art must give us pleasure, or else it is bad art, or we are abnormally blind. To architecture as an art and the joy it brings we are in general too callous. It is the constant proximity of architecture during our entire conscious existence that has blinded us in this way. We forget that it is an art of here and now, because it is with us every day, and because we have to have houses to live in we are too apt to think of them solely as abiding places. Therefore we think of architecture as some vague, learned thing dealing with French cathedrals or Italian palaces or Greek temples, not with New York or Chicago streets or Los Angeles suburbs, and this fallacious doctrine has strengthened in us until our eyes are dulled and our minds are atrophied to all the beauty that is being created around us today, and we lose all the fine deep pleasure that we might otherwise experience from our ordinary surroundings.

This pleasure is of several kinds and comes from several different sources. Many of us have felt its call and, unknowing, turned away, perhaps perplexed. We feel it vaguely and accept it as something vague; with strange lack of curiosity we have never tried to find out why we choose some streets to walk on and shun others. We can be sure that this vague feeling, if it is real and worth while, will not die on analysis, like a flower picked to pieces, but will rather, as we examine it, take on definiteness and poignancy and be reborn in all sorts of new ways.

First of all among the pleasures that architecture can give is that which anything beautiful brings to an understanding heart, which warms the whole being and sends one about his work gladder and stronger and better. Then there is the satisfaction that comes from the realization that a thing is perfectly fitted for the work it is to do, a satisfaction akin to that which the engineer feels in his locomotive, or a sailor in his vessel. Related to this is the universal delight in strength, the sense that a building is well built, neatly and exquisitely put together, and constructed in a suitable way to last. There is, besides, the pleasure that comes from the fact that good architecture is always a perfect expression of the time in which it was built, not only of that time's artistic skill but also, if the period is interpreted correctly, of its religion, its government, even of its economic and political theories. Still another pleasure arises from the perception of the specific emotional tone which each building sounds, from the austere power of an armory, the forthright efficiency of a good factory, the welcome serenity of a well-designed house, to the light playfulness of a smart café. And, last and greatest of all the pleasures to be found here, the best architecture brings us real inspiration, a feeling of awe-struck peace and reverence, a feeling of the immense glory and worth-whileness of things, that comes only in the presence of something very great indeed.

All these different pleasures and more are open to one who will walk our streets with a seeing eye and even an elementary knowledge of what architecture is, what it is striving for, how and under what laws it works. And this knowledge we can possess at a trifling cost of time and study, but to our great advantage. We must first gain a clearer understanding of precisely what architecture is; then we can obtain such a knowledge of it as to enjoy it to the utmost with no lack of spontaneity in our appreciation.

The first kind of pleasure we have mentioned is that which comes to one from anything beautiful. It is one of the hardest of all to analyze, for it is the deepest, and it goes so far into difficult questions of psychology that we can only give examples and analogies. For the pure beauty of architecture is in many ways similar to the pure beauty of music or painting or poetry. It is a pleasure primarily of the senses, but in the educated man it touches through this sensuous appeal an immense category of intellectual thoughts and emotions. It is a pleasure primarily exterior, but through exterior qualities it touches the deepest in us. It is a thing of rhythm, of balance, of form. It comes from the perception of anything which fulfills certain innate qualities of beauty that are well-nigh universal. It exists irrespective of styles, even of critical discriminations; a man feels it in looking at the Greek Parthenon, at the medieval Cathedral of Amiens, at the Classic Revival Capitol at Washington, or at the modern city hall at Hilversum. He may feel it as thrillingly in a Colonial farmhouse or in a factory as in a great cathedral. The confirmed modernist in music, if he is at all candid with himself, feels it in a Bach fugue; the confirmed secessionist in painting feels it in the glorious composition of a Tintoretto or the blazing color of a Rubens. Similarly, the confirmed traditionalist in architecture may feel it in the quiet loveliness of Frank Lloyd Wright's own house, Taliesin. It is a universal pleasure, the capacity for which is inborn in every normal person, and it is always aroused by the perception of anything that fulfills certain requirements of form for which the mind is constantly athirst. It is the satisfaction of this thirst that is at the very base of all artistic pleasure, and it will therefore be necessary to understand at least the fundamentals of these requirements of form in order to have any really intelligent appreciation of architecture.

The study of the "why" of the sense of beauty is the domain of aesthetics, a highly specialized body of knowledge, for, from Greek times on to the present, philosophers and psychologists have been striving for explanations of this universal emotion. The most important aesthetic theories may be divided into three major classes— formal, expressionist, and psychological. The first group is associated chiefly with classic art and classic thought; the second with romanticism and medievalism; the third with modern science.

According to aesthetic theorists of the first type, visual beauty is entirely a matter of form, or form plus color. Essentially, it is a pleasure in geometrical relationships, shapes, some of which innately please. Such aestheticians have frequently tried to seek in actual mathematical ratios the secret of beauty—the "golden section" and the like. It has led academic designers to harp on the strictest possible following of "exact" proportions in columns and windows and the relation of breadth and length and height. To Plato, beauty resulted when an object approached the "ideal" object—the ideal which included within it all the possible variations of actuality. At sight of such an approach, the soul was filled with pain and bliss—pain at the memory of a lost "ideal" world, where perfection was all-pervasive; bliss at the recall of it. Yet even to Plato the matter was largely one of form, and the question of whether or not an object approached the ideal—was beautiful—was chiefly a matter of its simple shape relations.

To the aesthetic critics of the second type, the shape or form is beautiful not so much in itself as because of what it means or expresses. Thus, to Hegel, that is most beautiful which expresses the noblest thoughts in the most perfect manner; to Schopenhauer it is that which best incarnates the eternal struggle between desire and actuality, between energy and matter; to Ruskin it is that which most embodies aspiration toward the divine, or best represents or expresses "nature"—the thoughts and creations of God. This second type of aesthetic theory often slips over into religious speculation or sociological and ethical interpretation.

The third, the psychological, type of aesthetic thinking has itself several different aspects, as the emphasis of psychology shifts from the physiological to the psychical. Thus to one school of recent critics visual beauty is a mere matter of easy, simple, rhythmical eye movements; to another it may be the result of early, well-nigh universal infant emotions, only recoverable through psychoanalytic procedures; to still another—a growing school today—beauty is the pleasurable result of the observer's identification of himself with the observed object (what the German aestheticians call *Einfühlung*), so that, in a way, he lives its life, rises with the tower or the soaring vault, supports weights easily and gracefully with the well-designed column or arch, is serene and relaxed with the long horizontals of roof eaves or terrace walls.

These doctrines are manifestly not all mutually exclusive; they are, rather, attempts to explain beauty from different points of view —intellectual, mystical, emotional, or scientific. The experience itself remains, and, whatever our explanation of its causes may be, beauty, whatever you may call it, and in architecture the beauty of

buildings and towns and villages, goes on enriching the lives of those
sensitive to it.

But there are more sides to the satisfactions that buildings can
give than those derived from its mere external shapes. There is, for
instance, the pleasure arising from the perception that a building is
supremely suited to its purpose. Everyone has at some time been
irritated by a house which, though superficially pretty, was nevertheless so built that the kitchen odors penetrated everywhere; or,
perhaps, by a theater full of charm and color where one could not
hear; or by a city hall where every office that one seeks seems to be at
the far end of long and tortuous corridors. In buildings such as these
the architect has failed, at least partially, and the irritation arises as
much from his failure as from the inconvenience of the building itself. On the other hand, there is always a soothing satisfaction from
a library where the appearance of the building itself expresses what
use each part serves; or from a station where entrance leads to waiting room, and waiting room to ticket office, and ticket office to
trains, directly and clearly. There is a somewhat similar satisfaction
from a bridge where every stone and every girder seems to do its
work perfectly, and where each smallest part is necessary. It is a
growing understanding of the importance of these aspects—fitness
and structure—which has marked the best architectural thought of
the twentieth century and caused a veritable revolution in architectural forms. During the last half of the nineteenth century and the
early years of the twentieth, many factors in the industrial and
cultural life of the Western world had combined to separate the
architect and the engineer, and to make architects forget construction and engineers forget appearance. More and more the architect,
using forms borrowed from past times, had come to consider
architecture as merely a sort of exterior and interior dress, a kind of
mere "prettying up" of necessary buildings. Scholarship in knowledge of past styles had often come to replace true creative imagination in design; ingenuity in developing symmetry or other *a priori*
visual patterns had often replaced the search for real convenience in
arrangement or real expressiveness of effect. Construction had often
become a purely secondary consideration, and materials were used

without understanding of their qualities. Steel, concrete, cheap and easily available glass—all the results of industrial development—were used, not in ways to bring out their superb potentialities, but merely to imitate the past or to cheapen buildings thoughtlessly. The result had been an architecture increasingly divorced from the actual bustling industrial world of the day, increasingly unreal, and the plaything of wealthy aesthetes.

Manifestly this could not continue; new conditions clamored for attention, for architectural expression. The new revolutionary architecture that arose as a result necessarily stressed the qualities which the earlier period had neglected—modernity, convenience, construction, the appropriate use of modern fabricated materials. The new school of thought was often called *functionalism*, because of its emphasis on these qualities.

For architecture is a science as well as an art, and the architect must not only build beautifully but must also see that his buildings are strong and durable and efficient, that they are proof against the weather, and that they fulfill all the practical purposes for which they were built. Good architecture, therefore, must always be sane and practical. Architecture is not only an art of cathedrals and tombs and monuments—though even these must be built to stand and endure—but it is also an art that deals with every phase of the most ordinary businesses of men. Our houses must be as convenient and roomy as possible. Office buildings must be economical, with the greatest possible renting space, and they must be provided with all the necessary elevators and toilet rooms and heating apparatus. Factories—for even factories may be architecture—must have fresh air and floods of light, and be so constructed as to minimize noise and vibration. Theaters must be so arranged that from every seat there will be an unobstructed view of the stage, and no echoes or undue reverberation to destroy the sound, and so planned that in case of accident the theater can be emptied in the shortest possible time.

When one considers that architecture embraces every one of these points and more; that plumbing and heating and electric wiring and ventilation and the design of concrete and steel columns and girders all come under its control, it is not likely that he will accuse it of being an art esoteric and aloof. Indeed, it is of all the arts the one that touches life at the greatest number of points. The architect must always be in our midst, hard-headed, clear-thinking, careful, to fill our daily structural needs, whatever they are; to build dwellings and shops and airports and factories and theaters and churches; and to see that each is as useful and well built as science can make it, and that it is crowned with beauty and made a source of constant delight.

Yet in a sense this is not altogether a correct statement. It is not that the architect plans for convenience, designs construction for strength, and then composes the whole for beauty. These are not entirely separate processes, nor is architecture composed of three unrelated factors—convenience, strength, and beauty. It is, rather, that all three considerations are *always* present in the architect's mind, just as all three aspects should be inextricably integrated in the final building. Each type of interior space has its own implications as to the structural system and the special materials best suited for its construction; each type of structural system has its own characteristic shapes that help determine the appearance; and each building material has its own appropriate colors and textures. All work together to create the final effect of the completed building; its beauty is therefore a matter dependent on convenience and structural strength as well as on geometric or arbitrary design. In great works of architecture these three factors are absolutely made one. This is one of the most powerful reasons for the richness of aesthetic experience that flows from architecture; this integration gives reality, seriousness, and power to the whole and makes architecture eternally different, say, from scene painting or pure sculpture.

Let us see how the three aspects of architecture that we have just been discussing—which the Roman Vitruvius, in the time of Augustus, first listed, and which Sir Henry Wotton quaintly called "commoditie, firmeness, and delight"—are bound together in an actual structure. Let us take, for instance, the entrance hall of the International Building in Rockefeller Center designed by Harrison & Fouilhoux, and Reinhard & Hofmeister, associated (Plate I). A large, light, impressive area was desired, with escalators to the exhibition hall above, and with wide passages on either side to the elevators behind. The spirit of the whole problem dictated height. The desire for daylight created the tall windows. The entire building concept made steel skeleton construction a necessity. Efficiency of maintenance, and the fact that many people would use the area and often bring in outside dirt, demanded that all surfaces should be hard, smooth, and easy to clean. Out of these requirements, by a judicious choice of materials (marbles, terrazzo, metals), by the imaginative expression of the construction, and by the use of pleasing proportions, an interior was created that is impressive but not heavy; lavish without ostentation; harmonious in color and form; thoroughly expressive of its purpose, its construction type, and the spirit of the civilization that produced it. The columns, H-shaped in plan, follow and express the steel section of the actual structural columns within their rich marble casing; they serve also as lighting elements by the use of concealed lights. The metal sheen of the escalators expresses their mechanical nature, their basic metallic construction. The glass of show windows around gives a useful variety, a pleasant gleam of reflecting surface. The brass-barred dark terrazzo floor conceals dirt, is easily washed, and gives a solid base to the whole composition; the marble used for the wainscoting and column facing is in big sheets to express its non-structural character, and its colors and design are so arranged as to mark the basic harmonies of the whole design.

Here, a difference in purpose or plan would have created different kinds of shapes and other materials, a different structural system (say the use, for instance, of vaults), and architectural forms entirely different from the basic rectangularity of what exists. One can say of any truly competent work of architecture that a change in any one of the three Vitruvian factors—use, construction, aesthetic design—necessarily entails changes equally far-reaching in the other two.

Indeed, one element of the unique beauty that sometimes resides in such a building is the fact that the entire form springs so directly from the particular needs it is built to house and from its structure.

Mirroring these needs and these ways, buildings must inevitably mirror the economic system, the industrial milieu, that gave them birth; and the particular ideals of beauty apparent in their design mirror equally well the kind of culture their makers enjoyed.

It is this which makes the peculiarly exciting quality of the chaotic mass of buildings that crowd lower Manhattan Island. Low tenements seen between tall office buildings; occasional old aristocratic mansions now drab and forlorn, filled with cheap restaurants or cheaper offices; square, many-windowed boxes; granite-faced bank buildings flaunting an ostentatious parade of applied richness; tall towers with the geometry of their steel decked out and concealed by fancy dress from Rome or the Middle Ages; occasional simpler, more direct buildings, whose designers saw in the new building ways some hints of a new and possibly more honest beauty—all tell their tale of a nation's struggles, of its worship of success and money power, of its desire to astound, of its genius for organization, of its youth and exuberance, of its greed, too, and that frenzied desire for get-rich-quick speculation which came to a welcome end, we hope, in the crash of 1929. It is all, indeed, a complete expression—almost too true for our pleasure—of a period's flamboyant vitality, of its respect for wealth, of its chaos and its sentimentalities; but it reflects, as well, its nostalgic search, beyond its own chaos, for order and for beauty; its frustrated turning to a past that was dead, in order to achieve a creativeness of which it was no longer master. . . . And yet on an autumn evening, when the white towers are pink in the afterglow, the lights are twinkling in the windows, and an October haze lies purple over all, hiding the borrowed finery so that only the basic shapes come through, it is magically fair, radiant with a beauty that is due not only to the soft and shimmering light but also to the ever present search for loveliness that distinguishes all men, to the skill of the engineers, the daring of the builders, and the constructive imagination of the architects who created them.

It is the combination of these three qualities—use, structure, design—which has made these buildings on the lower end of Manhattan Island so uncannily expressive of our American development. And architecture, because of this triple basis in practical needs, in construction, and in aesthetic idealism, has always been the art which most completely expresses the life of the people who produce it. In this fact lies the next pleasure one may obtain from architecture, the pleasure of reading in buildings the whole history of mankind, its struggles, its ideals, its religions. In the rise and fall of Roman architecture one may read the rise and fall of the Roman power, and in the continual use of Roman decorative forms for the four hundred years of the Renaissance and the Baroque one may feel some small measure of the powerful influence which the Roman genius has exerted throughout the world. Similarly, the architecture of the modern world is a revelation of its development. In almost all the countries of the Western world one can see how the political and industrial revolutions at the beginning of the nineteenth century produced a new sudden vitality in building; how the beginnings of scientific archaeology, coupled with those two heady new influences, gave birth to Classic Revival work in which the inspiration of the ancient world was creatively powerful, and the new railroad stations, exposition halls, warehouses, and factories which the nascent industrial culture required achieved valid architectural treatment. One can see, too, how, as the century wore on, exploitation and savage business competition—greed masquerading as enterprise—destroyed the older search for a better and a liberated world, gave rise to a new class of comparatively uneducated rich, created for them their ideal expression in architecture—grab-bag eclecticism—substituted ideas of cheapness for ideas of excellence, created slums, debauched the old concepts of beauty and had few of its own to offer in their place, made human labor a commodity and human lives a mere by-product of money-making—until sensitive and humane critics like Ruskin and Morris were sick and appalled. All this one may read in the chaos of the cities, in their ragged, squalid edges, in the ugly factories which ring them, in the befouled countrysides that surround them, in the false, ill-built gimcrackery of all too many of the buildings which crowd them. . . . Architecture could not lie, no matter how much the architects tried to ape an order and a dignity that was past.

And one may also read in buildings the gradual rise of protest

against these conditions, the growing attempts to build better low-
cost homes, the reaction of creative architects against the false tawdriness of the times. One may see this whole great culture of false
and inhuman exploitation of land and of men reaching a climax of
ostentatious construction in the years before 1929—producing a rash
of buildings in which the design and the decoration were as unreal
and untrue as the paper that financed them—until the whole
crashed in a welter of confused ruin. It is no accident that a new,
honest, creative, twentieth-century architecture which had been
gradually coming into being at the hands of a few pioneers—Sullivan, Wright, Otto Wagner of Vienna, Pieter Berlage and J. J. P.
Oud in Holland, Behrens and Gropius in Germany, the Perret
brothers, Le Corbusier, and Lurçat in France—had little chance of
more than piecemeal acceptance while the older dying culture was
supreme. And it is no accident that it is only since the crash of 1929
that this modern architecture has won almost universal acceptance,
and the trickle of work of the pioneers has broadened into a flood of
new creation, freer, more creative, more natural than the earlier
doctrinaire work, because it is no longer a mere protest; it is seeking
to express a new spirit.

In architecture, then, always keenly conscious of the influence of
the past, yet always supremely expressive of the present, there is a
continuous and vivid commentary on human existence. Whether in
the inscrutable immensity of the many-columned temples of Egypt,
in the virile delicacy of the refinement of the best Greek work, in
the rich and powerful splendor of Roman thermae, in the mysterious
aisles of a Gothic cathedral, in the free gaiety of a modern French
theater, or in the long lines of ranked window and skylight of a modern factory—in all these one with a seeing eye may discern the fascinating tale of human character and its aims and struggles. What
a treasure house of broadening and cultural knowledge architecture
becomes when it is seen in this light! Every building becomes eloquent of its own day and of all its background in the past.. Of course
it is only the archaeologist and the careful student of architectural
history who can enjoy this pleasure to the greatest extent, but it is
a simple matter for anyone to learn about the principal architectural

periods, how they arose and why they grew or died. Moreover, there is all the lure of romance in any such study of architecture, for it peoples the great monuments of the art with all the pageantry of the fascinating past. A true appreciation of architecture can only be gained by always studying it in relation to the history of the people who produced it, and to one gifted with such an appreciation every city becomes a living history of the past and the present, and sometimes even an indication of the future.

Another pleasure to be derived from architecture is that which comes from the perception of a building's emotional tone. For architecture is an emotional art, as truly emotional as music or painting or poetry. As an art it must have this emotional tone. Too often we forget this, and in such architectural appreciation as we attempt we adopt an attitude strangely cold and intellectual. It is hard for the average man to conceive of anything emotional in stone and steel and cement. Because architecture cannot tell stories or represent actual events, because it cannot work so directly on our sympathies as words or pictures, because (and perhaps this is the most important of all), although there are love poems and love stories and love pictures and love music, love architecture is rare, though not impossible —because of all these things we forget that there are a great number of emotions which architecture can express, and express with all the greater poignancy because of the abstract means at its disposal.

This poignancy is the result of the fact that in architecture the *form*, the element which acts directly upon the eye, and the *matter*, the element which acts upon the spirit or intellect, are so inextricably intertwined. Walter Pater, in his essay on the School of Giorgione, says that all art is constantly aspiring to the "perfect identification of form and matter." Music, in his opinion, is the art which most perfectly realizes this ideal. "In its ideal, consummate moments, the end is not distinct from the means, the form from the matter, the subject from the expression; they inhere in and completely saturate each other; and to it, therefore, to the condition of its perfect moments, all the arts may be supposed constantly to tend and aspire." It is precisely in this matter of the identification of the form and the matter, the subject and the expression, that architecture is most closely analogous to music. Architecture has been called "frozen music," not because of any mystical similarities between musical forms and architectural forms, or between musical rhythms and architectural rhythms, but because in both great architecture and great music it is impossible to conceive of the existence of the matter apart from the form. In this respect these two arts stand alone. For instance, the landscape or the figures which the painter paints have a real and definite existence outside the artist's work, and the same landscape under the same atmospheric conditions, or the same figures posed in the same positions, even similar purely geometric figures, would produce emotions at least partially the same, no matter how treated. But in architecture or in music, if the form is removed, the emotion which the form expresses is at once destroyed as well. A simple concrete example will show the truth of this assertion. Imagine a lofty-aisled Gothic cathedral. The light, mellowed by the glowing color of the stained-glass windows, is rich and soft; high piers soar up to the arching vault in the shadows overhead; on distant altars at the ends of long vistas through clustered shafts candles burn with a warm radiance; and the effect upon the beholder is an overpowering emotion of peace and quiet, of reverent awe. Then imagine the stained glass taken away, the clustered shafts, the pointed arches, the shadowed vault gone—the emotion has fled with them, for it is inherent in them, its existence is one with their existence, and the poignancy of the effect is directly due to this complete identification of the emotion with the forms which produce it.

It is true that the number of emotions which architecture can produce is limited, but those which it does arouse are usually of the highest and most beneficial kind. There is the impression of immense power, for instance. Surely everyone has felt it at some time in the presence of some great building—perhaps in the sunny courts of Thebes or Karnak, perhaps before the mighty vaults and serried arches of the Roman Colosseum (Plate II), perhaps under the high roofs of Rheims or Westminster, or perhaps, as one hurried through the narrow streets of lower New York, when he suddenly saw rising before him the massive arches of Brooklyn Bridge. It is a sort of fine pride, externalized and purified—a consciousness that in these, at least, mankind shall live; that these, at least, of his works shall endure and stand, as so many have, their thousand years and more. This sense of power is one of the commonest and most obvious of the architecturally inspired emotions, because most permanent buildings produce it to some extent. Building materials themselves —stone and brick and tile and well-worked wood—if properly treated will give this impression; it only remains for the architect to use them in a simple and expressive way, and his building will appear strong. Moreover, this emotion is dear to the heart of all mankind, for it serves to mitigate, at least to some degree, the hidden but all-pervasive sense of the poverty, the brevity, and the futility of the individual life.

Another emotion which architecture can produce is the emotion of peace, an emotion more subtle than the sense of power and more beneficent. Where heavy weight is strongly supported, where there is simplicity in design and a careful harmony of proportion, there is always a source of repose; wherever long horizontal lines dominate staccato verticals there is a subtle influence making for rest. One may at any time see a small crowd of people sitting around the base of the Boston Public Library, resting. People hurrying to or from the subway on 116th Street in New York will suddenly check their pace, confronted all at once with the imposing simplicity of long, white steps backed with the green of trees, and crowned with the dome and colonnade of the old Columbia Library. Indeed, wherever there is a really beautiful building in a little open space one is likely to find people slowing their hasty walk, sitting down if they can, resting. And why? Because there the mind of the architect has been at work; there good architecture is pouring over them the continuous blessing of its serenity.

There are lighter and more concrete emotions, too, which have their place in the architectural picture. The architect, as well as the musician or the painter, can express gaiety, playfulness, relaxation. There are theaters, for instance, that invite the passer-by to enter; their very proportions seem to give promise of a feast of enjoyment within. The best of these amusement places seem almost vocal, so full of gay abandon are they. Certain rococo interiors seem the essence of exquisite wit. Our exhibition architecture has a large amount of this quality; certain portions of the San Francisco Exposition of 1915, for example, were like solidified laughter. We must always remember that the architect is only a man; he need not always be solemn, nor need he forswear gaiety, provided only that the gaiety is appropriate and obtained in natural and unforced ways.

All good architecture should have this gift of expressiveness. Every building, every well-designed room, should carry in itself at least one message of cheer or rest or power. One should always study the buildings around with this in mind. Soon some will take on new values; whatever they are they will become vital with their message. A great number of others will remain as before—vague, grey, lifeless things. In the buildings which seem alive with some message the architect has succeeded; they are true works of art. In all the others the architect has failed in one of his most important duties.

Another emotion which architecture can give should be supreme in dwellings—the sense of warm human living, of quiet fellowship, of relaxed sociability. Here, one says, before some house—here people, real people, live. Before another, the same observer can only say— here people pose, here they are trying to be what they are not, trying to give a false impression. In some rooms one feels chiefly the stultifying impersonal hand of a commercial decorator; in others the deadening touch of the slavish following of a current fashion craze; in still others one feels instead the warmth, the reality, of individual persons living warmly together . . . which is the best? The architect has here one of his great creative opportunities; the house he builds or the interior he arranges or suggests forms the people who live in it as inevitably as they, in turn, form it, and the expression, the emotional tone, which he helps confer upon the building will go on helping or hindering as long as it exists.

By far the most important of all the pleasures which architecture can produce is the deep joy of true and noble inspiration—that big sense of awe and reverence that comes only when something has struck deep at the foundations of our souls. It is the feeling that thrills one as he enters from a blustering autumn day into the dim, tremendous quiet of Notre Dame at Paris; it is the joy which sings in the gorgeous glow of the richness of St. Mark's at Venice. It is most frequently associated with religious buildings, such as St. Peter's in Rome, or Westminster Abbey, but it is by no means confined to these. Nor is it limited to buildings of large size. It can come from small structures as well: for it would be a cold person, indeed, who did not thrill as he turned a corner in Athens and suddenly saw rising in front of him out of squalid slums the little Monument of Lysikrates, so delicate, so perfect, so shining with a candid purity in the midst of all that drabness.

This inspirational quality is as independent of a building's age as it is of its size; it is a result of perfection, and it may exist in a building a year old as strongly as in one a thousand times its age. When one lifts the leather curtains of the door of St. Peter's and enters for the first time the hushed immensity of its great interior, the inspiration of its nobility sweeps over one like a compelling tide; but exactly the same emotion may overwhelm one in the concourse of the Pennsylvania Station in New York—that great strong-vaulted interior which swallows up its crowd, stills their tumult, and dignifies them—until suddenly the knowledge sweeps over one that its vaults are only lath and plaster, and not the true vaults they pretend to be. One wonders then what the hall of a Roman bath is doing in a modern railroad station in New York, and one's pleasure is dimmed. . . . Yet architectural forms, as forms, are so powerful over the sensitive observer that, for the moment, pure composition and design—pure form—have their way with him. For the moment, until the unreality of the whole creation sweeps over him, he feels a thrill of awe, a sudden keen realization of the worth-whileness of life and the extraordinary potentialities of mankind.

Architecture has always this crowning revelation as its end, and when it strikes this note it has succeeded in saying its greatest word. When, as you stand before some building, or in some grand interior, you feel rising within you this wave of thrilling inspiration, this emotion of quiet reverence—if at the same time all is so truly real, so actually what it seems, that no disturbing questions arise—then you may rest assured that you are in the presence of something truly great, a veritable architectural masterpiece. Such a joy as this can never be taught or learned; for, just as it takes professional giants to design buildings that produce it, so those alone can experience it fully who keep their souls unspoiled and sensitive and their sensibilities alert and keen, those who know what faith and reverence are and have not lost amid the turmoil of modern life the thin clear music of the soul's singing.

These, then, are the gifts that architecture is always ready to give you freely, will you but keep your minds active and your eyes open. Begin at once, whether you think you know anything about architecture or not. Study the building you work in and try to decide whether it pleases you, and why. As you leave your home, look back, and see if it is a residence you are proud to live in; if it expresses in some way the joy you feel in returning to it; if it looks inviting, comfortable, homelike, beautiful. And on your daily round of business, wherever it may take you, by library or school or apartment house or church or farmhouse or villa, look at the buildings, be they good or bad, with a new interest, and know that in the emotions they arouse in you there is an immense store of vivid and broadening pleasure awaiting your enjoyment. As you do this, either there will gradually grow over you a grey feeling of fatigue and displeasure when you pass street after street of thousand-windowed boxes with rusty tin cornices atop and horribly ornamented hallways below— the homes of thousands upon thousands of city dwellers—or you may feel a glow of pleasure or a quiet restfulness or even awe where some really beautiful structure rears its walls.

When even this measure of appreciation is yours, you may know that you have begun to open the great book of architecture; on every successive page you will find more and more of interest and value. And the pleasure you get from your growing appreciation will not be its only result, for you will have joined the continually growing number of those who realize the enormous value of good architecture, and in place of the terrible architectural blunders of which we have been too often guilty you will demand architectural master-pieces. Thus you will be helping in the task of the gradual elevation of the standard of our national taste, and so adding to the health, the happiness, and the spiritual enrichment of yourselves and the Americans of the future.

2

ARCHITECTURE
AND
CONSTRUCTION

SINCE ARCHITECTURE is an integration of construction, use, and design, it follows, of course, that construction methods and materials have a profound effect upon both the arrangement and the appearance of buildings. And it is equally true that one's possible enjoyment of buildings is vastly enriched by at least a basic understanding of some of the principles of construction. In fact, construction has been almost a controlling element in some types of architecture—Gothic cathedrals and much contemporary building, for example—so that any true appreciation of them entails a knowledge of the construction that underlies and conditions their forms. The processes of construction have always fascinated mankind; crowds of passers-by probably watched the great stones of Egyptian temples eased into place by enormous gangs of workers just as avidly as today they watch steam shovels and pneumatic drills bite into the earth or derricks lift heavy steel high in the air.

Many animals have been and are skilled constructors in forming their nests or dens, but apparently it remained for mankind to invent constructive methods, to approach construction creatively instead of as a blind instinctive reaction to the reproduction of its kind. In this continuing study of how to build, and what to build with, men have in the past developed three basic kinds of building and several classes of building material.

The three methods of construction resulted from man's efforts to roof over enclosed areas as a shelter for himself, his tombs, or his gods; they are the *post and lintel*, the *arch* or *vault*, and the *truss*. These terms are almost self-explanatory. The first, post-and-lintel, or wall-and-lintel, construction, entails merely the bridging over or covering over of generally vertical supports (either continuous, like walls, or isolated and small in size, like posts or columns) with one or more flat horizontal beams or lintels, big enough to carry whatever loads are imposed upon them. Post-and-lintel construction in stone characterizes most Egyptian architecture; in stone or brick and wood, it is typical of much Greek architecture and of the greater number of small buildings of many periods; in concrete or steel, it is the governing constructive method of many large buildings today.

The arch was the result of the effort to bridge over an opening with many pieces of material, each smaller than the width of the opening. It developed first in countries where stone was rare and expensive and good wood hard to obtain, and where the chief building material was brick. This was especially true of the Tigro-Euphrates Valley; men there at least 4000 years ago discovered that, if the bricks used for covering were made wedge-shaped and arranged in a vertical semicircle, each piece would be held rigidly in place by those on either side and the whole would form a strong arch or tunnel. Thus the arch and vault were born. The Mesopotamian people used arches and vaults extensively for thousands of years—first for tombs, for drains, and for similar hidden and buried constructions, later for gates and halls. The Etruscans knew the arch and vault; the Romans made of these constructions one of their chief architectural features; and in the Far East the Chinese—perhaps through distant early European influence—vaulted city gateways and occasional temple halls. From Rome, arch and vault building descended to the Middle Ages and the Renaissance, to become one of the most beautiful and varied of structural methods. In recent times the extensive use of wood and steel—both generally more suited to post-and-lintel than to arched construction—has severely restricted its use, but the growing popularity of concrete construction is gradually bringing arched forms back into use again, particularly for bridges, great market halls, and various types of large industrial buildings.

Arches have one particular feature that has vastly influenced building design—their outward thrust. Because of the wedge-shaped pieces of which most arches are built, and because of their curved shape, there is always a tendency for them to spread and to open sideways and so collapse. Just as a house built of cards leaned slanting against each other will stand only so long as the lower edges of the cards are prevented from slipping, so an arch or a vault is strong only when it is prevented from spreading at the base. This outward push is called the *thrust*; it has always to be considered in design, and must be counterbalanced by heavy buttresses, by the counter-thrust of an adjacent arch, or by tie rods. In modern concrete vaults the thrust is minimized by the integral, monolithic type of the construction, and by the incorporating of judiciously disposed steel reinforcing rods in the thickness of the vault itself.

Trussed construction depends essentially on the geometrical fact that, in a triangle, the length of any side cannot be changed without changing the angles at the corners; conversely, if the lengths of the sides remain constant, the shape of the triangle is preserved. Thus, in a simple gabled roof, if the pairs of rafters—the roof beams—are not tied together at the bottom, they tend to spread and push the walls out; eventually, unless the walls are very strong, the roof will collapse. But if a tie beam is placed across the building, connecting the lower ends of opposite rafters, the roof will be strong and rigid. This triangle, formed by each pair of rafters and the tie beam connecting them, cannot change in form unless one of the beams breaks; if they are strong enough, the whole is necessarily held in place and exerts only vertical weight on the walls or posts which support it. Such a triangle is the fundamental truss form, and all true trusses, however large and complicated, are merely combinations of these rigid triangular forms. Trusses have been of vast use in bridges and in roofing over wide spans.

It is a stange fact that, with all their genius in geometry, the ancient Greeks seem never to have discovered the truss principle; similarly, the architects of China and Japan never realized its possibilities and, like the Greeks, held up their roofs by elaborate and wasteful combinations of simple horizontal and vertical members. Trusses (not always strictly scientific) were used extensively by the Romans, however, and in the Western world they have been com-

PLATE I

F. S. Lincoln

International Building,
Rockefeller Center: lobby
Harrison, Fouilhoux & Abramovitz
and Reinhard & Hofmeister, architects

PLATE II

Colosseum, Rome

Bonwit Teller Building,
New York
Warren & Wetmore,
architects

PLATE III

ily News Building, New York. John Mead Howells,
ymond Hood, and André Fouilhoux, architects

PLATE IV

St. Peter's, Rome: interior
Bramante, Michelangelo, Bernini, and others, architects

mon architectural features ever since. The builders of the Gothic period were especially skillful in designing magnificent trusses of wood, often richly carved and painted, for great barns, castle halls, and church roofs. The open-timber roof of Westminster Hall in London (Plate XVII) is characteristic of the type. Today, steel and concrete as well as wood are frequently used for trusses, and the greater number of steel bridges as well as vast numbers of factories, armories, halls, and so on make use of them (see Plate XVII). Since trusses over wide spans often concentrate enormous weights at the points where they are supported, special attention has to be given to the walls or columns at these points to see that they are sufficiently strong and rigid.

There is another classification of construction, cutting across the triple division of post and lintel, arch, and truss. It is the division of buildings into *bearing-wall* and *framed* construction, and is especially pertinent to an understanding of buildings today. In bearing-wall structures, the walls that keep out the weather or divide the various areas of the plan also support the entire weight of floors and roofs. In framed construction this is not so; the walls are frequently mere protective or dividing screens, carrying no weight except their own; all the major weights of floor and roof, and sometimes even of the walls themselves, are borne by a framework of posts and beams, girders and braces, trusses, or arches, specially designed to carry them. Thus the simplest form of framed construction is represented by the savage's skin-covered or thatched hut or the Indian tepee; the modern steel-framed office building, hotel, or city hall is an example of its complex modern forms (see Plates II and III).

In some cases frames are exposed, as they were in medieval half-timber houses, where the alternation of dark timbers and the wall filling of brick or plaster is one of the chief factors in their beauty; in recent times as well, concrete frames are often apparent, as in much of the work of the Perret brothers in France, and the observer is instantly aware of the rhythms of support and screen. Yet in most cases today, especially when the frame is of metal, necessities of economy or of protecting the frame against fire or weather have forced the complete covering of the frame, as in our average

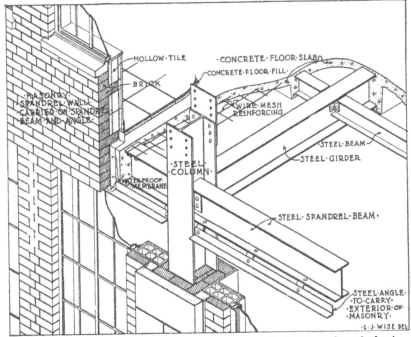

·HOLLOW·TILE·   ·CONCRETE·FLOOR·SLAB·
·CONCRETE·FLOOR·FILL·
·BRICK·
·MASONRY·
·SPANDREL·WALL·
·CARRIED·ON·SPANDREL·
·BEAM·AND·ANGLE·
·WIRE·MESH·
·REINFORCING·
·STEEL·BEAM·
·STEEL·GIRDER·
·STEEL·
·COLUMN·
·WATERPROOF·
·MEMBRANE·
·STEEL·SPANDREL·BEAM·
·STEEL·ANGLE·
·TO·CARRY·
·EXTERIOR·OF·
·MASONRY·
·G·J·WISE·DEL·

Architecture through the Ages

FIGURE 1. DIAGRAM OF TYPICAL STEEL-FRAME

FIRE-PROOF CONSTRUCTION

This cut-away diagram shows how all the steel is covered with masonry as fireproofing, and how all the weight of walls and floors is carried by the steel frame.

large city buildings (see Figure 1). The result has been that frequently the architect has forgotten the true structural nature of a framed building, and tried to use in its design the heavy forms, the great arches, and the cornices appropriate only to bearing-wall constructions; the immediate loss of expressiveness, of honesty, of integral quality is obvious.

For the type of construction affects design in many more ways than in the details of the exterior, or in the obvious questions of whether or not a frame is exposed. In bearing-wall construction, for instance, walls are naturally thick to carry the loads they bear and are as continuous and unbroken as possible. Openings are few and relatively small; if wide openings are required, they are strongly arched. Moldings and other decorations tend to partake of the power and the thickness of the walls they enliven. Such an Italian Renaissance palace as the Riccardi in Florence (Plate XXI) is characteristic, and generally all the greatest Renaissance buildings throughout Europe display the same spirit. Part of their enduring beauty lies in this truth to structure, this solidity and power.

In framed construction, on the other hand, the exterior walls, being mere protective screens without structural functions, are as thin as possible in order to reduce the weights on the frame. They can be made of any appropriate weather-resisting material; tile, metals, marble veneers, even glass are as fitted for this use as the older traditional brick and stone. If desired, openings can fill the entire area from column to column and the entire height from beam to beam. Decorations—carvings or moldings—naturally reflect the slim lightness of the construction. To attempt to force them into the old patterns appropriate to bearing-wall construction is not only to violate the integral nature of good architecture but also to deprive the world of the new, characteristic kinds of beauty which modern construction, modern materials, and modern industry make possible. Our pleasure in such a Gothic interior as that of Ste. Chapelle in Paris arises largely from the perfect manner in which it expresses its stone-framed construction. The ribbed vaults, the slim colonnettes that carry the lines of the vaults down to the floor, the magnificent sweep of glass windows, the elimination of wall areas, the delicacy of moldings—these elements all arise naturally from the construction and form with it a completely integrated and harmonious whole. And today similarly integrated and harmonious structures can arise when we accept as frankly as did the Gothic architects the splendid implications of the construction we use.

Even when brick and stone are used for the exteriors of framed buildings, they can be treated honestly in accordance with their non-structural, protective, surfacing functions. Brick can be laid on end, or with definite patterns, or with all the joints running continuously from top to bottom; or a light-colored brick can be laid in mortar of the same color, so that the effect is that of a clean, unbroken surface. Stone can be used in large, thin slabs, and, as in brickwork, joints can be continuous to give a reticulated pattern; where moldings or other decorations are used, they can avoid any suggestion of thickness in the wall (see Plate II). It is to avoid giving this thick-wall impression, and to emphasize the feeling that the outside covering of a building is one continuous surface membrane, that architects today so frequently place the glass surface of windows as close as possible to the plane of the walls.

In general form and plan, too, constructive systems deeply influence design. Thus post-and-lintel buildings generally have many parallel walls or rows of posts or columns and tend toward simple rectangular shapes, as in the case of Egyptian or Greek temples. Structures in which arches and vaults play pre-eminent parts always base their design on the development of adequate buttressing to relieve arch thrusts, as in the case of the great Roman baths or the Gothic cathedrals. In arched construction there is much greater freedom of mass design than when post-and-lintel construction is used; buildings may have some parts much higher than others, and domes and barrel roofs may cap the whole. Wider and higher interiors, of great variety of shape, may develop highly complex plans, in which support and buttress and wide span all combine to give impressions of tremendous and varied interior spaces, as, for instance, in Santa Sophia in Istanbul (Plate XVI), St. Mark's in Venice, the Pantheon (Plate XVIII) or St. Peter's (Plate IV) in Rome.

Similarly, bearing-wall and framed structures have their own characteristic plan types and generate characteristic shape envelopes. Bearing-wall buildings typically are combinations of simple rectangular rooms separated by thick partitions and develop simple masses with long stretches of continuous wall and unified roof lines. Framed constructions, on the other hand, are most free in their plans, because the partitions, being merely dividing screens, can be curved or straight, continuous or with breaks, and placed wherever desired or even made wholly or partially movable. The structural frame will demand regularly spaced posts, often widely separated, and, especially in the case of steel-framed structures, economy and ease of construction will tend to develop a building that consists of a multitude of similar cells; the basic form both in width and height can be broken in or out wherever a division between the cells occurs. This quasi-cellular character is obvious in steel frames before the walls are built; it is apparent, too, in the rectangular setbacks, the basic geometrical character, of many tall business buildings (see Plate III).

The determination of the design by the construction carries through into the smallest details. Each constructive method, each material, has its own characteristic proportions, its own rhythms. Thus openings in the older bearing-wall structures are usually tall and relatively narrow, like the doors and windows of the Renaissance, whereas more modern materials and framed construction often develop openings that are long and relatively low, like many shop windows, or the strip windows of some recent houses and schools, or the bands of doors that are common in theaters, shops, or office buildings. And the almost universal use of steel-framed construction for the larger buildings of cities has generated an almost universal rhythm of bay spacing, that is, the distance between the supporting columns—a distance that economy has set somewhere between fifteen and twenty-five feet. One can see this everywhere in the downtown sections of American cities; attempts to conceal it by basing exterior aspect on the closer supports of earlier styles nearly always fail, because a basic confusion arises to plague the designer and fog the clarity of the design.

Two other types of construction demand a briefer mention— suspended construction and corbeled or cantilevered construction. In the first of these, major weights of roof and floor are carried by hanging them from above, rather than building them up solidly from beneath. When it is realized that steel, for example, in long lengths is stronger in *tension* than in *compression*, the occasional desirability of the system becomes obvious. Of course the total weight has somewhere to be taken down to a firm foundation; this is accomplished by building up towers, pylons, or posts from which the structure is hung by means of cables or rods, or by building a great arch or arches from which the weights are hung. There has also been projected a house—the "Dymaxion House," designed by Buckminster Fuller—built around and hung from a central mast-like structure, held vertical by stays or shrouds.

The greatest use of suspended construction has been in suspension bridges, but enclosed structures sometimes make use of the system; the future will probably see many more.

Corbeled or cantilevered construction is that in which major portions of a building are bracketed or corbeled out beyond the posts that support them; the corbels or beams which do the bracketing are called cantilevers. In modern uses of the system, the cantilever is usually a continuation of a beam, girder, or truss, which rests on a post or column somewhere in its length. If its inner end is prevented from rising in the air, either because of the weight upon it, or because of its being tied down into the ground, and if it is strong enough not to break at the point of support, considerable weight can be carried on its outer, unsupported end. By connecting a series of such cantilevers, a continuous wall can be carried far outside the line of columns; this is the essence of cantilevered construction.

Many half-timber houses made use of this method, projecting the upper parts boldly beyond the line of the walls below. The beetling upper stories of some of the houses of late medieval England and Germany and Switzerland are one of the most striking characteristics of many towns in those countries.

Today, cantilevered construction in steel or reinforced concrete is frequently used where continuous bands of windows are desired. Show windows of unlimited length are made possible by cantilevering the walls above them, and more and more it has been found the most practical and economical way of building certain types of factory where floods of daylight are required.

From these various methods of construction most of our buildings take their basic forms. We might make a sort of table of the various methods and the qualities of plan and exterior aspect appropriate to them which it may be helpful to bear in mind as one examines the buildings around him. It would run something like this:

Post-and-Lintel and Wall-and-Lintel Construction

PLAN	ASPECT
Continuous, usually parallel walls and rows of posts	Generally simple cubical or parallel masses, or combinations of them
Square corners; general rectangularity	Columns or posts over each other; strongly marked horizontal or vertical lines to express the construction
Many similar sized rooms	
	Openings usually one over another

EXAMPLES

Egyptian temples
Greek temples (Plate IX)
The typical Colonial house plan
The typical modern office building (Plate III)

Arched and Vaulted Construction

PLAN	ASPECT
Widely spaced supports	Arches—round, segmental, or pointed—prominent in the design
Buttresses at right angles to the general wall line to take the thrust of cross arches	Continuous heavy walls where thrusts are continuous, as in a dome or a barrel vault; often contrasting with swelling curves of vault or dome above
One or many large interior unbroken areas	
Great variety in plan	Exterior buttresses create vertical accents between arches, at building corners, etc.
Direction of heavy walls dependent on direction of arch or vault thrusts	Openings few and large
	Great variety of general mass possible

EXAMPLES

Roman baths, both outside and in
The Pantheon at Rome
Santa Sophia at Istanbul (Plates XIII and XVI)
French Gothic cathedrals such as Amiens (Plate XXIII)

EXAMPLES (*Continued*)

Several important modern European market halls,
like those at Rheims or Leipzig (Plate XIX)
Several recent American hangars, especially some
at U.S. Navy bases

Trussed Construction

PLAN	ASPECT
Wide, unbroken interiors	High curved or gabled roofs
Walls often thin and open, with posts under truss ends	Variety in roof forms, as different types of truss are developed for specific purposes
Great variety of interior form possible	General lightness and openness

EXAMPLES

Westminster Hall (Plate XVII)
Many English late Gothic churches
Many wooden and steel bridges (not suspension
bridges)
Most large convention halls, sports arenas, and exhibition buildings
Many recent factories, especially for large-scale,
mass-production industries like the manufacture
of automobiles or airplanes (Plate XVII)

Bearing-Wall Construction

PLAN	ASPECT
Heavy, unbroken, continuous walls, with relatively narrow windows and doors, often rhythmically spaced	Thick walls give deep reveals at openings; these give wide, deep shadows
Ratio of wall area to enclosed space, large	General mass form tends toward simplicity
Large interiors have thick walls around them; small interiors may have thinner walls, since weights are less	General expression of weight, permanence, power
	Supporting quality of walls emphasized in accent on horizontal spread at base
	Ratio of wall to opening, high
	Boldly projecting cornices, moldings, and decoration

Post-and-Lintel:
   Greek temples (Plate IX)
   French châteaux
   The Lincoln Memorial in Washington
   The greater number of small houses built today
      in brick, stone, or concrete

Arched or Vaulted:
   The Pantheon at Rome (Plate XVIII)
   Many early Romanesque churches, such as St.
      Sernin at Toulouse
   St. Peter's at Rome (Plate IV)
   Occasional modern concrete vaulted warehouses
      and the like

Framed Construction

POST-AND-LINTEL:

PLAN	ASPECT
Slim supports, spaced with some regularity, often in regular series	Regularity of supports and beams produces masses of rectangular outline, or combinations of such masses
Thin walls, sometimes connecting supports, sometimes independent of them	Regularity of supports and beams produces a general plaidlike basic exterior pattern
Large openings	When frames are exposed, contrast of frame and screen material gives interest
Free, open plans	Possible over-all "membrane-like" exterior surface
	Great possible variety in wall and partition materials

EXAMPLES

Half-timber houses, common in England, France,
   and Germany in the late Gothic period (Figure 16)
Many seventeenth-century American Colonial
   houses

The greater number of recent factories
Many recent houses, especially in California
The typical large modern business building, loft
    building, or department store

ARCHED CONSTRUCTION:

PLAN	ASPECT
Lines of arched frame establish rows of posts or columns	The arched frame determines all major architectural lines
Buttresses, often quite deep, to take arch thrusts	Buttresses and flying buttresses accent the structural pattern
Great possible variety in plan shape	Little solid wall
	Enormous windows
Walls minimized, both in length and thickness	Accent on verticality
Openings very large	Arched frames accented by moldings, as in Gothic vault ribs

EXAMPLES

A few late Roman structures show this system in
embryo, for example, the Baths of Caracalla at
Rome

Any developed Gothic vaulted church; the most
perfect expression was probably achieved in the
mid-thirteenth century, in France, as in Amiens
Cathedral (Plate XXIII) or Ste. Chapelle in
Paris

Mont St. Michel shows the picturesque variety of
mass and the accented verticals this type of construction naturally produces

Suspended Construction

EXAMPLES

Suspension bridges; especially revealing of the light
grace of such a structural system are the Oak-
land Bay Bridge in San Francisco, or the Bronx-
Whitestone Bridge in New York

Occasional fair or exposition buildings

Tents

Corbeled or Cantilevered Construction

EXAMPLES

The Philadelphia Savings Fund Building in Philadelphia

Many balconies, porch roofs, and window shelters in modern houses

Occasional concrete warehouses and factories; one of the finest examples is the Van Nelle plant—factory and warehouses—in Rotterdam

There is nothing dogmatic in this table. You may make your own, for your interpretation of the common-sense forms that result naturally from any type of construction may differ from mine. But what *is* important is a realization that each type *does* have some architectural forms which fit it and some which do not; that plan and the appearance of a building, both inside and out, are conditioned by the construction used, just as the choice of construction is in turn influenced by the qualities desired in the plan and in the aesthetic effect.

Seen thus, as an integration of construction and design form, architecture is bound to take on new life and new meaning. Once we are conscious of this constructive side of architecture, we can realize in buildings new values of reality; we can see in them man's struggle to construct, man's pride in his constructions. Buildings will no longer seem mere arbitrary conglomerations of forms or materials but creations embodying their own discipline, the result of a logic devastatingly compelling. And one will soon tire of the merely pretty buildings that have nothing to say; more and more come to value and to love those which speak boldly and well of the way they were built and the materials of which they were made.

3

PLANNING

ARCHITECTURE, we have said, is a triple-sided art, aiming at "commoditie, firmeness, and delight"—utility, strength, beauty. We have already seen how deeply construction and design are implicated, how they affect each other at every point. It is the same with the quality of convenience or utility, and it becomes necessary to examine this side also, in order to understand the true nature of architecture and the true bases of beauty in buildings.

Planning is essentially the art and science of the arrangement of the parts of a building, or of buildings in a group, so that they serve the purpose for which the whole was designed and at the same time create seemly, harmonious, and beautiful spaces. For, although architectural planning is mainly concerned with utility and strength, it must not be imagined that the true architect is sociologist when he plans, engineer when he constructs, and artist only when he composes and decorates. The true architect is all three all the time, and he must keep his artistic imagination as busy when he is planning, so that his plans may build beautifully, as he keeps his structural sense when he decorates, in order that his work may be unified and the forms harmonious and expressive.

Thus planning is not the dull puzzle that it is often considered. The word suggests strange and incomprehensible diagrams of black lines and white areas, and lines of black dots or white lines on a blueprint. Planning means much more than a "plan" or many "plans," for planning is the distribution of all the varied parts of a building, rooms, corridors, and the like, with regard, first, to utility and, second, to beauty. A "plan" is merely a diagram to show the arrangement of parts arrived at by means of this imaginative arrangement.

Planning is a subject that touches modern life at every point and has always so touched life. The designer of a hospital must know absolutely the requirements of a hospital, how it is managed, what its equipment is, how the parts of it are related. An architect may spend hours in a newspaper office with a notebook, watching, watching, absorbing the methods of administration, because he has the problem before him of laying out a newspaper office. In order to plan proper apartment houses, or private residences, the architect must know just how the people live who are to inhabit them, and what are their greatest needs. And so it goes in the case of all kinds of buildings; the planner must keep in the closest and most practical touch with the life around. It is this which gives planning, when it is rightly understood, such an appealing and fascinating interest, for every building offers a different problem, the solution of which requires a constantly changing knowledge of people and affairs. Seen in this light, even a plan—a despised diagram—may take on new life and interest.

A plan is a horizontal section through a building, taken at any desired level. It is as though some giant were to take a knife, cut square through a building in a horizontal direction, and lift off the upper portion. What he saw when he looked down would be a plan of that building. Walls would be solid lines of greater or less thickness according as the walls were thick or thin. Doorways would be blank spaces between spaces of wall; windows would be similar blank spaces with one or more thin lines, the section of the glass and the sill below; columns would be solid circles, and so on. The whole arrangement of the building would be revealed at a glance—the relationship of all the rooms and corridors to each other, all the openings, the doors, the windows, the courts, everything.

The architect's best method, therefore, of presenting the results of his application of the science of planning to the particular problem of the building in hand, is the plan. In a way it is an abstraction; it is a diagram, but more than any other means at his disposal it makes clear the results of his skill and the design in his mind to the builder and to the layman as well. To the architect a plan of building is often as valuable as photographs or sketches, for by the relation of thick walls and thin, wide rooms and narrow, columns and piers, he can at a glance gain a complete idea of the whole construction of the building, as well as its arrangement.

The plan—that is, the actual arrangement, not the diagram that expresses it—has another function of great aesthetic importance; it determines the order in which an observer progresses through a building, and thus determines the order in which the visual experiences produced by the different rooms or areas impinge upon him. As we shall see later, this is of enormous importance, for architecture is an art in time as well as in space. The sequences of exterior view, entrance, vestibule or hall, room, and so on in great buildings have an ordered and inevitable quality as definite as do the successive movements of a symphony or a quartet. To displace this order, or to have no order, is to have an architecture merely fragmentary. Now it can easily be realized that this order of experiences is determined by the plan. One enters *here*, because the architect has planned the door; one goes on to *there*, because the architect has made it either the necessary, or the easiest, thing for one to do. He has made it so by the arrangement of his plan. A good plan guides one almost unconsciously; the well-planned structure needs few directional signs. Now the *here* and the *there* are successive parts of one continuing and changing aesthetic whole. The architect has planned so that one naturally receives these experiences in the order in which they should be received. He is both the composer and the conductor of the architectural symphony; the plan determines the sequence and the tempo of the whole.

A plan, like any diagram, must be looked at with imagination. The observer, if he wishes to gain the total value of the plan, must build in his imagination walls over the solid places, columns over the dots or circles; he must imagine doors hung in the doorways, and windows placed complete; he must try to imagine the ceiling overhead, and the lighting; he may then walk from hall to room, or through the towering interiors, master of the building from its plan. In architectural plans certain conventions have come to be employed to help the imagination. A dotted line from one support to another usually indicates an arch or beam above; thus in the plan of a Gothic church the crisscross dotted lines indicate the intersections of the arches which form the ribs of the vaulting. A dotted circle in a square indicates a dome overhead, and even the design of beamed ceilings is sometimes indicated on a plan in dotted lines. Furniture may or may not be shown, according to the purpose for which the plan is to be used. Often the projecting base of the walls is indicated by a single line just outside the solid portion, and the bases of columns are similarly shown. Border lines may often be drawn around rooms to emphasize their shape, and arrows or axis lines may be used to bring out main entrances or lines of important communication. The materials of which the whole is built are also frequently indicated on the plan by means of different symbols or by notes. With all these aids a plan becomes a very important record of what a building is and an invaluable indication of its structure.

The science of planning demands first of all a careful analysis of the uses of a building as a whole, be it house, store, factory, or city hall, and an analysis of the uses of all the several portions of which the building is composed. These may be classified briefly as follows:

Public Rooms. This class consists of those areas which are open to the public, or at least to a large number of people. In governmental buildings they are represented by public offices and the like, in theaters by the auditorium and foyer, and in houses by the reception room, or even, by stretching the meaning of the word public, by the living room.

Private Rooms. This class consists of those rooms given up to the particular use of the people for whom the building is designed. Such rooms are private offices and libraries, studies, bedrooms, and so on.

Means of Communication. This important class consists of corridors, vestibules, halls, staircases, elevators, rotundas, and the like. All these are of importance architecturally, because on their right design and arrangement depends a great deal of the building's convenience, and their aesthetic effectiveness is tremendously important, particularly in public buildings, because so many people are constantly using them. They also serve to set the character of the building's interior—lavish or modest, serious or gay, public or private.

Service. This class consists of all those parts of a building that minister to the humbler wants of man, such as toilets, closets, boiler rooms, fuel rooms, storerooms, pantries, and kitchens, as well as those minor rooms made necessary for the maintenance of the building and the convenience of the personnel, such as dressing rooms in a theater, sacristies and robing rooms in churches, and the like.

The first thing, then, that the architect has to do in designing a building is to classify the different rooms which the client requires under some such heads as the foregoing. In some cases he may also have to decide, himself, what rooms are needed, but usually the client has very definite notions of his own on that point. This preliminary classification has a very important place in the science of planning, for the classification of any room may determine its position; service rooms demand positions that are subordinate but at the same time conducive to efficiency, public rooms demand positions readily accessible, and so forth. And such a classification is by no means always an easy matter. A dining room is usually a private area, but in a family that entertains a great deal it may come to have almost a public significance. Similarly, a living room may be at one time a private area and at another time a public area, and its position has to be considered with regard to both functions.

Once this first classification has been made, another must follow, a classification of the rooms with regard to their importance. In general the public rooms are the most important, but this is not always the case. In some houses, for instance, it is the private portion that needs emphasis; the public room—the reception room, if it exists at all—is a very minor room somewhere near the door. This classification of rooms with regard to their importance is even more necessary than the first classification in arriving at the actual plan of a building, for it determines at once what rooms shall occupy the most prominent positions.

For there are important positions and unimportant positions, and this is the key of the whole matter. The most important position of all is exactly opposite the main entrance. This should be self-evident, for the position opposite the entrance has these unique characteristics: first, it can be approached without a single turn; and, second, it is the first thing that strikes the eye of one entering.

Herein lies the importance of what architects term an "axis"; it is not only the most direct method of proceeding through a building—usually a straight line—but also the direction in which a person looks. What he sees, then, directly opposite—that is, in an "axial position"—is something he cannot help seeing, and it behooves an architect to design a view that is balanced and beautiful. A careful study of such things creates the power of good formal planning. Formal planning is frequently symmetrical; there is in it a conscious search everywhere for stressed axes with strong points of interest at their ends, for complete balance of one side against the other, for right-angle turns, for strongly marked and geometrically shaped areas, for placing important elements opposite each other—mantels opposite doors, windows opposite windows, and so on. Thus, in formal planning, if there are two rooms of equal importance, an importance greater than that of any of the rest of the building, the most important positions for them are at the two ends of a broad, straight corridor which has the main entrance on one of its sides in the middle. This arrangement allows both rooms to be approached and entered with but one turn and also places them at the ends of the important vista of the corridor. If there are three main rooms of nearly equal importance, the most used or the most decorative may be placed across a corridor, opposite the main entrance, with the other two at the corridor's ends, or the three may be placed on three sides of a square or circle, with the entrance on the fourth side.

The importance of the axis depends not upon mystical metaphysics but upon the simplest of facts already hinted at. The axis is merely an abstraction of the simplest line of sight, and also of the simplest line of approach. An open, well-defined axis, leading to an interesting and important room or feature, means an open, well-defined symmetrical view, with an interesting feature as its climax; such a view is always more powerful than a view that is absolutely lacking in this orderly character—that is, than a view in a plan that has not been well studied with regard to axis. A well-defined axis usually signifies simplicity and directness as well, for it is always easier to walk in a straight line than to turn many corners. Behind the architect's desire for symmetry in formal planning lie those two important considerations: *interior effect,* and *directness of access.*

The effect of good formal planning is necessarily powerful, usually impersonal, monumental, studied. It may, however, become too self-conscious and artificial. It is especially suited to public and religious buildings, and to buildings used by large crowds of people, who find its directness time-saving and efficient. Yet there are many persons who find formal planning usually inhuman and repellent and cold; they demand a beauty with more variety, more of the accidentally charming. In certain periods most of the people have preferred formality, as was the case with the ancient Romans, the Italians of the Renaissance, the French academic designers of the period of Louis XIV, and the Chinese. At other times the majority have preferred less symmetrical and studied buildings, such as Gothic monasteries or English Tudor mansions or the almost artificial formal informality of Japanese gardens.

In informal planning, the architect tries for free balance rather than for symmetry, but the importance of the axis both as line of direction and line of sight remains. The good informal plan may be as carefully studied as the formal plan, but the variety of the whole conceals the careful balance, which is felt rather than consciously seen. Curved axes may be used; that is, the line of progress will be curved rather than straight, and the view which the observer will have as he moves along will change constantly. There may be balance of great rooms along one side against views outdoors on the other; variety may be furnished by all sorts of little unexpected touches of color or shape or climax.

At the present time informal planning is by far the most common type, the type generally preferred by the best designers. Yet just as formality in planning can be abused, and formal symmetry attained at the sacrifice of true utility (hence, because of the integral nature of architecture, at the sacrifice of the highest architectural beauty), just so, in some buildings, informality can be abused and achieved only as the result of a similar forcing. Thus, when the program of a building calls for one highly stressed element only, or when it requires two parts of equal importance and equal size (such, for example, as two courtrooms in a small courthouse), then natural logic suggests a symmetrical formal scheme just as inevitably as the program of the usual small house suggests one that is informal. We can never say arbitrarily that formality is better than informality, or informality more logical than formality; many elements will enter into a correct choice—the program of the building, its relation to its site and neighboring buildings, the spirit of the community, the emotional effect desired. What is desirable is that the architect approach the design, and the observer the completed building, naturally, log-

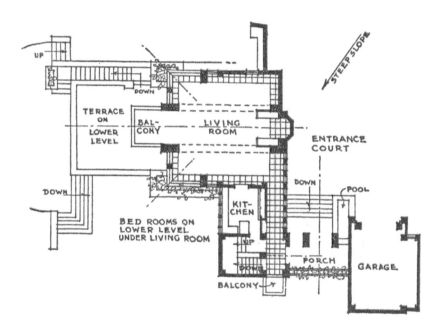

FIGURE 2. FREEMAN HOUSE, LOS ANGELES, CALIFORNIA

FRANK LLOYD WRIGHT, ARCHITECT

A house built on a steep slope, with entrance at the upper level. The careful attention to strong axial composition is obvious. Note the way the porch axis takes in the wide view. The axis of the door is blocked by a pier, so that one is turned into the corridor. The axis of the corridor is blocked by the fireplace pier, which turns one to the left into the living room. The strong diagonal axes through the corner windows relate the room to the outside and attract one's eye as soon as the living room is entered. Although the living room is square, a strong sense of length is given by the developed axis through the fireplace and emphasized by the balcony and the girders above (shown in dotted lines). The house is constructed of square concrete block; the pavement of the corridor and the border of the living room recalls this and ties in with the walls.

ically, and with no foreordained bias toward either the formal or the informal; the building itself should be the deciding factor in the choice.

Nor is a certain amount of formality always illogical in modern houses. It is interesting to note how often the plans of Frank Lloyd Wright, for instance, have strong notes of formality and careful balance, how carefully he studies and emphasizes important axes, how a subtle but essentially formal order is nearly always a marked trait (see Figure 2). And, similarly, it is significant that in the very midst of such a free plan as that of Mies Van der Rohe's Tugendhat house in Brünn, Czechoslovakia, one of the epoch-making works of contemporary design, the climax of the whole is a great sheet of onyx, formally placed and establishing a sudden sharp note of axial symmetry (see Figure 3).

It may be interesting to see how these notes of formality and informality work out in actual practice. As an example of the more formal treatment, let us take a house designed in 1916 by Murphy & Dana in New Haven. The plan of its main portion is shown in Figure 4. Here there were to be arranged a library, a reception room, a dining room, a study, and a stair hall. The house was to be used for much entertaining, so that the reception room had to be large, and arrangements were required for throwing the greater part of the first floor together. The library, on the other hand, was to be kept private, as a family living room. The problem was solved as the plan shows. When a guest enters the front door, which is on a landing raised three steps above the rest of the floor, he is confronted immediately by the wide arch that leads to the reception room, on the axis of the door and hall and in the middle of a symmetrically paneled hall. The reception room opens through three large windows onto a brick terrace so that there is immediately an interesting view on the axis—arch, room, window, terrace, and garden behind. The reception room itself is a large and rather formal room with a fireplace at the center of one end and a wide doorway in the center of the other, which leads into the dining room. The dining room has its fireplace directly opposite this door and opposite the reception-room fireplace. When dining room and reception

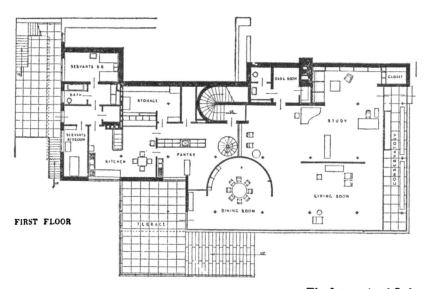

SECOND FLOOR

FIRST FLOOR

The International Style

FIGURE 3. TUGENDHAT HOUSE, BRNO, CZECHOSLOVAKIA
L. MIES VAN DER ROHE, ARCHITECT

A plan of great and subtle brilliance, with the dividing screens and partitions kept largely independent of the steel supporting columns. The progress from the upper entrance, through the vestibule, and down the stairs to the living room is clear and strongly articulated; the climax is a rich onyx panel placed to accent the formal reception area.

room are thrown into one, this strongly marked axis through them both, with the fireplaces—each room's most interesting architectural feature—at the ends, binds both rooms into one whole and produces at once a spacious, quiet dignity. Now this axis is crossed by the axis of the front door at a point exactly in the middle of the reception room, so that anyone near the center of the reception room commands four different, interesting, yet studied and composed views: the dining-room fireplace, the reception-room fireplace, the front door and stairs, and the brick terrace and garden. Such a result could never have been obtained in an unsymmetrical plan.

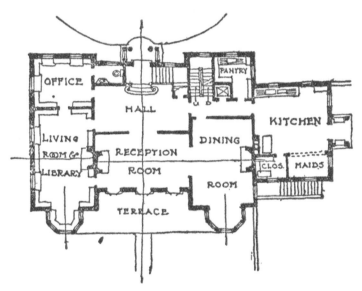

FIGURE 4. HOUSE IN NEW HAVEN, CONNECTICUT
MURPHY & DANA, ARCHITECTS

A characteristic plan of an eclectic Georgian house, carefully arranged
for axial openness and formal grandeur.

The program of this house is, in a sense, a conservative one, and leads almost inevitably to a conservative, rather formal type of plan. Let us take another example, a more "modern" program, and see how application of the same principles leads to forms quite different (see Figure 5). Let us imagine a young couple with limited means and two children. They have at most one servant, but they like to entertain informally. Friends are continually coming and going. The family loves sun and air and space and wants the largest and most flexible arrangement of its living quarters. It needs at least a two-car garage, with space for a guest's car as well as for its own, and, since the people who live in the house are likely to want to use their car at any moment in any weather, they want the garage attached to the house. To simplify the problem, we shall imagine a flat lot, with the entrance road or street on its northerly side.

The first floor of such a house must obviously be built around the living room. This must be flexible; it should have a separate dining portion, a reading portion, and a portion for general use, each so arranged as to give a sense of cozy intimacy, yet all together forming a spacious unity. Each part should command the greatest possible amount of south light, and at least in part seem to open out on and almost be a part of the open space beyond.

The entrance hall should be as small and direct as possible, and should have opening off it capacious coat closets and a lavatory, and also if possible the garage. The kitchen should be as small as possible, to reduce steps and cleaning time, and should be carefully studied for the utmost efficiency of storage and working facilities; its connection with the dining space should be direct, and communication through a sliding panel or part of a cabinet should be furnished so that trays may be pushed through from one space to the other.

Upstairs, bedrooms may be comparatively small, but bathrooms or combined bath and dressing rooms ought to be larger than the usual ones. The mechanical necessities for clothes storage and dressing space for each room should be concentrated, so that the bedroom becomes primarily an airy, open, uncluttered sleeping space, with cross ventilation and large window areas. There should also be a pleasant tiled living terrace, opening from the second floor or arranged above it, protected from north and west winds, private enough for sun-bathing, and large enough to be a delightful outdoor living room.

Such a house will manifestly be vastly different from the house shown in Figure 4. Notice, however, that the same principles of planning are still at work. The idea of the axis, as the direct line of

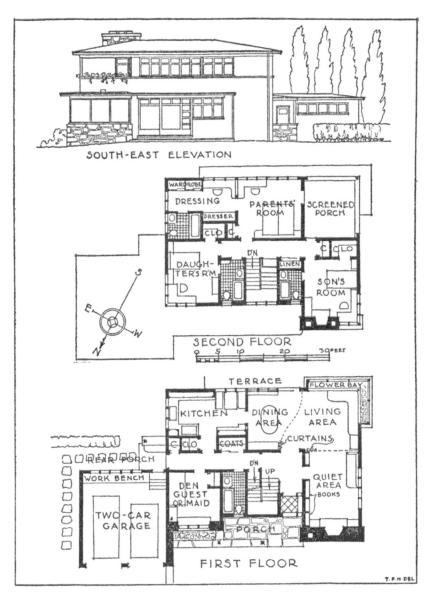

FIGURE 5. A HOUSE OF TODAY

A house designed for flexible living in accordance with a definite program. The living-dining area is arranged so that the quiet area may be either kept separate or thrown into the general living space, and curtains can be drawn to shut off the dining area. A breakfast alcove is in the kitchen area for informal meals when desired. The rooms are carefully oriented for sun and view, and the house is closely related to the garden to the south by large windows. Stone walls and hedges give privacy in the garden and shut off the garage court and the service entrance.

approach and the direct view, is still a controlling one, but its use is complicated by more numerous minor axes and by a study of various unsymmetrical but carefully balanced views. From the door the entrance is direct and open, and from every point in the living room the views are pleasant as well as naturally and purposefully planned. Windows are arranged to give the most view and the most south sun; in the dining space the window takes advantage of the pleasant morning easterly exposure.

Necessarily, too, this house with its broken outline, its large concentrated glass areas, and its flat roof terrace—all the results of careful planning developed from the program set—is going to have an outward aspect far different from that of the other house, and any attempt to force it into any historical style is bound to result in compromise or absurdity. Thus it may be seen that planning is integrally bound up with appearance and therefore with style.

If axes are so important in simple houses, it may readily be appreciated how essential they become in public buildings, where impressiveness is one of the great ends to be achieved and where directness of approach for the many people who are to use the building is indispensable. It is one of the chief faults of much mid-nineteenth-century American architecture that this important question of planning was so neglected. Building after building still exists, which, though beautiful without, has no coherent plan, no strongly marked axis, no impressive interior. The courthouse at Springfield, Massachusetts, by H. H. Richardson, is an example; the conception of the picturesque exterior, with its turrets and gables, has been the ruling idea, and the plan is chaotic, with the various necessary rooms scattered anywhere. In time this lack of planning sense became almost a tradition in American architecture; our country is filled with courthouses, city halls, and post offices in which the exterior design has absolutely controlled the interior arrangement, to the utter loss of both convenience and interior effect, and in which entrances are mean, corridors narrow and dark, and stairs ill placed and crooked.

During the last sixty years our planning has improved. Crowding practical problems of the swift circulation of large masses of people, a growing demand for economical and efficient functioning in all types of structure, and increasing knowledge of what people want and how they react have combined to force attention upon all matters of practical, direct planning. A surer sense of what is truly monumental and a restudy of the qualities inherent in the long tradition of classical design have given us a new grasp of the aesthetic problems involved. Let us take, as an example, the Nebraska state capitol, designed by the late B. G. Goodhue (plan, Figure 6; Plate V). Here is an extraordinary integration of use, structure, and effect, achieved by a plan of great but natural formality, magnificently composed.

The whole mass expresses the plan directly. The high vault of the entrance corridor leads directly to the higher mass of the domed central rotunda; from this the two legislative chambers—house and senate—project in similar higher masses, one on each side. Note how convenient and direct it all is. The public can approach through the great main doorway, down the handsome vaulted corridor, and in the central rotunda find the entrances, equally stressed, to the public portions of the legislative chambers on either side or to the state's highest court at the rear. The masses of the two legislative chambers themselves project out to the exterior side walls, so that the members of the legislature may approach by their own private entrances and find their house and senate coatrooms, lounges, and committee rooms, conveniently situated and leading out efficiently in the wings that surround the four courts. These courts are beautiful compositions which let light and air into the very middle of the large structure. Here is formal planning of a high order, symmetry with variety, and the whole gained not at the sacrifice of usefulness but with the most careful attention to convenience.

Nor is this all; in the Nebraska capitol the architect has integrated his construction and his effect as closely as he has integrated utility and effect. The building is in a way structurally conservative; it is a bearing-wall building with the minimum of steel frame, and all its major interior areas are vaulted with thin tile vaults. Vault thrusts and weights have largely dictated the size and thickness of walls, piers, and columns; there is little false work or furring merely to create false impressions, yet the proportions seem perfect. The whole

has a firm reality, a power in its integrated beauty, that the all too
common make-believe plaster vaults and false great piers of lath
and plaster around a thin steel column could never achieve. The
formal symmetry of the plan is here the result of true architectural
thinking, and that is what makes the Nebraska capitol perhaps the
finest twentieth-century governmental building in the country.

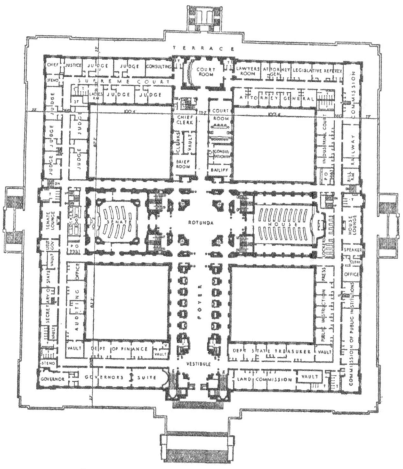

FIGURE 6. NEBRASKA STATE CAPITOL, LINCOLN, NEBRASKA
B. G. GOODHUE, ARCHITECT (*American Architect*)

A plan of superb and logical formality, where every element in the arrangement is
designed for a specific purpose and in close accordance with the structural system.
In this building the integration of use, construction, and effect is well-nigh perfect.

Imagine, then, that an architect who is planning a building has embodied in his plan all the foregoing principles. He has decided which are his most important rooms and has placed them in the most important positions, and he has decided on the axes which they determine. He must now begin to study the plan in more detail, so that each portion of the building shall be fitted to perform its purpose in the best and simplest way. To do this, he must keep fixed fast in his mind the actual use that each smallest portion is to receive; he must know just how this use will affect his plan, and what arrangements it demands. That, again, is a question of the relationship of the parts of the building. It is merely carrying the method of the architect's preliminary analysis one step further and applying it, not to the building as a whole, but to each separate portion of the building. In this study he will think in terms, not of *rooms*, but of *activities*. The building itself is thought of not as a collection of box-like enclosures—rooms—but rather as an aggregation of areas where certain activities take place. It is only when the spaces for these activities have been thoroughly studied and arranged for maximum usefulness that the question of whether they should be "rooms" in the conventional sense arises.

The designer will probably begin this detailed analysis with a consideration of the most important areas—the public areas. Now these have certain definite requirements, which it is well to keep in mind. The first requirement, of course, is safety. Safety in a public area means more than strength of construction. It means safety of health, it means liberal exits in case of fire or panic, and it embraces a number of questions of heating, of ventilating, of arrangement. The second requirement is convenience, fitness for use. That is, in a lecture hall or a theater, each person should be able to command an unobstructed view of the stage, and the hall should be so planned that each person can hear without effort. In a public office, convenience demands that each person shall be able to enter, to attend to his business, and to leave in the easiest possible manner. In a library, convenience demands such a relation of parts that anyone may enter, obtain the desired book, read it in comfort, and depart with little effort and delay, yet always be under the librarian's control. And so on for every kind of public area; the architect must imagine its every use, and make arrangements for it.

The following questions which may affect the planning of the building will then arise in the design of the public areas:

1. How many persons will use the area? The answer to this question will decide the number and size of entrances and exits and the amount of corridor space necessary to take care of these people.

2. How long and how continuously will it be used? The answer to this will settle the amount of ventilation necessary. It will determine whether or not public toilets should be near at hand, and if so how many are needed. The type of doors is also important. Revolving doors are suited to those situations where egress and ingress are continuous, but wide banks of swinging doors are desirable where crowds have to be handled in a short period, as in a theater.

3. Exactly what is its purpose? The answer to this will determine whether it shall have coatrooms; it will decide whether there is to be a banked or level floor, or a stage, and, if so, of what kind and size; and it may bring up the whole question of acoustics, a science in itself so complex that only the merest reference to it is possible here. Acoustics may often be the governing feature in the shape, size, and materials of a room. If the area under consideration is a suite of public offices, the answer to this question will decide their exact relation to each other, the relative size of their public and private portions, the number of doors, and sometimes the exact force and direction of the lighting.

This outline will make plain at once the intimacy of the connection between planning and life; it should also show how absolutely the architect is governed by the needs of the building he is designing, and how the arrangement of a good building is a direct result of these factors.

When the architect has solved these questions on the use of the public portions of the building, he may turn to the next great question, closely related to the others, the question of corridors and halls and other means of circulation. Here he is less bound down by complex problems of particular use than he is in the design of the public areas themselves, but even in corridor design he must always keep dominant the factors of safety and convenience. Corridors should always be as straight as possible, and always wide, airy, and light. A cramped, close corridor, lighted by electricity in mid-day, is an inexcusable feature where room is plentiful and money not stinted. A corridor with steps that are unexpected, or with changes in level that are not expressed in the design in such a way that their existence may be readily grasped from a distance, may be dangerous; in a panic such a corridor has often been the cause of many deaths. Even in corridor design the architect must keep the matter of use clear in his mind.

We have already considered the importance of corridors, rotundas, and the like in giving impressiveness and grandeur to a building, and the bearing of this on planning. Stairs are also of tremendous importance. Their practical usefulness is self-evident and so should be the qualities their very function makes desirable: directness, simplicity, such a slope and steps as will be comfortable to ascend or descend, light—everyone knows from experience the danger and discomfort of a dark stair—and ease of access to all portions of the floors it connects. The aesthetic importance of stairs is less evident, but experience and open eyes will soon show it. There is an appeal about a beautiful and well-planned stair that impresses unconsciously the most callous observer, and stairs in general have a powerful emotional and dynamic character—they are, in fact, a common psychoanalytic symbol. A good stair is an invitation to ascend, it suggests all kinds of interesting features above, it fills one with the zeal of the explorer and an instinctive love of the unknown; whereas a poorly designed stair, crowded into a dark corner, repels. There is, besides, an innate grace in the relation between the sloping and the level lines of the railing or balustrade that can be lovely. Curved stairs are a delightful feature which the French, like the American designers of the early Republic, have been particularly skillful in using.

Even in the simplest stairs of our houses these values are apparent. The straightforward stairs of the Colonial houses of our ancestors bear eloquent witness, climbing direct and true with carved newel and twisted baluster to a broad landing lighted by a wide and often beautifully decorated window near the top. Such a stair gives at once the impression of fine large rooms to live in on the floors above. It serves not a little to give that impression of dignified homeliness which is so well-nigh universal in those houses. Where sometimes the second floor is the main floor, or *piano nobile*, of the building, stairs are of even greater importance. For example, take the great stairhall of the Opéra at Paris (Plate VI). Its great flights, with easy steps and sweeping balustrades, though perhaps over-ornamented and ostentatious, give at once an effect of majesty, an impression of being built for crowds of spectators, that is usually lacking in our American theaters, where patrons in the cheaper seats are forced to climb interminable dreary stairs that are rough, uncouth, uninviting, ugly. In the Paris Opéra, with a truer application of the principle of democracy, the topmost galleries open on this same great stair; all the spectators are considered one great beauty-loving crowd. Or take the Boston Public Library, with that majestic wide flight leading up between the two guardian lions, and then dividing into two symmetrical flights that climb by painted wall to the marble arcade above; this is a staircase that is not only convenient but also one of the most beautiful features of a beautiful building as well. The stair correctly planned and conveniently arranged is one of the most salient examples of how architecture takes necessary requirements and converts them into objects of beauty and delight.

Today, escalators and elevators have largely replaced stairs as the chief method of vertical communication, especially in public buildings. The effects on architecture have been tremendous, for not only have elevators made possible the many-storied structure, they have also changed entirely the habits of the public. Accustomed now to a life of level walking, with all major changes in height above the ground taken care of by mechanical means, people have come to resent stairs and to avoid their use wherever possible. Where land is relatively cheap and building lots large, the one-story house is increasingly popular; where land is expensive, people increasingly prefer apartments—each on one floor—to little narrow high houses with their necessary stairs. And in public buildings designers are striving more and more to put the chief rooms, the most used portions, as close to the ground level as possible, to avoid great flights of exterior steps or monumental stairs within. Where many levels of important public rooms occur, elevators or escalators serve to carry visitors up and down.

In an integrated architecture, this enormous practical importance of escalators and elevators would suggest a like aesthetic importance. Yet how seldom does one find a building in which the design of these important features is treated as more than a purely utilitarian necessity! Architects generally have been too conservative, too lacking in imagination, to take advantage of this new opportunity, and elevators get tucked into corners or arranged in banks in dark narrow lobbies. Even in skyscrapers, where the necessary elevators occupy a large area of floor space, this is too often true. In the tallest building in New York, for instance, the elevators can be reached only by making several right-angle turns; the banks open on narrow, short lobbies, some in one direction and others at right angles; even the lavish marbles that line the walls cannot hide the creative poverty of the design or make these lobbies seem other than funereal, like corridors in a columbarium. And in the more recent structures of Rockefeller Center, as well, handsome, open, easy to find—in other words, truly architectural—elevator arrangements are the exception.

This need not be so; there are buildings in which the reverse is the case. But to achieve true efficiency and beauty in elevator arrangement requires of the architect the same unconventional imagination in approaching this modern problem that the architects of the Baroque period applied to the design of stairs. It is a fact that the practical requirements of elevators are stringent, that economy is a "must" in modern structures; yet to the great architect such limitations are often needed stimuli to new creativeness, added opportunities for a new beauty. The day will come when this is realized, and elevator and elevator lobby design and arrangement will come to have an aesthetic importance to match their economic and practical necessity. In the Chrysler Building in New York, for example, one may see a logical, open arrangement—the beauty of its plan, alas, concealed by an ostentatious garishness of treatment. And in a quieter way the Time and Life Building in Rockefeller

PLATE V

Gottscho-Schleisner

Nebraska State Capitol, Lincoln, Nebraska: exterior
B. G. Goodhue, architect

Gottscho-Schleisner

Nebraska State Capitol: corridor

J. B. Franco

Nebraska State Capitol: rotunda

PLATE VI

Opéra, Paris: stairs
Charles Garnier, architect

PLATE VII

Cushing-Gellatly; from *Design of Modern Interiors*

House in Lincoln, Massachusetts:
living-dining room
G. Holmes Perkins, architect

House at Miquon, Pennsylvania:
bed-dressing room
Kenneth Day, architect

Robert M. Damora; from *Design of Modern Interiors*

PLATE VIII

United States Capitol, Washington, D. C.
Thornton, Latrobe, Bulfinch, and Walter, architects

Center demonstrates the trend toward greater simplicity and beauty achieved without loss of economy or practical efficiency.

Escalator design has been an easier problem, for basically escalator forms have great similarity to the forms of stairs, so that in their placing and treatment a less original and revolutionary attitude is necessary. The escalators in the lobby of the International Building at Rockefeller Center (Plate I), already discussed in Chapter 2, are superb in material, finish, and effect, and many recent department stores and railroad stations have examples almost as good.

Two classes of areas remain to be considered—private rooms and service spaces. In these the architect has problems to solve that are no less complex than those of public rooms and circulation areas, and the good architect will use as busy an imagination and as careful a judgment here as in the more public spaces. He will see that the private rooms are accessible to those who use them and that every requirement of comfort or use has been met. He will see that privacy, where desired, is preserved, that each space has just the right outlook for its purpose, and that each is properly related to its dependencies and to the hall which serves it. The architect's care must extend to every humblest room; he must see that his arrangement of service rooms makes the building easy to run. He must be thousand-minded; he must think with the minds of the owner, the cook, the chambermaid, the janitor, the boiler tender, the coal heaver.

Let us take, for example, the problem presented by a modern bedroom and its appurtenances. A century and a half ago a bedroom was usually just a large rectangle with adequate windows and a fireplace for heating. Sanitary requirements, washing facilities, and clothes storage were all taken care of by means of pieces of furniture set in the room where desired. Much service was necessary to fetch and carry water, slops, and waste, and to keep dustless and clean the multitude of surfaces the varied furniture possessed. If, in the winter, one wished fresh air at night, he dressed in an arctic temperature and broke the ice in the pitcher in order to wash, or else waited for a maid or a valet to come up, close the windows, and light a fire.

Today the architect's problem is far different. We demand bathrooms and closets. And the imaginative and conscientious architect has only begun his work when he has incorporated these into his plan; he then has to ask himself and his client a whole series of much more detailed questions. Exactly how is this bedroom to be used: Does it serve as an upstairs living room? Is it the place where the household accounts are made up and bills paid? Does it serve as a sewing or mending room? Is it the emotional center of the family

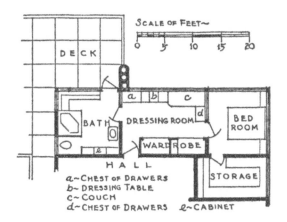

Plate VII shows a view looking into the bedroom from the dressing room. The bedroom is kept to a minimum; the dressing room serves as boudoir and sitting room; the bathroom is larger than usual, and there is a large connecting exterior deck.

The Modern House in America

FIGURE 7. HOUSE IN MIQUON, PENNSYLVANIA: THE MASTER'S SUITE
KENNETH DAY, ARCHITECT

life? Is it a twentieth-century boudoir? What clothes have to be stored there—a man's? a woman's? both? Do the occupants dress in the bathroom or the bedroom? How many persons use the bathroom—usually? on party occasions? Are twin beds or a double bed desired? Ideally, there should be no taboos whatsoever in the nature of these questions which the architect asks himself or his client. Are the occupants people of strict, old-fashioned ideas of privacy, or have they a freer, more liberated attitude toward the body and its functions? These considerations will all affect the planning of a family's sleeping, bathing, and dressing areas; they will determine the relative sizes of the parts, the elaborateness of the clothing storage arrangements, the accessibility of the bathroom to the hall, the question of whether the bathroom is itself subdivided into separate compartments for the various fixtures, the aesthetic character of the bedroom, its outlook and orientation, its heating and ventilation, the arrangement of its furniture. And all these factors not only have to be arranged efficiently but also must be integrated into a whole of charm and beauty and harmoniously related to the entire structure.

Thus the modern "bedroom" is a far different thing from the simple rectangle of the Colonial house, and to attempt to force it into conventional old-fashioned lines can produce only compromise and confusion. Screen partitions, glass divisions, built-in furniture, windows freely placed to give desirable light and views—these all combine in the best recent houses to give in these intimate areas both a convenience and a beauty, a true livability, that the older houses never possessed (see Figure 7 and Plate VII).

The careful asking and answering of questions of similar scope have revolutionized the design of kitchen and eating areas. Today domestic service is a problem of growing difficulty; servants are fewer, and those who act in that capacity are of a higher type, who demand treatment not as mere servants but as human beings practicing a skilled profession. Kitchens must be designed for efficiency of working, but they must also have sun, air, and if possible a view. In many cases they should be so arranged as to allow a mother working there to supervise her young children as they play. As far as possible, color and outlook should make this room as beautiful to be in as any room in the house, and not simply a forgotten area for drudgery. Where there are servants, their bedrooms and living areas must have the space and the pleasantness compatible with human beings, and not be mere cells for slaves or prisoners.

The question—at the forefront in house design today—of a full, separate dining room versus a dining alcove or a dining area in the living room can only be answered in each individual case by a similar asking of relevant questions, a similar imaginative grasp of the relative demands for space in the living room or for separateness and size in the eating area. Whichever way the questions are answered, there remain the problems of ease of service, of proper outlook, and of orientation. Some persons prefer sun at breakfast, some like to have sunset and late light at dinner or supper; for the former the eating area should have an eastern exposure, and for the latter it should face west.

Similarly, as has already been noted, a living room is far more than a mere large well-lighted space; it is a place of multifarious activities, and each activity should be considered in its design (Plate VII). Thus a study of detailed functions has to be made of every area in a building, and the demands of all satisfied as far as possible, balanced against each other, and at last integrated into one harmonious and beautiful whole; for a good building is never merely a conglomeration of separate and well-functioning parts but, like any work of art, also a single unit, consistent and integrated, where every part helps the others and the whole. If the architect can produce this and persuade his client to accept the plan he has created with so much care and forethought and imagination, he not only will have helped to produce a beautiful building but also will have made it possible for everyone connected with the building to lead more efficient and useful lives.

But good planning must accomplish more than this: it must make an arrangement that is not only practical to build and easy to run but also strong. And such a requirement demands a tremendous amount of study. The architect has to see to it that all his supports are heavy enough and so spaced as to permit the simple and easy construction of the floor or roof above; he must also see that chimneys run as directly as possible, and that plumbing, heating, and all the elaborate apparatus of modern mechanical equipment are simply located.

The use of steel supports and skeleton construction has revolutionized modern planning. It has enabled the bridging of long spans; it has reduced the size of supporting piers; it has largely eliminated heavy walls. But its technique is so complex that steel is usually designed by specialists—structural engineers—and the result frequently is a mechanical framework of equally spaced columns between which the architect or planner fits his partitions as best he may. Now this is obviously an incomplete, disorganized way of working, and the result—especially in many hotels, apartment houses, and commercial buildings—is an incoherent arrangement that resembles a picture puzzle rather than a creative organism.

Yet this need not be. Steel and reinforced concrete construction have set the architect free from many of the hampering restrictions of wood and masonry construction and have allowed him to create such light and airy buildings as the world has never known. They have made possible the soaring heights and jagged outlines of our cities, the glittering openness of the last modern industrial buildings. Why, then, has steel seemed sometimes to bring into the building art so many falsities, so many compromises? The answer seems to lie in the fact that not until recently has steel been used in ways suited to it. The inertia of popular taste and the traditionalism of architects have conspired to force steel-supported buildings into plan types unsuited for this kind of construction (plans based on the old types developed in masonry); the unnatural arrangements of units that have resulted from this misuse of steel are true to neither tradition nor material. This is not good architecture; it is merely a set of mechanical tricks. A good plan is never a tricky plan; a good plan is simple and straightforward, with no faking of material or method of construction.

Moreover, steel construction, as was indicated in Chapter 2, like concrete construction, has its own characteristic plans. There is a beauty in the geometry of normal steel construction which is new and characteristic, and this holds as true in planning as it does in exterior appearance. It has also rendered possible a new kind of plan, admirably fitted to express its nature—a plan where all the supports stand clearly exposed, creating their own pattern, and the purely dividing partitions run completely independent of the supports, superimposing, as it were, their own additional motifs upon the structural basis. It is a sort of architectural counterpoint; the use pattern developed by the partitions and the structural pattern of the supports run along together, separated but related, distinct yet harmonious. This type of planning is especially notable in such works of Mies Van der Rohe as the Tugendhat house (Figure 3) and in many of the houses by Le Corbusier, but it is common, though less stressed, in much other contemporary design—such, for instance, as the lobby of the central building at Rockefeller Center.

Yet this contrapuntal type of relating use and structure is by no means universal today. Many architects feel, instead, that the greatest harmony, the greatest repose, the truest expression, come only when the two patterns of use and construction have been so thoroughly studied that they merge at last into one. The other system, they find, leads too often into a kind of fantastic modern rococo, into arbitrary whimsicalities of planning with little meaning, into complexities that often conceal sacrifices in real usefulness. The perfect integration of use and structure had characterized the greatest past architecture; why should it be different today? Frank Lloyd Wright has always stood for this integration, and in the best American architecture today—as, for example, in the best recent houses on the Pacific Coast—it is the integrated system of design that is more and more the rule.

But, whichever system is adopted, the good plan always expresses the construction; small house or large, cathedral or town hall or parliament building, the plan should reveal at least the essence of the way it is built. Heavy walls should run through where the weight is heavy, and the main divisions of the plan should follow these main constructional lines. Arches should be amply buttressed, and the plan should reveal the buttress. Notice the plan of Amiens Cathedral (Figure 8), and see how the heavy cross buttresses at the sides are placed where they best do their work, with their long axis parallel to the cross thrust of the vaults. And note how around the apse the great main buttresses are used to divide the chapels; how the crossing of nave and transept is emphasized by the heavier piers that are necessary to carry the great square vault above them. It is a perfect plan; every part does its work simply and easily, and every part is made to work in as many ways as possible.

This is an ideal that every plan should strive to emulate. There should be a constructional reason for every important feature, and a practical reason behind each constructional feature. Breaks in the outside wall should indicate changes in function within, and important structural walls should separate important rooms, if possible.

This is an ideal that is impossible of absolute realization, particularly in small houses, where the demands are so complex and the construction so simple; but it is an ideal that is always in the architect's mind consciously or unconsciously, and it is an ideal that has had a tremendous power in the development of architectural forms throughout the ages.

FIGURE 8. AMIENS CATHEDRAL

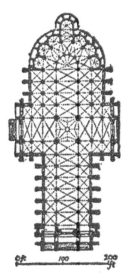

A plan resulting largely from the careful organization of structure to shelter actual necessities and express a great popular religious movement. Vault thrusts condition the buttresses which project at the sides, and the regular spacing of the piers within is developed from the vaulting system. The richness of the east end, with radiating chapels, aisles, and apse, results from the liturgical needs of the medieval church.

Planning has still a third requirement to fulfill. Besides finding scientific solutions for the problems of building for practical use and for constructional simplicity and strength, it must incorporate beauty. Indeed, in planning, as in every other branch of the art of architecture, the question of beauty is so implicated and bound up with all the other questions that confront the architect that it is impossible to consider them entirely apart. It will therefore not be necessary to consider the subject at any very great length here.

There is one point, however, that must be insisted upon, and that is the fact that the architect's solution of the plan determines absolutely the general character of the outside appearance of a building and its interior effect. The reverse is also true. If an architect, or his client, decides that a certain type of exterior or interior design is required for a proposed building, by reason of the adjacent buildings, or the character of the site, or tradition, or for any other reason, then this choice is bound to exercise enormous influence over the planning of the building. The layman often forgets this. He thinks of the walls and roof of a house merely as a shell, and the interior arrangement as a separate and unrelated kernel. He may desire for the exterior a simple Colonial house, and for the interior a complex contemporary arrangement of rooms which is directly contrary to the straightforward Colonial simplicity. And then he wonders why his architect, in striving to meet both demands, creates a result that satisfies neither. If every educated man and woman in the country truly realized the absolute interdependence of planning and exterior design, there would at once develop a sane tradition of popular criticism of architecture—a development that would raise our architectural standards more than any other one thing.

This interdependence of planning and design is equally important in the interiors, and perhaps more so, for there even more strongly the arrangement not only suggests but actually creates interior effect. This has already been referred to at some length, but it cannot be stated too often or too strongly. Our country has been filled with houses that are mean and gaudy within, just because the designer has attempted to produce effects his plan contradicted; he has made elaborate doors lead only to narrow and congested halls, or he has treated tiny rooms with miniature columns and entablatures all complete, thinking thereby to gain an effect of grandeur.

The good architect, on the other hand, will not try to force effects his plan does not warrant, nor will a client, if he is wise, attempt to make him do so. The architect will always keep in mind the interior effect he wishes to produce, be it grand or modest, and he will make his plan with this idea clearly before him. He will see that the effect is suitable to the purpose of the room, and will not attempt to give us living rooms like the state reception rooms of an eighteenth-century palace, or dining rooms too coldly monumental, or churches like barns, or great public halls that are bare and undignified. He will plan always to give an interior effect that is absolutely in harmony with the use of the interior, with the plan, and with the exterior.

It should be evident by this time how infinitely complex is the science of planning. It is like some of those mathematical problems which algebra cannot solve because there are too many variables, problems that yield only to calculus. In the case of planning the variables are four: practicability, constructional demands, exterior effect, and interior effect. And they ought all to be always in the architect's mind at once—not at one point one of them, at another point another—for every smallest detail of a plan must be considered from all four standpoints. And it is this fourfold attitude that the good architect always adopts.

Architectural planning is thus by no means the uninteresting and abstruse matter that it is usually considered, without importance save as a humdrum matter of convenience. On the contrary, it is at the very foundation of all good architecture; for the plan determines the character of the building outside and in, and it is good planning, as well as good design, which has made, and still makes, the great buildings of the world not only suitable for their purpose but also beautiful for our eyes, and strong to endure. The art of architecture, when founded on great planning, is the greatest, the widest, and the most practical and useful of all the arts.

4

FORM IN
ARCHITECTURE

THERE IS no greater obstacle to the appreciation of architecture than the fog of criticism that hangs all about it. The architects themselves are largely to blame for this. Forced into close contact with its infinite complexity, they have been so occupied with questions of style and of structure that their minds have become obsessed with these, to the almost complete neglect of the broad, basic criteria of criticism which underlie all styles and all methods of construction. The critics have in general followed in their steps. There are histories of architecture galore, and books and lectures supporting this, that, or the other point of view; but the amount of serious and simple architectural criticism has been small indeed. Conditions have improved little even in this critical and self-consciously discriminating day. A few books have striven to pierce the fog and show the real values of a building, but in too many cases an attempt at broadmindedness has led to an almost complete lack of discrimination. The popular magazines devoted to building and landscape gardening too often murmur, through an intellectual vacuum, of the charm of this or the charm of that, and beautiful photographs strive in vain to take the place of real criticism in telling the reader what is good and bad in architecture.

For there is a good and bad in architecture as in all the arts. Popular taste may wax and wane; it has demanded Gothic arches and Greek columns, and now it demands new and creative forms; but beneath all this change there is a substratum of what seems to be universal law. Architecture, as an art of form and color, can as surely be criticized according to the approved criteria of form and color as any of its sister arts, and it is on these laws that all criticism of architecture must be based.

It is not our purpose to go into the origin of these criteria. That is the concern of the psychologist and the philosopher. Whatever may be their basis, the fact remains that certain qualities seem to be possessed by all works of painting or sculpture or architecture which the consensus of opinion of mankind has judged beautiful. Not only are these qualities and the "laws" derived from them deducible in painting and sculpture and architecture (the arts of form and color), but the working of the same laws, or laws closely analogous to them, can also be found in the arts of sound—in good literature and good music. They seem to be general rules, in accordance with which a man's mind always works when he strives to create something which shall have that quality which makes it pleasing to his senses—the quality of beauty—or when he tries to think about that which has appealed to him as beautiful.

The first of these laws is so universal and so important that compliance with it has often been recognized as the sole necessity of beauty. Pythagoras and Aristotle voiced it in Greece over two thousand years ago, and almost every philosopher since has recorded it and restated it when dealing with the subject of beauty. Beauty, according to these authorities, is a characteristic of any object, itself composed of varied elements, which produces a *unity* of effects upon the sensations of the beholder. It sounds simple enough, this formula, but as it is examined its meaning will become so full, and so far-reaching, that the simplicity of the phrasing will seem deceptive. Even so, this definition covers only a small part of the whole field of what men call beautiful; it neglects the entire emotional and associative value of beauty. It considers beauty merely as an external quality, as a matter purely of the senses rather than of the emotions. Allowing for the one-sidedness of this definition, however, it will still be necessary to discover its meaning and its application to architecture, particularly as we are dealing in this chapter with architecture purely as form.

What is unity? Unity is the quality of an object by which it appears as definitely and organically one single thing. It is possessed by any building that at once strikes the beholder as a single composition. No matter how complex the parts of a building may be, or how large the whole, if the parts take their place at once as component portions of the whole, the building is unified and is thus far a good building. As an example of a complex yet unified building, take the United States Capitol at Washington (Plate VIII). The Capitol was built at several different periods, with several distinct parts—the two end wings, the central block, the portions that connect them, and the dome—and with each part itself composed of many varied elements—columns, windows, doors, pediments, balustrades. Each of these, in turn, might be analyzed into its own several elements, moldings, spots of brightness and shadow, carved ornament, until the building is seen to be composed of thousands of pieces of carved or cut stone, and myriad openings through the stone, each stone and each opening contributing its own special note of dark or light to the whole. Nevertheless, in spite of all this complexity, this enormous number of differing parts, when the whole is seen there is no sense of confusion, or multiplicity, and the great dome above seems to bind the whole into one mighty composition. The skill of the architects who worked successively on the building—Thornton, Hallet, Latrobe, Bulfinch, Walter—has been equal in each case to the task. By keeping the main lines simple, and by judicious repetition of the main motifs—pediments, colonnades, and steps—these architects have succeeded in making a unity out of complexity and so have produced a building that fulfills perfectly the first and perhaps most important requirement of beauty. It is a living expression in stone of our country's motto, *E pluribus unum*.

And yet how easy it is to lose this unity! In New York stands a lavish building whose twenty-four-story height is surrounded by a stone façade of eight stages of Ionic colonnades—three stories to each stage. Forget, for the moment, the manifest deception in such a treatment, and its denial of steel structure and office function. Consider it only for its unity or lack of it. Let us grant that the material is rich, the execution perfect, the ornament graceful despite its archaeological origin. Let us grant that the Ionic columns and their entablatures are in themselves beautiful, studied, and refined. It might seem that this continued repetition would create unity, but in reality how different is the case! Far from producing unity, this repetition of the same order, stage over stage, produces only an ostentatious and monotonous confusion, and the building—sawn into pieces by the cornices that cut across it every three stories—appears not one but several buildings, piled interminably upon each other. Accordingly, all other things aside, however costly its materials and delicate its details, this building through its lack of unity fails of beauty. The failure in this case is made all the more evident by the contrast presented by the lovely simplicity of the neighboring Colonial St. Paul's Chapel, where the simple lines, dignified colonnade, and graceful spire create a unified harmony.

FIGURE 9. NATIONAL GALLERY, LONDON

A building that is unimpressive despite its great length because of over-complexity and insufficient climax.

As an even better example of the loss of unity and its disastrous results, take a still simpler structure, the National Gallery in London (Figure 9). This building is particularly suited for comparison with the Capitol at Washington, because it uses so many of the same motifs—domes, columns, and a pediment. Indeed, it has fewer motifs and simpler elements. In place of the many windows of the other building, it has long stretches of cut-stone wall, one of the strongest and most dignified forms that can be used in architecture. Yet, even with this simple and dignified series of forms at his disposal, the architect has failed to give unity to the building. In place of the great dome of our national Capitol there is a small excrescence above the main entrance, a dome so small in size and so puny in design that it becomes not the building's crowning glory but rather an ugly superfluity, a useless appendage, which, instead of binding the whole building together by its compelling grandeur, seems only to add to the confusion. The same lack of unity, the same indecision, appears in the whole front. Standing as it does at the head of Trafalgar Square, one of the most important sites in London, this building should have a magnificent dignity. In reality, its central eight-columned portico is small and meager in effect, and its pediment above too low; like the dome, it completely fails to center one's interest, or even adequately to suggest the purpose for which it was built. On either side of its ineffective columns the design is still worse; there is a stretch of wall, and then a sudden ornamented projection with columns and cornice, as if the wall were to end here in this strongly marked end pavilion. But no, it stretches on beyond, to fade away in another pavilion similar to the first but much weaker, and still farther on it appears once more in a third and final pavilion, the weakest of all, the indecisive close of an indecisive building. Despite the simplicity of its motifs, the building is a hodgepodge—wall, pavilion, wall, pavilion, ineffective and meager entrance, puny and insufficient dome. Because of its lack of unity, this home of one of the world's greatest art collections is a building that laymen pass by without a second glance and architects think of with scorn.

All these buildings, good and bad, have a certain amount of complexity, and they must have this complexity, not only for practical but for aesthetic reasons as well. Absolute unity, were such a thing possible, might excite wonder, amazement, awe, but never that intimate pleasure that is one of the signs of beauty. For instance, let the reader think of that monument of prehistoric effort, Stonehenge. If it is beautiful, it is beautiful only in so far as it has complexity. Where the lintel stones remain in place, the result is more beautiful than where only the upright piers are left; where several of these stand side by side, in some semblance of order, the result is more beautiful than where one is left upright, alone, forbidding. And the variety of the plan—circle within circle, altar stone and approach avenue—these complexities are of the very essence of its beauty. The simplest obelisk is beautiful, not because of its simplicity, but because of the subtle relationships between the several parts of it—the width at the base, the width near the top, the slope of the sides, the relations between the height of the pyramidal part at the top and the part below. There is great complexity of form in an obelisk, simple as it appears, and complexity in aesthetic discussion always refers to complexity of form and not of function or number. Let the reader try to imagine something totally without complexity, as large or small as he pleases. It is impossible; on the one side is the geometric point—a pure abstraction—and on the other infinity, equally an abstraction. The nearest approach to such a concept possible to the human imagination is conceivably a huge colorless sphere hanging in nothingness. Surely that would not excite in one the pleasurable warmth of beauty. The feelings at such a vision might be feelings of terror, of awe, of wonder, perhaps even of religious reverence, rather than of beauty.

Unity and variety, then, are both necessary to beauty, in architecture as in everything else. Variety is a practical essential in architecture; the architect need not be concerned over that. A host of requirements necessitates windows, doors, chimneys, porches, roofs. The disposition of the rooms and the several parts of even the simplest building requires projections or variations of the exterior. Even in tombs or commemorative monuments inscriptions and ornament necessitate a certain complexity. It is impossible, therefore, for any architect to design a building without variety. His greatest aesthetic problem is the binding of all the various units into a single work, the correlating of all, so that each shall perform its required aesthetic service, so that each shall bear its proper relationship to every other element and to the whole work. How, then, may he do this?

The best way to answer this question, so important to one who attempts to appreciate architecture, as well as to the designer, is to find out the dominant qualities that are common to all beautiful and unified buildings. This has often been done, and the results have been so uniform that they have been codified into laws, or, perhaps more correctly, rules of artistic composition. Once these are understood and applied, sound criticism of architecture as pure form is the inevitable result; it is necessary, therefore, that they be carefully considered. The rules of composition applicable to architecture, in brief, are balance, rhythm, good proportion, climax, harmony, and functional expression of both purpose and structure. It is a strange fact that, except for the last one, functional expression, which belongs peculiarly to architecture, these laws are the same as those which govern the other arts; on them one might base valid criticism of literature, of music, or of painting. But it is their application to architecture which is of primary importance to us here. Let us examine them by applying them to buildings.

The first aesthetic law, the law of *balance*, may be stated as follows: Every building should be so composed that the parts of it on either side of an imaginary line, expressed in some manner in the design, shall be of apparently equal weight. The basis for the beauty inherent in balance is both physiological and associative. In a balanced building the observant eye, traveling over the surface, finds its path easily, from one side to the other, and always back to the center of balance; there is no eye strain, no frustrated eye wandering. The resultant sense of visual balance is associated almost unconsciously with the sense of physical balance; a pleasant feeling of reposeful equilibrium inevitably arises.

Since the simplest application of this law may be seen in symmetrical buildings, it will be well to consider these first and leave the more difficult applications in so-called picturesque and non-symmetrical buildings till later. Symmetry—the exact correspondence of the two halves of a building—can exist only when a building is in perfect balance. This is self-evident, but it is not all. Symmetrical buildings may themselves be divided into classes, corresponding to several different schemes of design, each of them more or less complex. The simpler schemes are the more universally successful; it becomes increasingly difficult to manage the whole composition as motifs are added, for the increasing complexity makes it difficult for the eye to seize at once the inherent balance, which is such a large element in the beauty of the whole.

The simplest of these symmetrical masses, of course, is the plain rectangular front, with or without a gable. Such a front may be seen in any Greek temple—the Parthenon, for example, or the temple of Theseus at Athens (Plate IX). The latter is chosen for illustration because in mass, at least, it exists in nearly its original form. The front of this temple consists simply of a row of six columns, crowned with a low gable—a pediment. The symmetry is perfect, and hence the balance; the axis of balance, the pivot, as it were, is just sufficiently expressed by the peak of the gable above and the door below. The Greek architect, by a slight upcurving in the lines of the steps on which the columns stand, by the almost invisible sloping inward of the columns, and by the subtle narrowing of the spaces between the corner columns and those next to them, has done everything to emphasize this balance. The whole accordingly is reposeful, satisfying, and beautiful.

A second scheme, a shade more complex, consists of a simple rectangular form—in the middle, usually, but not always—long and low in effect, with a smaller but strongly accented form at each end. It is seen to perfection in the post office on Eighth Avenue in New York, designed by McKim, Mead & White—a long open colonnade, stopped at each end against a projecting feature or pavilion of heavy masonry. In a slightly more subtle form the same scheme is seen in the Palazzo Vendramini at Venice (Plate IX). In this case the end pavilions are treated exactly like the portions between them, with the exception of the coupling of the columns on either side of the end windows, and the flat wall that shows between these coupled columns. These little changes at the ends of the building give it at once a dignity and a distinction that it could never have had if the end bays had been the same as those between. Without this additional weight at the corners the building would have had an undistinguished, indecisive air. There would always have been the feeling that there was no reason for the building to end where it did, that it might just as well have been two or four or six windows larger. The same thing is true of the New York Post Office; a colonnade of that length without strong end pavilions to stop it would have been disastrously amorphous, beginning nowhere, ending nowhere.

The aesthetic value of these end features in a large and complex building can be seen in the apparent weakness of so many modern

American loft buildings, especially when they are designed to produce monumental effects quite without relation to their actual use
and their actual structure. Symmetry they may have, but demand for
light and show window space has reduced the walls to mere piers
of terra cotta or brick; economy in the use of steel necessitates the
regular spacing of these piers, so that all too many such structures
seem mere unfinished shells—slices of building, as it were, sawed in
sections out of some huge composition and dumped hit or miss in
our streets.

There are dangers too, however, in the use of end pavilions. The
main danger is that they may become too large for the whole, large
enough to distract the attention from the central portion of the
building, and yet not large enough to be the main features of the
design, as they are in Notre Dame in Paris (Figure 10), or the
Cathedral of Cologne, or St. Patrick's Cathedral in New York,
designed ninety years ago by Renwick and Sands. This is a fault that
spoils great numbers of American churches; the towers, which ought
to dominate, have been reduced and spread apart, with a mediocre
porch between, so that the final result is confusion—three units of
equal aesthetic weight crowded together, all fighting for the observer's attention.

This scheme of tripartite symmetry is closely allied to the next
scheme, also of three units. In this scheme the central unit is much
more strongly emphasized; it is usually higher and broader than the
rest of the building, so that the effect, instead of being that of a unit
repeated several times in the middle, and stopped at the ends by
heavier units, is that of a strong unit in the middle, with weaker
elements at each side. The effect of the two schemes might be compared to two families out walking; in the first the father and mother
walk on opposite sides of the road, with all the children hand in hand
between them, and in the second the father is alone in the middle,
with a child or two on either side of him.

This last scheme is a favorite one for the smaller types of formal
building. It is illustrated by many Colonial houses, such as the
Craigie (Longfellow) house in Cambridge, Massachusetts, and by
endless small libraries, where the dominant central portion suggests

the welcome of the entrance, and the less dominant portions on either side the various rooms to which the entrance leads. The United States Forest Products Laboratory, at Madison, Wisconsin, by Holabird & Root, is an example of the same treatment applied to a large modern building. In this scheme the danger is that the side portions will become unduly important, through size or decorative treatment, so that the effect of the center is lost and confusion results.

A fourth symmetrical scheme is well illustrated by the United States Capitol (Plate VIII). It consists of a main central portion, subsidiary connecting links, and at the ends strongly marked pavilions. It might almost be considered a combination of the two foregoing types. It is the most monumental of all, and constitutes perhaps the most successful manner of treating large and important formal buildings. Hundreds of examples suggest themselves—the colonnade of the Louvre, the lovely City Hall in New York, many of our best state capitols, and, on a smaller

FIGURE 10. NOTRE DAME, PARIS

A façade of great power because of its perfect balance and the beautiful relationship of its parts.

scale, many of the great monumental mansions of eighteenth-century England. Here again the central portion, to be successful, must be strongly dominant. If the end portions become equal to the center in apparent weight, the eye will be tempted to fix on any of the three as the important feature of the building, will strive to fix the axis of balance at the end instead of in the center, and confusion will result.

The reader will notice that in the successful examples of every scheme, except perhaps the second, the axis of balance is strongly accented by the dominant central portion. In the case of the second scheme, illustrated by the New York Post Office and the Vendramini Palace (Plate IX), or by St. Patrick's Cathedral, the ends are heavily and equally weighted, and consequently so strong is the sense of balance that the axis of balance need not be so heavily stressed. Yet even in this second scheme some little accent in the center is desirable; in the Vendramini Palace, for instance, it is given by the door. The longer the central bar in this second scheme, the more definite becomes the need for this accent to prevent the eye from wandering.

All the best symmetrical buildings can be grouped under one of these four heads. The moment a building becomes so complex that its motifs will not fall into any of these four groupings—in other words, when the system of the building divides into more than five distinct motifs—the probabilities are all against its being a success. There is a limit to what the human eye can perceive and the human mind apprehend in a moment, and the basic composition of a beautiful building must stand forth as beautiful on the most cursory ob-

FIGURE 11. CHARTRES
CATHEDRAL

An excellent example of balance achieved by dissimilar towers carefully related.

servation. This accounts for the ineffectiveness of the National Gallery in London; its system of walls and triple end pavilions is too complex to be grasped at first glance. To avoid confusion, the main divisions of any building must not be so many in number as to make it difficult instantly to understand their system.

It is a more difficult matter to understand the application of the law of balance to non-symmetrical buildings. At first sight a non-symmetrical building may appear to be out of balance, yet beauty cannot be denied it. What a tiresome place this earth would be if every building in it were absolutely symmetrical! We should lose Chartres Cathedral (Figure 11), for instance, and Amiens, and most of the early French Renaissance châteaux, as well as countless lovely modern houses and country churches and myriad other buildings—and to be denied all those buildings gifted with that free and appealing charm which we term "the picturesque," where the lack of symmetry is the direct and logical result of an efficient plan, would be an unimaginable loss.

The simplest class of non-symmetrical buildings is that in which the axis is very clearly felt, in which there exists a kind of free, though not absolute, symmetry. Chartres and Amiens are examples. In both the lack of symmetry is in certain details, rather than in scheme. If well carried out this scheme is always successful, but balance and beauty result only when the mass of the two unsymmetrical parts is kept almost the same. For instance, in Chartres Cathedral, one of the most beautiful buildings of this type, balance is preserved and beauty made certain by the fact that the greater sturdiness and solidity of the older tower on the right is compensated for by the added height of the lighter, more airy tower. The present aspect of the front of Rouen Cathedral, on the other hand, shows the unfortunate effect of this quasi symmetry when wrongly handled. Whatever is thought of the glorious doorways and the lacy late Gothic openwork all over the central portion, it is certainly true that as a whole the front is not perfectly beautiful, for the heavy mass of the famous "butter tower" on one side, with nothing adequate as a counterweight on the other side of a front otherwise symmetrical, throws the whole out of balance and consequently produces a strong feeling of dissatisfaction, of restlessness, whenever the whole is considered as one single work of art rather than as a combination of exquisite details.

In these cases of non-symmetrical but nearly symmetrical buildings, the balance is obvious, but in the more complicated "picturesque" buildings the problem becomes more difficult. It is impossible to codify these "picturesque" buildings as most symmetrical buildings have been codified; they are too different from one another, and the possible schemes of design are infinite. Yet it is absolutely essential that every beautiful building have balance, whether the structure is symmetrical or not.

The question of balance in non-symmetrical buildings is especially important today, for the last three decades have witnessed a widespread trend toward informal, non-symmetrical design, even for public buildings. This has already been mentioned in connection with formal and informal plans. The average architect of thirty years ago in America or Europe would naturally think in terms of formal arrangements; he would make a building symmetrical unless there were compelling reasons to do otherwise. Today the position is reversed, and the best architects would tend to design an unsymmetrical building unless the conditions of the plan problem or the site made symmetry logically inevitable. Therefore the subtle balance existing in good non-symmetrical structures demands study, and if one is to appreciate the beauty of much that is being built today he must understand something about this complex problem.

A   B

FIGURE 12. A SMALL LIBRARY: ALTERNATE ELEVATIONS

Elevation A shows balance between dissimilar elements by the correct placing of the center of balance and its accenting by means of flag pole, door, and porch. Elevation B, with the door moved away from the natural center of balance, shows the restless diffusion of interest and the unpleasant and clashing duality which result from lack of balance.

The best that can be done is to indicate and to illustrate a few of the basic principles that govern balance in these informal buildings. First, the axis of balance must be expressed in some way, by a door, a balcony, a porch, or some other interesting feature. This, perhaps, is the most important point of all. If the axis of balance is so expressed, the eye will be drawn to it at once and, resting on it, will feel that the masses on each side of it are approximately equal. A sense of repose results at once, and consequently the building appears beautiful.

Let us take an example: the front, shall we say, of a small library building (Figure 12). In this case (A) the porch, with its interest of step and door and richer material, attracts the eye at once; when the eye comes to rest there, the mass of building on either side seems equal, and balance is the result. The narrower, projecting mass of the left wing balances the longer, simpler arm of the building with its greater leverage. Then notice the awkward, unbalanced result (B) if the door is shifted far out on the arm at the right. The eye is still attracted first to the porch, but now it finds a long mass of building to the left and an obviously puny portion to the right, with only sky beyond. The balance is lost, and no exquisiteness of detail or proportion can conceal the error in basic composition.

Of course this is an extremely simple case; it is given merely as a hint to stimulate further observation. In reality the architect must keep in mind not only the front but the sides and the rear as well. He must imagine the building as it appears to a person walking all around it, with reference to all existing trees, or slopes of ground, or shrubs near by. From every possible view a really good building must have balance, and this accounts for the comparative failure of some of our informal American country houses. They seem manifestly designed to be viewed from only one point, or two; from these points they are good, perfect in balance and composition, but from other points the same buildings are a mere hodgepodge and lack that little accent on the center of balance given by a chimney or window group, a porch slab or balcony, or some similar element of interest, which would have made the whole seem balanced and in repose. That is why the architect as a rule is so suspicious of the "built picturesque," that is, a building where the informality is forced and unnatural; on one side it is likely to be in almost too studied a balance, on another a mere confusion of changing line and restless mass.

There are a few points about the balancing of masses that it is well to make clear. First, there is in this matter an artistic analogy to the law of leverage. That is, a heavy member close to that interesting feature which expresses the center of balance—the pivot, as it were—will counterbalance and be balanced by a long, low, lighter member farther from that point. Second, the shapes and positions of the masses themselves affect the balance. For example, a member that projects always seems heavier than a receding member. That is, in a building of the L type, with one arm longer than the other, the best place for the center of interest is on the long side near the angle, for then the projecting wing, nearer the eye, seems heavier than the rest, and requires a longer portion to balance it. A high mass usually appears proportionately heavier than a low mass. Dudok's city hall in Hilversum, Holland, is a superb example of informal balance (see Plate X). Note how the tower acts to hold all the complex forms together, and how the boldly projecting slab over the entrance leads the attention to the wide, welcoming doorway.

But the question of architectural balance is more complex than any consideration of mere mass. There is balance of interest as well. A highly ornamented spot will draw the attention more than a plain area. Sudden changes of linear direction, especially where continuous horizontal lines are received against verticals (as can be seen in many of the department stores of Eric Mendelsohn), also are attention-compelling (see Plate X). And there is, moreover, an interest of function to consider, as shown for instance in the fact that a door will attract more interest than a window of the same size, because it suggests motion in and out—it is "inviting." Piers or columns apparently carrying heavy weights, if rightly designed, are more impressive than those carrying little or none. Rooms, terraces, or porches for social living and dining are more interesting than service areas; rooms or areas for public, religious, or recreational use are more interesting than those devoted solely to commerce or individual advantage. Finally, there is balance of line—of curve against curve, of vertical against horizontal. The balance of curved lines reacting on each other lies behind the exciting beauty of much Baroque architecture; that of vertical against horizontal distinguishes the work of many contemporary architects. Out of such complexities the architect seeks perfect three-dimensional balance. And there is one more consideration in the balance of nonsymmetrical buildings: their composition must be, and should appear, *reasonable*; their balance should be achieved in reasonable ways. The merely erratic, the romantically picturesque, however cleverly balanced by artificial tricks or false emphases, soon cloys.

The second great aesthetic law, the law of *rhythm*, may be stated thus: Every beautiful building should be so composed that its units shall bear some rhythmic relation to one another. The term "rhythm" is applied to architecture in a very broad sense. In most cases there does not exist through a building any set repetition of groups of the same form without a break. There are exceptions, such as the Colosseum in Rome (Plate II), where the continued repetition of the same rhythmical form, the same *measure* almost, consisting of the broad, dark mass of the arch, with the smaller, lighter mass of masonry between, broken by the projecting engaged columns, gives a tremendous and overwhelming dignity. In the interior of a Gothic cathedral, Amiens for instance (see Plate XXIII), there is the same dignity produced by the repetition of a rhythmical measure of the same sort, broad arch and narrow pier, only in this case the unit is in three tiers, and each tier varies in rhythmical structure from the others. First, low down, there is the broad arch that leads from nave to side aisle. Above this is a narrow band of arcading, the triforium gallery; and above that the great clerestory window, which in vertical divisions corresponds with the triforium but dominates because of its richness. Each of these complex units is repeated the whole length of the nave, and in the wonderful rhythmical effect that results lies one reason for the poetry of the whole.

This matter of rhythm is one of the features in which certain persons have tried to find an absolute analogy between architecture and music, but this is an analogy that must not be pushed too far or too seriously. Architecture is analogous to music, but the analogy is in "the intellectual vagueness, the emotional certainty" of both arts, as J. A. Symonds put it, and in the abstract character of the forms used, rather than in any mere tricks of technique or any hidden and mystical twinship of form.

To try to find musical analogies to architectural forms is amusing and stimulating, but to overdo it, to try to distinguish actual chords and pitches and complex musical rhythms in architecture, so that a symphony might be built, or St. Peter's played, that is an absurdity and jeopardizes the particular charm of both arts. No, architecture has been called "frozen music" not because there are scales and chords and measures and rests in great buildings, but because both arts strive to obtain emotional effects of the same sort—that is, emotional effects of the graver, deeper, vaguer, less distinctly discriminated, and more sublime sorts—by means which are abstract, which exist by reason of their own virtue, and in which representation of actual sights and sounds bears but a secondary place.

Furthermore, if we are to look for an accurate analogy to most architectural rhythm, we shall find it in the rhythm of good prose rather than in that of music. Architecture has more the rhythm of a Gregorian chant, or of plainsong, than of a Beethoven symphony; it has more the rhythm of the flowing English of Whitman than of the poetry of Burns or Keats. This is a point that must be insisted on, because, if an attempt is made to find in every beautiful building the absolute metrical scheme of music or poetry, disappointment can be the only result. For an analogy to help in the better understanding of rhythm in architecture, therefore, we must turn to prose. Take such an essay as Pater's "Giorgione," for instance, or a page from Henry James's *The Golden Bowl*. When a sentence from either is read aloud, it falls naturally into groups of syllables, phrases, and clauses, freely balancing each other, each leading gracefully into the next, the whole effect rising in waves of sound into climaxes, or melting softly into rests. The rhythm of a good building is much the same, except that in place of syllables we have all the play of light and shadow and color over its various surfaces and openings. As the sentence divides itself into freely balancing phrases and clauses, so the building divides itself into freely balancing units—porches, doors, projecting wings, or sometimes even the mere pleasing alternation of window and wall. As in the sentence the phrases lead gradually and gracefully from one to another, so the units of the good building lead one to another. As the sentence has its climaxes and its rests, so the lights and darks of a building surge into climaxes and soften into quiet. The Capitol at Washington (Plate VIII) might be considered a building with three climaxes—the three great porticoes—and two rests, the simpler wings between them. The White

House has at each end a simple element of wall and window that changes in the middle to a climax produced by the insistent alternation of light and dark in the strongly projecting colonnade in the center.

But this is not the whole point. All the different phrases, or units, into which a building seems to separate, may themselves be strongly rhythmical. So the repeated alternation of light and dark in colonnades is rhythmic; so, too, is any repeated change of wall and window. The ornamental details of a building usually have the most strongly felt, the most strictly metrical rhythm of all. The reason the cornice with brackets has always been so popular lies in the fact that the strong rhythmic repetition, over and over again, of the light brackets and the shadows between binds together into one whole all the looser rhythms of the building it crowns, as the insistent bass of a Spanish dance binds together its flowing melodies. For the same reason, in a complex building of varied rhythm unity is produced by the repetition here and there of units with strong rhythmical character—for example, groups of windows spaced equally, or colonnades of the same number of columns, or sometimes merely bands of repeated ornament—with the result that the eye everywhere glimpses some element that sets, as it were, one rhythmic tone for the whole building.

Vertical rhythms, or rhythms of height, are important also. They can be created by horizontal cornices, bands of windows, breaks in the outline, or setbacks and are of peculiar importance in towers and high buildings. These rhythms are often repetitions of units varying from each other by some easily recognizable difference in size, rather than exact repetitions—as, for example, in the distance between the setbacks of a high building, or in the height of each, which may increase or decrease as they rise. These are progressive rather than regular rhythms. The beauty, or lack of it, in many modern city buildings is often caused by rhythm, or lack of it, in setback design. The Daily News Building in New York, by Howells and Hood (Plate III), well illustrates the beauty of such progressive rhythms. Many ordinary loft and office buildings are ugly just because rhythm has been neglected in their design; a sheer wall is car-

ried up on the front as high as the law allows, then follow a series of
equal setbacks of one or two stories each, brought out to the very
limit of permissible volume, and out of these suddenly rises a vertical
tower covering the largest permissible area of the lot. There is no
rhythm in such a design, no unifying pattern tying together the three
separate parts; nor can any surface treatment of any kind, however
rich or careful, cure this underlying fault. Such a building, designed
not by creative imagination but by the mere vagaries of a building
code, is scarcely architecture at all.

The rhythmical tastes of different architectural periods have varied
enormously, just as they have in music. Some have been distinguished
by a desire for definitely regular, simple, light rhythms, like those in
Greek temples and Greek ornament. Some, like the Italian Renaissance, have created architectural rhythms of strongly stressed regular-
ity; the buildings have a simple rhythmical majesty arising from this
definite repetition of motifs—windows, pilasters, or arcades. Palladio's basilica at Vicenza is an excellent example; both vertically and
horizontally its rhythmical repetitions are superb. The Baroque, on
the other hand, sought for freer patterns of rhythm, loved the strongest contrasts, liked to build up from simplicity to almost turbulent
climaxes of architecture and sculpture at doors or climax points.
Rococo rhythms are quieter again but infinitely varied; there is an
almost Mozartean quality in the best Louis XV or Bavarian rococo
interiors.

Today in music we take delight in rhythms of great complexity—
free, often syncopated, but definite. And good modern painting and
architecture often have rhythmical complexities of a not too dissimilar type. The pictures of the late Dutch painter Mondrian illustrate this; his abstract patterns of verticals and horizontals are full
of a subtle rhythm—progressions from small to large or from large
to small, staccato notes of bright color, quieter portions almost
monotonous. The best buildings of today frequently have a similar
kind of free, abstract rhythm. There are often areas of quiet wall—
long bands of glass, broken by rhythmical sash bars—then the strong
staccato note of a tall glass stair window. The buildings of Eric
Mendelsohn and of Dudok are particularly brilliant in their subtle

handling of these modern rhythms; long, repeated horizontals are received against strong verticals, or there is a free play of shadows made by projecting porches and window hoods which creates an all-over rhythmic pattern (see Plate X). Mies Van der Rohe's rhythms are more suave and flowing but equally definite, and it is a winning and beautiful rhythmic simplicity which distinguishes the work of Frank Lloyd Wright.

Rhythm, as repetition, is destined to become more and more a characteristic of modern buildings, as prefabricated units come into greater use. These, like the common, inexpensive, stock wood and steel windows of today, will necessarily be based on standard dimensions, and buildings will show in a more and more obvious way the repetition of these motifs and these sizes. But rhythms too unbroken can become merely boring or, if too long continued, actually harassing, as anyone who sits too long at a radio can testify. Prefabrication, of itself, therefore, will be no guarantee of beauty in buildings, even beauty of rhythm; it will still be the task of the designer and the architect to take these rhythmical units, to compose them, to vary them, to make of them a whole structure which shall be a thing of beauty. Like all the conditioning of modern industrialism, these rhythmical building units of the present and the future are an opportunity for new beauty, not a guarantee of it.

Architecture is a three-dimensional art. In plans, therefore, there is a rhythm, just as there is in the external aspect of buildings. One not only looks at a building from the outside; he also walks through it, lives in it, works in it. And, as one walks through any structure, the changing visual pattern of what he observes will be determined, as we have seen, by the plan. A series of posts or columns that is rhythmical in *plan* will appear to him as a rhythmical repetition of the post or column in *time*; often he cannot see all the piers at once, but as he walks down the nave of a Gothic cathedral, for instance, the time repetition of pier, arch, pier, arch, becomes one of the most striking of his artistic experiences. That is why no photograph can ever do justice to a building; outside or in, an actual building can be thoroughly understood or appreciated only by a continued progress— toward it, away from it, through it. . . . And the quality of this experience is the result of the *plan*, more than of anything else. Hence the necessity of careful rhythmical design in planning.

Examples should suggest themselves immediately—a colonnade through which one walks, like the oval colonnades Bernini curved around the piazza of St. Peter's, with the columns flashing rhythmically by as one walks; or the repeated fireproofed steel columns in the lobby of the central building in Rockefeller Center; or the forty-eight great wooden posts forming the gorgeously impressive central structure of the United States Government Building at the San Francisco Fair of 1939-40. But these are all equal rhythms; good planning, especially the planning of the Egyptians, the Romans, the Baroque designers, and our best architects today, makes use also of progressive, or unequal, rhythms.

In the typical Egyptian temple plan there is a continual progress from large to small, from high to low, from light to dark—pylon, court, hypostyle hall, smaller halls, and finally the small holy-of-holies, the climax shrine. Roman and Baroque designers preferred the progress from small to large, and complicated and enriched the experience by alternations: small vestibule, larger foyer, perhaps a narrow arch leading to a long hall, then a smaller anteroom, and finally the great hall—throne room, library, or salon—to which the whole series of sequences leads. It is this alternation in size, in richness, in dark and light, coupled with the definite progression, which creates the powerful dramatic effects which the Baroque period so loved. In the Nebraska state capitol (Figure 6; Plate V) there is a somewhat similar use of alternating progressive rhythms—arched porch, simple door, shallow vestibule, domed lobby, long vaulted corridor, the arched and vaulted areas surrounding the rotunda, then the breadth and height and rich color of the rotunda as the climax. Rhythms more subtle but equally strong, fascinating in their change and balance, governed the placing of glittering metal supports and rich marble screen walls in Mies Van der Rohe's German Building of the Barcelona Exposition of 1928 (Plate XII). Frank Lloyd Wright's houses, in plan as in exterior and interior aspect, are full of dominant rhythms and rhythmical changes, both regular and progressive.

Let the reader, then, as he goes about his daily tasks or his recreation, look for this quality in the buildings he enters. Too many of them, alas, are rhythmically amorphous, stupid, and either monotonous or a confusion. But in some he will become aware of rhythms in plan carefully and creatively designed; the building will seem alive, purposeful, pleasing; it is here that the architects have risen to their task, have taken advantage of the practical and structural necessities of the building program, and have created a work of living art.

Closely allied to this question of rhythm is the next great law of building beautifully, the law of *proportion*. According to this law, a beautiful building should be well proportioned. The apparent vagueness of the law will disappear as its terms are defined and amplified; it cannot be stated in more definite form here without becoming unduly long.

Good proportion, broadly speaking, is the quality possessed by any building the several parts of which are so related as to give a pleasing impression. It is primarily a quality of the relationship of all the units in a building, rather than a quality of the units themselves. Indeed, it might be truly stated that within certain very wide limits there can be in a single element of a building no such thing as good proportion beyond the natural dimensions for it dictated by common sense. For instance, in some cases a high, narrow window, like the great clerestory windows of Amiens, is in perfect proportion, but imagine the awkwardness of such a window in the basement story of a long, low building. It would look hopelessly out of proportion.

It has been claimed that a feeling of good proportion is produced when the parts of a building are in simple arithmetical ratios—like extreme and mean proportion (the "golden section"), or the ratio of two to three, or two to four—and with this in mind attempts have been made to codify arithmetically or geometrically what good proportion is. This idea was especially prevalent in the period of the later Renaissance and the Baroque. The French academicists were enamored of it; it became part of the official architectural doctrine of the Academie Royale d'Architecture under Louis XIV, and is set out at length in François Blondel's superb official textbook for the

academy, *Cours d'architecture*. To Blondel, the rules of good proportion in architecture were as fixed and invariable as the rules of harmony in music. He argued that, just as only precise exactitude of
string lengths can achieve the perfect musical chord, the slightest
deviation producing discord instead of harmony, so in architecture
only fixed, precise, and absolute arithmetical ratios can give perfect
architectural proportion. In the more realistic eighteenth century
many critics arose to combat this dogma, but there were also those
who continued to support it, and the controversy raged on till the
time of the French Revolution, producing some very quaint literature. Even today the idea still finds supporters; the doctrine of
"dynamic symmetry" rampant a few years ago is but a more complicated attempt at the same kind of approach.

Thus it has been claimed that the typical Gothic cathedral is
based on the equilateral triangle, that Greek temples were designed
according to complex geometric principles, that the height of the
best door is exactly twice its width, and so forth; but these things
can be considered true only to a limited extent. It is better to consider architectural proportion, as its name suggests, as the relationship between the diverse ratios of height and breadth, and so on, of
all the units of a building taken together, rather than as any innate
beauty in simple ratios themselves. The architect may have definite
ideas of ratio in his mental background, but the best design is always produced by the constant free adjustment of size and ratio in
the units of a building until the whole takes shape as a single, beautiful object, until "good proportion" is secured. Yet it is true that
sometimes the use of a basic module—some fixed linear dimension
—as a controlling unit in plan and elevation may simplify this
process. It is this larger side of the subject of proportion, this question of the relationship of various units, doors, windows, and the
like, to each other and to the whole, that the observer of architecture must keep in mind, rather than the ratios of the units themselves. In a good building each unit, however beautiful in itself, is
in reality only a part of the whole, and it is as such that it should
always be judged.

As we have noted in discussing rhythm, an increasing use of pre-

PLATE IX

Theseum, Athens

Vendramini Palace, Venice
Pietro Lombardi, architect

PLATE X

City Hall, Hilversum, Holland. W. M. Dudok, architect

From Wendingen

Schocken Store, Chemnitz. Eric Mendelsohn, architect

Museum of Modern Art

PLATE XI

Public Library, Boston. McKim, Mead & White, architects

Panthéon, Paris. J. J. Soufflot, architect

PLATE XII

Museum of Modern Art

German Pavilion, Barcelona Exposition
L. Mies Van der Rohe, architect

Author

Country House, Marin County, California
William W. Wurster, architect

fabricated units in building, as well as the development of structures entirely based on such units, will undoubtedly affect architecture profoundly. It will, for instance, make strict modular design almost a necessity, for each building will have to be in multiples of the standard prefabricated frame member or wall panel. As a result, these buildings will have a definiteness of proportion, a clarity, that is new. It is all the more important that the designers of these fabricated units see to it that the units themselves are beautiful in proportion.

A corollary of the principle of good proportion is the requirement of good scale. Scale, in architecture, is that quality by which the observer gains some conception of the actual size of a building or any of its parts. Good scale enables a structure to appear its true size almost at first glance. Bad or forced scale is that treatment which aims to make the whole appear larger, or smaller, than it really is; it is essentially a kind of architectural trickery. The normal size of a building is denoted in many ways, by general shape, by the number of units of which it is formed, and by similar elements of general composition, but it is still more definitely set by details that have a specific reference to human beings or human actions. Railings and balustrades, for instance, have normal heights that vary, say, between 2'–6'' and 3'–6'', depending on their use. People are used to these heights, and whenever they see such a feature on a building they instinctively grasp its size and, by an unconscious measuring of it against the height and breadth of the building, gain an idea of the size of the whole. If, however, the railing they see is not of the normal height, but only 1'–0'' or, at the other extreme, as it sometimes is in Italian Baroque buildings, 6'–0'' or 8'–0'' high, their whole judgment of the size of the structure is falsified; the building has false scale. When on further acquaintance the observer discovers the true size, he is likely to feel more disillusioned than amused, more tricked than surprised. The conscious use of false scale by occasional Baroque architects (the front of St. Peter's at Rome is an excellent example) is merely a sort of architectural joke, like the trick fountains they often erected in villa gardens.

Steps also are invaluable as scale indicators. The adult has climbed so many stairs in his life that he is hard to fool on the size of steps or stairs. It is for this reason, among others, that many architects like to have a strongly marked flight of steps at a building entrance. Other elements that give scale to buildings are sculpture, inscriptions, lamps, and the like; certain structural elements, like the height of stone courses, the size of bricks, and the width of brick joints, also help in the appreciation of size. Even larger structural elements enter in; so standardized have our modern city story heights and column spacings become, that we judge a structure's dimensions almost instinctively by them.

There are many types of scale, appropriate to many types of building. Heroic scale, for example, is that in which a building is made to seem as large or as impersonally or superpersonally imposing as possible; it is suited, of course, only to buildings for public use or for memorials and monuments. Intimate scale, on the other hand, seeks to minimize size, to relate everything to the individual as an individual; it is found in many houses and in some cafés, restaurants, and theaters. Yet it takes a sure hand to design consciously in heroic scale, or in intimate scale; too often the attempted heroic becomes the vulgar grandiose, like the front of the Grand Central Station in New York, and the attempted intimate becomes puny and picayune, like the Adam decoration of many hotels today. The true heroic and the true intimate in scale should flow normally from the conditions of the problem, without conscious trickery.

When proportion and scale are regarded in this larger light, it will at once be evident that they are closely related to the next great aesthetic consideration, the law that a building must be *harmonious* to be beautiful. Indeed, if harmony were merely a matter of proportional harmony, we might consider the subject already covered; but harmony in a building covers a wider field than the mere harmonious proportion of the various parts. There must be harmony of expression as well, and to a certain extent harmony of style. In a word, in a beautiful building, *not a single element must be so designed as to appear disturbingly distinct and alone and separate from the whole, for the moment this occurs unity is lost, and without unity there can be no beauty.* Harmony, then, is threefold, harmony of proportion, harmony of expression, and harmony of style.

By harmony of expression is meant a harmony of the apparent

forms of a building with its purpose or use as well as with its structural nature. For instance, in a building built for intimacy, privacy, or seclusion, such as a small country cottage, it would be manifestly silly to have an enormous and richly developed doorway to suggest the entrance or exit of large crowds of people. On the other hand, buildings to be used for congregations of people should have entrances large, inviting, and important. It is the one blot upon the beauty of many of the loveliest of the English cathedrals that, despite all their tremendous length and all their richness, their feeling of size and of spiritual invitation is contradicted by the forbidding impression given by the tiny doorways through which they are entered.

Harmony of form and structure is a more difficult and subtle matter. It is the quality that gives a building "honesty," as the romantic critics call it. It obviously produces only discord to attempt to clothe the slim, strong elegance of a modern steel structure in the massive forms of ancient masonry buildings, or to pile the weighty pyramids of Egypt or heavy Gothic buttresses upon the slenderness of steel columns. In such buildings the spirit of the two systems—the steel and its enclosure—is too different; however much the designer may try to hide the structure, its insistent rhythms will be apparent and will confound the result, will set glaringly evident to any sensitive eye the conflict between the underlying skeleton and the superficial clothing of unsuitable romantic costume. Yet how often the attempt is made! A walk on almost any city street will reveal a dozen examples—great stone piers, pilasters, engaged columns, or Gothic buttresses suddenly cut off and apparently resting with absurd insecurity upon sheets of plate glass. . . . Or what shall we say of the Yale University Library, with its vast bookstack tower, as massive looking as a medieval donjon or castle keep, held high in air by elaborate steel stilts, and its catalogue room like an English late Gothic church, all its catalogue cases and library machinery hidden as far as can be in the "side chapels"? What possible sentimental "atmosphere," what pseudo "charm," what possible lavishness of detail could ever compensate for such an utter disharmony of form with both use and structure?

By harmony of style is meant a harmony in the detailed shapes, the

ornament (if any), and the materials of a building. All must belong
to the same general category, and none be discordant with the others.
The simplest examples are to be found in the harmony resulting
from the use of details of but one historic "style" in buildings—the
harmony possessed inevitably by the French thirteenth-century
cathedrals, for instance, or the fifteenth-century rusticated palaces
of Florence. But harmony of style today transcends all questions of
authentic historical "styles"; stylistic purity is vastly different from
aesthetic harmony. That has been proved during the era of eclecticism which is rapidly passing. McKim, Mead, & White's Boston
Public Library (Plate XI) owes its reposeful beauty not to any historical style rigidly chosen and adhered to, but to the harmony of
feeling inherent in every line from the quiet expanse of the tile roof
to the strong, simple base. Each detail, each smallest molding, falls
happily into place, without strain.

This problem of harmony of style becomes daily more difficult.
The eclecticism of the last years of the nineteenth century and the
first decade of the twentieth has blunted our sense of fine discrimination, has buried our sensitiveness to the actual aesthetic meaning
of detail beneath a slag heap of too much half knowledge; it has
made us superficial. And now this half knowledge covers not only
past styles, Greek and Roman and Gothic and Renaissance and Chinese, but also all the varying so-called "modern" styles—the dynamic
lines of Mendelsohn, the richness and erratic over-charged detail of
the "modernistic" of the Paris 1925 exposition, the delicate and
decadent neo-Baroque of Vienna, and the stripped and stark as-
ceticism of the International Style of Gropius and Le Corbusier. We
suffer from an indigestion of too much superficial knowledge, and
the true harmony of style in our buildings is too often lost.

It seems then that, under conditions as they are today, true harmony of style is best achieved by forgetting "styles" altogether and
letting the detail forms flow naturally from their purpose and their
material. It is interesting, for example, to realize how beautifully
some of the most radically modern Dutch architecture harmonizes
with the older seventeenth- and eighteenth-century buildings that
surround it. This is a natural harmony, the result of certain continu-

ing ways of living, certain continuing tastes, a certain persistence in the use of the same local building materials. Both the modern and the older buildings make great use of glass in larger openings than are common elsewhere in Europe. Both are full of bright colors— doors vermilion or bright blue or yellow, for instance. Both are distinguished by an exquisite use of bricks and tile. Both surround themselves wherever possible with tiny brilliant gardens. And even in plan types the native, the national, tradition produces similar features in both. The result is that the contemporary buildings, growing naturally from materials and ways of life today, are completely at home with—harmonious with—the buildings of two centuries ago, which developed with a similar naturalness and were as expressive of their time as the new and radical work is of its own culture today.

By contrast, the unnatural attempt to gain harmony with older surroundings by parroting them is frequently doomed to failure. With all the scholarship they possess, antiquarian architects build so-called Colonial houses in old towns; to the sensitive observer these seem often to stand out more blatantly from their surroundings, to appear more obtrusively different from and alien to their neighbors, than if the attempt to copy the past had not been made. Modern demands show through the antiquarian forms; the need for larger windows, for bathrooms, for elaborate service facilities, for that more stringent and compelling economy in time and money which distinguishes most construction today, all contrive to set our efforts to be Colonial at naught. We love good Colonial architecture and the architecture of the early Republic, and we do well; at its best it is a noble kind of building. But we cannot build in the same way now, for our industry, our economy, our entire life patterns are different, and to attempt to do so is to produce only a travesty of Colonial and a travesty of today's architecture.

By all means let us preserve the precious American architectural heritage that has come down to us in hundreds of towns and cities; let us be reverential of all the beauty that has been created and careful to prevent its wanton and unnecessary destruction in the name of "progress" and at the hands of the real-estate speculator. But let us always remember that this beauty we admire was the result of men building naturally according to their skills, their needs, their times, and that the only way we can produce a living, harmonious town or city is by doing the same today.

Another aesthetic rule or canon remains to be considered—the law of *climax*. The necessity for some climax, some spot in a building more interesting than the rest, has already been suggested in the discussion of balance. The eye, as it wanders over a large building, grows tired if there is no single feature on which it can rest, and any eye exhaustion is fatal to beauty, just as mental exhaustion is fatal to beauty in a long piece of prose in which there is no climax on which the mind can fix.

And in architecture, considered as the design of an entire building, not just of a façade, the need for climax is especially great. We have already mentioned progressive rhythms and, in discussing planning, implied that one's passage through a building is not a hit-or-miss experience. Now the purpose of progressive rhythms is to lead one somewhere; the purpose of careful planning is to direct one's footsteps toward some end. That "somewhere," that "end," is, or should be, the climax of the plan. And the climax of the plan is frequently the climax of the entire structure. That spot to which one is led, and then stopped, must be beautiful enough, important enough, to justify the leading, or one feels cheated and the possibility of beauty disappears. If, on the other hand, this climax, this thing for which the building exists, is fine enough, big enough, strong enough, then a feeling of deep satisfaction arises; the building has performed its artistic task. There is true inspiration in the climax of great buildings—under the "eye" of the Pantheon dome (Plate XVIII), before the altar of Notre Dame, in the great official reception room of Dudok's city hall at Hilversum.

In houses and many minor buildings the need for climax is less obvious, but, however subtle, it is still present. A view through a great sheet of glass; a fireplace; a fine painting; an interesting vista from room to room—these all may be climaxes in house design. This climax effect is of the greatest importance, for it brings a sense of repose; there wandering ceases, albeit unconsciously. The secret of the beauty of many a house and many a room lies in its possession of a subtle but definite climax.

Like any complicated artistic composition, a great building may possess several climaxes, of greater or less importance. There may be climaxes on each of the four fronts of a rectangular building, for instance. Minor climaxes and spots of interest, developed through sculpture or planting, or change of material, or the sudden shadow of a projecting slab, may enhance minor pavilions or wings. Within the building, minor climaxes may crown every axial view, or terminate every corridor or passage. Everyone sensitive to the placing of furniture in a house or apartment knows this. But the principle of unity requires that minor climaxes be obviously minor, not interesting or important enough to stop one entirely, or to detract from the interest of the final climax, the most important climax, the artistic reason for the structure's entire existence. And normally this should coincide with either the symbolic or the actual purpose for which the building was erected. Thus the altar of a church, the proscenium of a theater, and the stage of a concert hall are natural climaxes, and to them all the rest should lead.

So the dome of the Capitol at Washington (Plate VIII) binds the whole complex building together because of its beautiful dominance. In the case of St. Peter's at Rome, that superlatively lovely dome fulfills a similar and still more difficult service, for here the greater portion of the exterior is bald, confused, and out of scale; yet all is passed over and forgiven because of the perfect beauty of the center of interest, the great dome.

A failure to fulfill this condition of beauty is one of the greatest faults of much modern American architecture. Lost in the multitude of windows which our modern exigencies demand, or entirely overwhelmed with ideas of bigness and grandeur, the American architect too often produces dreary monotony, when, if he had concentrated his richness on one spot, outside or in, to fix and delight the eye, he would have produced a truer and simpler beauty. If only our architects and builders had kept this idea always in mind, how different our streets would have been! Instead of that dreary succession of windows, windows, windows, set in walls covered, often, with meaningless and ill-applied ornament, there would have been an entire simplicity, with here and there an element of real beauty and grace—perhaps a doorway, perhaps merely one spot of sculpture or an accent of color or rich material, to center one's wandering interest. Then such a street would have been restful and charming, like some of the old alleys of Philadelphia, or the lovely-doored byways of Portsmouth or Salem.

The law of functional expression is closely related to harmony of expression and style, but it is a deeper matter. It is based on some deep-lying demand in the human mind that means and ends, causes and results, shall be inextricably intertwined—on some unconscious feeling that any willful confusion of this pattern is fatal to the sense of beauty. In a period when scientific examination of natural organisms is so dominant, when so much importance has been given to the finding of an organic system alike in the cosmos and in the progress and development of human society, it would seem natural that this matter of functional expression should have achieved a new and deeper value in architecture.

In fact, one entire school of modern architecture has been based upon making this the dominant, the most important, of all the laws of architecture and has founded upon it a new style, the so-called "International Style," the underlying thesis of which is that materials of construction and necessities of use should dictate and generate all architectural form, and that buildings should be stripped bare of all "unessential" trimmings. At times, in the writings of the extreme functionalists, it has been stated that design with beauty as an object should be rigorously eliminated from the architect's mind as something sentimental and hampering, and that buildings should be designed like machines, with no thought of anything save the materials of which they are made and the work they are to do.

One need not go so far as these extreme views to realize the immense value of this law of functional expression at a time when eclecticism is dying and new building materials are being developed almost daily. A new emphasis on the architectural value of functionalism leads naturally to an *organic* architecture which will give us buildings that are not only machines but an organic part of our whole life as well, with as much expression of the poetry of living and working as of its mechanics. Frank Lloyd Wright has realized and expressed this ideal more vitally than anyone else, both in his buildings and in his writings.

Seen thus, this law of functional expression is no Procrustean bed in which buildings are forced into stark and sterile mechanical forms dictated by engineering and economics, but a glad, creative, flowing, and flowering influence through which every new mechanical improvement, every new material, becomes an aid to architectural creation, a new opportunity for fresh and characteristic beauty. The new suave surfaces of enduring color in the synthetic plastics, the slim strength of metal supports, the rich variations of large unbroken sheets of veneered woods, the glittering and magical transparency of glass—these all are new means toward a new architectural delight. Similarly, changing modes and ideals of human life organically develop new and changing plan forms; the room as a four-sided rectangular box gives way to new expressions of enclosed space, with the outdoors and indoors wedded together by great sheets of clear glass, with space and movement within suggested by broad openings or the combination of elements formerly separated by walls. Yet nowhere need the expression of these new materials and uses supersede the other laws of form; it is part and parcel of them, an assistance in developing and following them and enshrining them in the material and concrete things buildings always are.

So far the analysis of these so-called laws of form has dealt with their applications in single buildings. But it is an important fact today that more and more the unit with which an architect has to deal is not just a single building, but a group—a school, a college, a housing group, for instance; or in other cases a park, a whole subdivision, a local neighborhood, an entire town. Some of the aspects of this development will be considered in more detail later, in Chapter 10. For the present, and considering the matter only from the aesthetic standpoint, it is interesting and significant that all these canons we have been analyzing—unity, variety, balance, rhythm, proportion, harmony, functional expression, climax—are as applicable to, and as important in, the design of groups of buildings as in the design of a single structure.

One must broaden the base of the analysis, of course, in learning how to apply these principles to groups; one must realize the balance of entire masses and not merely of building features; one must note the balance of structures in themselves and also with the areas between them. In rhythm, one must deal with the rhythms of whole houses, or the ends of blocks, rather than with those of columns or piers, or openings in a wall; in matters of climax, one must understand that, just as the group plan is more complex than the plan of a single structure, so more minor climaxes are possible and desirable —courts, gardened areas, seats, flagpoles, fine trees, beautiful views perhaps. Yet, just as in one building unity demands one climax to overshadow the others, so unity in a group demands one climax more powerful than all the others. It is part of the beauty of some New England and Ohio towns, and of many old European cities, that in each exists a common, a park, a market place, or a town square, to which the streets eventually lead and around which are situated the town's richest and most important public structures. Such an area becomes a true artistic climax and fulfills a human, practical function as well as an artistic purpose, for there is focused the whole social life of the people.

Open your eyes to your communities, then. Test them by the criteria that have been suggested. Look at the housing developments. See what real-estate promoters are building in the suburbs. In how many new groups of buildings—educational, civic, residential—do you find balance and rhythm, harmony and climax? If you find them frequently, congratulate yourselves on living in a beautiful town. If they are rare, remember it is partly the ordinary citizen who is to blame, for the builders try to give him what they think he wants. And remember that politically you have a vote, and that zoning, and city plan commissions, and subdivision regulations, and building laws, which do much to form and control the buildings in your community, are all political facts and issues and, in America, still subject to political—hence popular—control.

This discussion of the fundamental basis of aesthetic composition in architecture does not pretend to be final or complete. In such a personal thing as artistic pleasure there are bound to be wide differences of opinion. Even the so-called laws that have been stated may phrase themselves differently to different people, and other new requirements of beauty add themselves to the list. There can be no dogma stated to which all will agree; consequently the laws that are given above must be applied with latitude and freedom. They must be considered not as formulae but as mental stimulants; the truly appreciative critic of architecture will not stop with them but will use them as a basis for making his own decisions with regard to the buildings he attempts to evaluate.

After all, good and bad are relative terms; particularly in such a complex art as architecture, and in such a complex object as a building, it becomes dangerous to point to this as all good and that as all bad. The enjoyment of architecture is a personal matter, and the person who attempts for himself sincerely to form his own judgments about the buildings he sees, and to find reasons for his judgments in real and thoughtful convictions, is doing more for the growth of architectural taste than the one who accepts blindly the taste of the most competent critics. The reader must remember, too, that in this chapter but one side of the broad art of architecture has been treated; it has been considered as cold and bloodless form, void of other content. But just as architecture is more than bald form, just as it must be forms that clothe and express and grow out of human life, so architectural appreciation must include this human, subjective, and expressive side as well as the purely aesthetic. On the other hand, just as there can be no architecture without form, so architectural criticism, unless it be founded on a strong and sane aesthetic sense, becomes vague and sentimental. This chapter has tried to give a framework for that aesthetic sense, and it only remains for the reader to clothe the framework with his own personality and his own observations, until beauty is seen neither as a matter of geometric ratios, nor as one of vague and cloudy intuition, but rather as a definite organization of form.

5

THE ARCHITECT'S
MATERIALS

IT IS ONE of the characteristics of architecture that its component elements are in themselves few in number and simple in
structure. The very fact that all the beauty of a building lies in relationships of simple and easily comprehended parts has forced the
architect to study these relationships to the last degree, so that a
really great building has in it more absolute perfection of pure design
than has any other of man's works, with the possible exception of the
world's greatest music. The architect's expression is so concrete, his
imagination so bounded by the limitations of the materials with
which he works, that his creative art must be all the more forceful
and intense in order to make the desired effect upon the people who
may see or study the completed building. For to many persons a
building at first sight is only stones and mortar, and it lacks the charm
of human reference, of lovely face or alluring figure, to win the lazy
observer's superficial approval.

A building's appeal to the senses is produced by two things only,
the play of light and shade over its varied surfaces, and the color of
the materials of which it is composed. This play of light and shade,
in turn, is produced by the treatment of simple, surprisingly simple
elements, which are necessitated by the requirements of the building itself. The human mind always works up from the necessary to
the beautiful. Primitive man had to make a hut before he could
make it a delight to the eye. It is much the same now; the architect
must make a building before it can be a work of art, and one feels
instinctively that the most beautiful buildings are those in which the
necessities of the building are most clearly observed and most clearly
expressed. It follows, then, that the beautiful building is produced

by the arrangement, in accordance with the requirements of beauty, of elements primarily structural.

The first homes of mankind may well have been caves, the walls and roof of rough rock, smoothed crudely, perhaps, but with little of real architecture about them, despite attempts at mural decoration—those early evidences of a love of beauty that seems coextensive with humanity. Nor were the first primitive huts of bushes and rush and wattle of great architectural moment. Their lines were too simple and their requirements too limited to admit of great composition. They are, nevertheless, interesting to the architectural critic, because they show the elemental necessities of a building—walls, posts, beams, and roof: a roof to keep out the wind and the rain, and walls or posts to support the roof and give height inside, as well as to keep out the cold.

To this day, these two things, supports and roofs, are the most fundamental and the most important of the architect's materials, for they determine the whole shape and size of the building. Country house, office building, church, and factory all demand walls or posts, or both, and roofs, and the wall shapes and heights, the projections and recesses which a building requires necessarily determine a major part of its aesthetic composition and therefore its effect. Thus their importance is at once apparent; they are the framework of the whole artistic scheme of the building.

In modern buildings, as we have seen, the wall may have two functions. It may be a support, and it may be a screen to keep out the weather or to separate spaces within a building. Sometimes, especially in small buildings, it is both. In larger city structures and even many smaller buildings, the development of the steel skeleton has made the exterior wall a screen, supported on the steel and carrying nothing but its own weight; here it is a screen pure and simple.

When it is a support, the first necessity of a wall is the expression of its solidity, whatever the material—stone, brick, or wood-covered frame. The cut-stone wall, simply treated, with a spreading base to express broad foundations and a projecting cornice or coping to keep out the water, is the most obviously solid, the most monumental. Yet a wall of any material may have this quality. Take an old New England eighteenth-century farmhouse, nestling in lilac bushes under old elms. Its walls are of clapboards or wide shingles, grey and weather-beaten, but simple, straightforward, unassuming. Much of its beauty comes from this direct simplicity, this quiet, restful expanse of grey wood, so obviously designed for its purpose. Then compare with this some small town house of the 1870's, tricked out with jigsaw scrolls, its wall shingles carefully cut into patterns of scallops or wavy curves or zigzags, and the whole painted in contrasting colors of yellow and brown. Here the wall is lost; there is no repose, only a restless wandering of the eye. In a Gothic cathedral, such as Notre Dame, where at first sight the wall seems to be covered with ornament, clear spaces are left, and the decorative lines are all strongly structural in feeling, so that the expression of *wall* is given. There must always be this restful strength somewhere in every good building. The Panthéon in Paris (Plate XI) is an excellent example.

The same applies to brick walls; here also there must be quiet repose. Too obvious a pattern in the brickwork, too great variations of color, and too rough a texture, like the "skintled brick" so popular two decades ago, are bad, because by them the wall is broken up and its apparent strength reduced. Quiet patterns of subtle color tones, such as were used in much English Tudor work—Hampton Court Palace, for instance—are pleasing; they vary the monotony without detracting from the strength: but they must be unobtrusive. For the same reason it is dangerous to mix brick and stone, or brick and terra cotta, to such an extent that the unity of the wall is marred. Accents of stone in a brick wall may be good when they are in important structural positions—keystones over arches, for example, or architraves (frames) around openings, or courses of stone at the corners of a building (quoins), or wall caps or cornices or bases—for if rightly treated they appear to strengthen the wall. Sometimes even a panel of stone set in an important position is interesting, but the hit-or-miss insertion of panels and garlands and shields that is so much practiced by our less conscientious architects and real-estate builders is productive of nothing but confusion. Better, every time, a monotonous but sincere and simple wall than an ostentatious eyesore. The trend today is toward the simplest treatment of brickwork, using colors as uniform as possible and mortar joints not too wide or obtrusive, and letting the bond—that is, the manner in which the bricks are laid—give interest. Advanced architectural taste delights in the beauty of pure geometric forms, of clean and untroubled surfaces, and therefore prefers quiet walls that will accent this strong simplicity.

For the same reason the paneling of stone walls is full of dangers for the designer unless the paneling is kept quiet and unobtrusive. Simple, shallow panels are often effective, because their delicate lines seem to emphasize the strength and solidity of the wall, but the moment the panels become coarse and are framed by too heavy moldings, the restfulness of the wall is gone. Paneling in walls of wood is quite another matter, for the structural qualities of wood, the comparatively small size of the pieces obtainable, and the fact that wood warps and shrinks continually demand for it some such treatment as paneling to express these qualities. Wood paneling, therefore, is a correct expression of the material and is good in general, but even in wood the panels should not be too deeply sunk or too heavily molded.

Modern industrial science has been busy with woods and glues, as well as with metals, and has produced ways of using thin continuous veneers glued together into waterproof sheets. This waterproof plywood does not appreciably expand and contract with changes in moisture content; its use therefore makes paneling of the old type unnecessary, and we can now have outdoor wooden wall surfaces as continuous and unbroken as the size of the available sheets will permit. In practice, this size has been standardized generally at 4' x 8'; where joints between panels occur, they are covered with thin covering strips or are slightly molded. Many recent wooden houses add interest in their basic design by the careful patterning of these divisions.

All walls, then, should be treated so that both their function and their structure are expressed. They should be ornamented sparingly, and such ornament as they have should be carefully designed so as not to diminish their apparent strength. Repose is an absolute necessity. Emphasized caps they may have as copings to keep out moisture or as an eaves cornice, and accented bases to express foundation; the corners or the borders of openings may be accented by moldings or bands of differing materials; they may even be paneled, provided the paneling be delicate and quiet—but a wall can never be beautiful without that quiet dignity and that restful simplicity which only careful proportion and sincere expression can give.

In many modern buildings, however, the wall is no longer a support. What freedom of design, of materials, is at once open to the architect! Sheets of colored marble, thin slabs of stone with joints running continuously from top to bottom, sheets of copper or bronze, even the glittering loveliness of glass, all become proper materials for our modern screen walls. And great freedom of treatment is possible, as well. The fireproofing layer of brick or concrete which surrounds the steel columns or girders may be accented with one type of material or one color, and the areas between filled with other substances; or the whole may be treated as one simple envelope of plain or patterned surface.

Yet how seldom are these possibilities realized! A walk through any city street reveals one steel-framed building after another with coverings designed as though they were heavy masonry walls carrying tons and tons of weight, like the stone walls of Florentine palaces. Heavy arches, which hold up only their own weight; deep rustications, in a wall twelve inches thick; careful stone jointing, imitating the use of heavy, thick supporting units—these are too often the futile and expensive ways in which the unimaginative architect, blind to the new beauty of which he could be master, turns sentimentally to the past and confuses alike the structure of the building and our pleasure in it. How much pleasanter, more real, more truly satisfying are the buildings in which the true function shows, as for instance in the Bonwit Teller Building in New York (Plate II), designed by Warren & Wetmore, with its suave stretches of quiet walls built of large slabs of stone—unbroken surfaces that accent the design. Naturally many monumental buildings, churches, and smaller buildings generally are still built with walls that do support the floors and roofs, and in them the appearance of strength and solidity is logical; but by far the greater number of modern commercial buildings, hotels, and the larger apartment houses are held up by their steel skeletons alone.

A walk through any of our cities will reveal a woeful lack of regard for good wall design. In this country we are improving in this respect little by little, and the value of restful wall is coming to be more and more appreciated, but we have still far to go. For one building like the Ethical Culture Meeting House, designed by Robert Kohn, in New York, with all its stalwart, strong-walled dignity, or the simple, restful masses of such a house as Frank Lloyd Wright's own Taliesin, in Wisconsin, there are thousands which add to the nervousness of our life and our mental exhaustion by forcing upon us immense areas of meaningless ornament. It is no wonder that we have grown to appreciate, perhaps with even too great an enthusiasm, the simple, unassuming English cottage in a Cotswold valley, or the rugged houses of our own bleak New England countryside; for in them, at least—in the crude half-timbering or stuccoed masonry or ·hand-wrought shingle—there is more than the mellow beauty of age and sentiment: there is the true charm and clear repose of unbroken areas of simple wall.

The matter of roofs is more complex. At some time the cave or the rush hut which was his first home became insufficient for primitive man, and he discovered that he could lay tree trunks flat on earthen walls and thus make himself a flat roof. Ever since, there have been two main classes of roofs: flat roofs, and roofs with sloping sides. Assyrian bas-reliefs show us domed houses recalling the conical form of the primitive hut. Egyptian roofs, on the other hand, seem always to have been flat.

The two classes of roofs have widely differing uses. The flat roof was developed chiefly among peoples living in hot, dry countries. It furnished a most useful, airy outdoor living room. As such we find it used universally in nearly all the countries of the Moslem East, as it is in the Indian pueblos of the American Southwest. In colder climates where outdoor life has less charm, and in countries where there is excessive rainfall or heavy snow that must be disposed of quickly, we find the sloping roof most frequently used.

The simplest sloping roof is the gable roof, but this is capable of endless modifications, running the whole gamut from the dignified formality of the low roof of the Greek temple, with its gables—pediments—decorated with sculpture, to the fantastic and romantic effect of a German medieval village, with its myriad steep roofs and peaked gables. In the north of England—in Yorkshire—the stone-built houses nestle low and sturdy to the ground; the gables are low and the roofs comparatively flat. The effect is completely in harmony with the rolling moor and the bleak, wind-swept uplands. In Switzerland the same solidity, the same strength, and the same kinship with wild and bleak nature is given to the chalets by the same wide and gently sloping roofs. That is the reason a Swiss chalet, so lovely, so perfect in its place, seems always so fantastic and meaningless when set down in flat, more civilized regions.

For roofs, so essential to our protection from the wildness and occasional hostility of nature, have for that reason an especially close relation to natural conditions. Heat, dryness, heavy rains, heavy snows—these all condition roof design, both in materials and in shape. In hot, dry climates flat roofs are natural. In countries with heavy rain as a dominant condition, roofs are very steep, to throw it off rapidly. Thus one finds such steep slopes alike in the damp climate of Indonesia and other islands in the Southwest Pacific, in many African huts, in western and southern England, in Germany and Denmark. Where heavy snows occur, the problem is different and lower roof slopes are indicated. On these a thick blanket of snow, though heavy, is a marvelous conserver of heat, an excellent insulator. A steep roof in this case, moreover, would allow snow to slide down in masses in freezing and thawing weather, and would be a definite danger. Hence roofs in countries of heavy snowfall are usually of medium pitch, well under forty-five degrees—steep enough so that water will flow off readily as the snow melts, but flat enough so that the greater part of the snow will remain on the roof throughout the winter. Roofs of this gentler slope are the rule in Alpine countries, in Chinese hill towns, in Norway and Sweden. It is significant that the settlers of New England at first built the steep roofs they were accustomed to in England; later, as they learned the severity of the winters, they gradually flattened the slope until the roofs of the typical New England farmhouse of the early nineteenth century have a pitch that varies from about thirty-five to forty degrees.

Materials, too, affect roof slopes. Tiles and stone or marble slabs require roofs of moderate slope; they are heavy and on slopes too

FIGURE 13. A GAMBREL-ROOF HOUSE, KENNEBUNK, MAINE

steep have a tendency to slip. Thatch requires a steep slope to shed water as rapidly as possible. Wood shingles are among the most adaptable of roofing materials, good for steep slopes and slopes more moderate, but if the pitch is too slight leaks will occur. Metal is even more adaptable than wood shingles; if rightly applied, with due allowance for its inevitable expansion and contraction, it is good for almost any slope, from the so-called flat roof up to that of the steepest spire.

There are a thousand varieties of gabled roofs, and their change and variety is a continual joy. Our broad New England gambrels—gabled roofs with a double slope—are the charm of many a fascinating old town. Small or large, there is about them all such a comforting solidity, such a simple and beautiful homeliness, that it is not strange they have been widely popular. It only needs the artist's touch in the relation of the slopes, so that they shall be neither too much the same nor yet too different, to make a gambrel roof an object of distinction to a whole community, like that of the Warner house in Portsmouth, New Hampshire, and that of the old town house here illustrated (Figure 13).

FIGURE 14. A HIPPED-ROOF HOUSE: NEWTON HALL, NEAR CAMBRIDGE, ENGLAND

Another type of roof that is coming more and more into use and is perhaps even more adaptable is the hipped roof. Here the roof slopes up from all four sides, instead of from two only, as does the gabled roof. The result is that the line of demarcation between roof and walls is a continual horizontal line on all four sides of the building, with no triangular wall space or gable. This at once produces great dignity and a restfulness of feeling that is tremendously valuable. The French châteaux of the Loire valley, perhaps the most lavish group of country houses in the world, nearly all have hipped roofs. Most of the Italian villas have this type, and so have many of the most beautiful Georgian mansions of England (Figure 14). The simplicity of the wall surfaces which these roofs produce, and the variety and charm of their own form—the difference, for example, between the actual slope of the roof itself, and the slopes of the intersections, or hips, between its adjacent sides—make a whole composition dignified and quiet, attractive and interesting, with just a shade of pleasant formality.

Because of the ease with which hipped roofs can be built over buildings with complicated plans and many projecting wings, they have proved especially well fitted for the free, informal planning of the suburban and country houses of today. The long sweep of the continuous eaves line has the stress on the horizontal which modern taste prefers, and the hipped roof also seems to harmonize better with the long horizontal bands of windows and the wide clear glass areas of the modern house than does the gable roof. Thus many of the houses of Frank Lloyd Wright have hipped roofs with wide spreading eaves, and numbers of the loveliest recent California houses owe some of their quiet and winning beauty to their long lines of projecting eaves and hipped roofs (Plate XII).

There are as many possible varieties of the hipped roof as there are of the gabled type. Where a building is varied in plan, the intersections of the roofs of various portions give great interest. The difference in expression, for instance, between the hipped copper roofs of the Columbia University buildings, low and simple, and the great slate roof of Chenonceaux, or between either of these and the quietness of Wright's Robey house, will give some idea of the adaptability of the form.

Today, however, partly because of our growing love of sun and outdoor life, and partly as a result of the development of appropriate and inexpensive roofing materials, the flat roof is becoming increasingly popular even in northern climates. With modern methods of insulation it may be made as warm in winter and cool in summer as any other type, and it avoids the waste space in top and corners that any pitched roof has. When the flat roof space can be used as a terrace, it may become a delightful, airy, outdoors room; if part of it is covered, so much the better—with some planting in boxes on the roof itself or along the top of the railing or coping, this may add to, and not detract from, the charm of the house. The flat roof, in fact, has become almost the badge of the "modern" style, but, like all style fads (in buildings as well as in clothes), it may be used well or ill, thoughtfully or carelessly, with or without reason. Like so many of the new results of new machines and new ways of living, it is a new means which the architect may use in his creation, but a means only and never an end in itself. Where slate or wood shingles seem the obvious and most inexpensive materials to use, where there is need for attic storage space and no real demand for a usable roof space, a flat roof may be as ostentatious an affectation as any other illogical fashion followed in defiance of need or reason.

Flat roofs that are to be used must have railings or parapets, and the careful design of these necessary elements gives "body" to the exterior of a house, as well as an apparent reason for the choice of the roof type. But if a flat roof is not to be used as a terrace or garden, and no railing or parapet is provided, the problem of its design at the edge, where it intersects the wall line, is both practically and aesthetically difficult. Certain of the earlier revolutionary modern architects, in their effort to achieve the simplest possible geometric shapes in buildings, often designed structures that looked like solid cubical blocks, with no differentiation between walls and roof where the two came together. At these intersections it proved almost impossible to avoid leaks, and often the sharp edge of the wall against the sky somehow seemed ineffective and weak instead of stark and strong. As a result, more of the recent flat-roofed houses have strongly projecting eaves, or at least an external gutter; this gives a welcome terminal band of shadow at the top of the wall, and at the same time furnishes a practical way of keeping water out of the building.

Last of all in our list of roof forms comes the curved vault, and especially the dome. These will be considered more in detail in the following chapter. The dome is perhaps the most monumentally beautiful element in all architecture, for its height, its appearance of breadth, and its solidity give it a unique position. It combines the soaring lightness of the spire with the solid strength and breadth of a Greek temple. Yet, like all precious things, it must not be misused. Its form suggests size, tremendous spaces covered, tremendous power and dignity (see Plate XIII). A small dome on a large building, unless it is a mere unaccented and minor feature, like the dome on the observatory tower of the Paris Sorbonne or the little domed cupolas that crown many early American church steeples, is almost a contradiction in terms. A glance at the National Gallery in London (Figure 9) will show the meanness of such a dome. Not that a small dome can never be good; there are many lovely domed tombs, but in every case where a building of that kind is beautiful the design is such that the dome is all-inclusive—there is no roof but the dome, so that relatively it seems large. In large buildings the dome must be large; it must dominate or fail. The truth of this may be seen in some of our early state capitols. The architects had realized the beauty of the form itself, but they had not grasped the fact that the dome necessarily must dominate; they made it too small. The dome is such a strong motif in design that to be effective it must be made the crown and head of all. A dome playing second fiddle is irrational, inconceivable, confusing, bad.

The charm of a dome seems to lie in its continuous and ever changing curvature, and also in the fact that it is the same seen from all sides. It is at once the most varied and the most unified form at the architect's command, and as such its fascination has laid hold of us all. It has built itself into our literature, even into our fairy lore.

> In Xanadu did Kubla Khan
> A stately pleasure-dome decree,

wrote Coleridge, and when an artist paints heaven, or some fairy city of his dreams, he paints it many-domed. That incomparable mausoleum, the Taj Mahal in Agra, Santa Sophia crowning the rising profile of Constantinople, St. Peter's seen from over the Campagna like an iridescent dream, St. Paul's rising grey and powerful out of the London smoke, the old Columbia University Library crowning its many-columned entrance so graciously and powerfully, all bear witness to the superlative importance the dome has held in the creative architecture of the world.

The dome still holds powerful sway over our imaginations. It is not without reason that our national Capitol is crowned with a mighty dome, and that so many of our state capitols have followed its example. And it is interesting to note that recent developments in reinforced concrete are bringing the dome back into current building design, particularly for large market halls, like that at Leipzig, and similar great open structures. Reinforced concrete half domes also have been used for many handsome modern band shells.

Such are the main types of roof in the architect's repertoire. Yet you may walk miles in our city streets and see no roof at all; even if you look down upon a city from the windows of an airplane, it is chiefly upon acres of waste roof space—acres of useless, forbidding blackness. True, we no longer need to build gables, or sloping roofs to shed the rain and snow, and the whole logic of our modern structural methods leads generally to rectangular, blocklike masses. But it is mere penury, mere catchpenny miserliness, that has allowed these areas to become the ugly waste they are, with their spider-legged water tanks precariously poised above, and their rusty vent pipes coming up anywhere, discharging their smell at just the worst possible level. . . . City roofs are a magnificent heritage, a great opportunity that we have failed to seize. It is there that the sun still shines when the streets are shadow-shrouded, there that the cleanest air blows, there that there is no danger of hurrying automobiles. There we might grow many kinds of greenery, we might have safe playgrounds or cozy sun traps. In the future, let us hope, city roofs will be designed, not left just to grow; they will have sheltered nooks and open sun-washed spaces, and they will be busy all day with playing children or resting adults. The city of the future will be a city with its roofs redeemed, made into objects of delight to the eye and of use to the community; a city whose roofs are its crown and not its disgrace.

But a building, as we have seen, must have more than walls and a roof; it must have means for entrance and exit, and means for admitting light and air; it must have doors and, in most cases, windows. The door is a development from the simple hole for entrance to a cave or a hut. As men began to build more skillfully, they came naturally to build these holes square, by putting two upright members at the sides and one on top horizontally. Eventually they began to decorate these three members, and the ornamented doorway was the result. Later, as they grew still more imaginative and daring, they began to widen the size of the opening, until a point was reached at which they could no longer procure a stone or wooden beam strong enough to span the door and support the wall above. At this point, then, they remained until some genius had the brilliant idea of placing two stones over the opening, inclined toward each other, resting on the sides of the door, and leaning on each other above in the middle, thus forming a triangular opening. After that they probably used three instead of two stones, and then more, until they had developed the arch. This we can only conjecture, for the history of the stone arch is lost in obscurity. The famous Lion Gate in the city walls of Mycenae is a modification of this triangular shape; instead of supporting the weight over the opening with stones leaning against each other, the builders bracketed or corbeled out each horizontal course of stone over the one below on each side, until they met in the middle; then, either from a love of decoration, or because of the tradition of square-headed doors, the builders put an ordinary beam or lintel of stone under the arch, and rested on that a triangular stone carved with two lions, which fills entirely the opening above. The more developed types of arch—semicircular, segmental, or pointed—have been favorite doorway forms ever since the arch came into common use.

The doorway or gateway, round or square, became early one of the chief places for decoration. Particularly was this the case in great buildings like temples or palaces. There may have been a desire in the builders to awe one approaching, to give notice to him of the divine or human majesty into whose presence he was entering, and for that reason the doorway was made the most tremendous and beautiful portion of the whole exterior. The medieval artists carved their church doorways with saints and virgins, virtues and vices, or set the Last Judgment streaming across above, surrounding the entrance with all the pageantry of beauty and fear of their wild and tender Christian mythology.

There is another reason, too, why the doorway should be emphasized. The doorway is the entrance, and the effect of a building should be such that one approaching would go instinctively to the door, rather than to a window or around the corner. For this reason the door is, often unconsciously, made the artistic magnet of the outside of a building, so that one is not confused by varied interests, but attracted inevitably, though unconsciously, to the door, the most beautiful feature of the whole. Our apartment house architects have grasped this bit of psychology only too well, but, alas, their idea of magnetic attractiveness is too often ostentation, their idea of beauty too often mere florid and ill-considered ornament. A badly designed, over-conspicuous door is like the clothing clerk in a slum store who seizes you by the arm as you pass, shouting, beseeching you to enter and buy. With what relief after such an experience you go to a high-class and well-served shop, or listen to low and modulated voices! It is with such a feeling of relief that one turns from the hideous monstrosities of many of our apartment house entrances to a truly noble doorway like the great doorway of the Pantheon.

The decoration of all doorways is of two types. It can be a frame around the opening (as in the Pantheon), with or without a cornice above, or it can emphasize the supporting character of the sides in some more definite way. The first scheme is the quieter of the two, and it can be just as monumental in effect; it is certainly the commoner. It can be seen in the metal or wooden trim of almost any modern doorway. The difference between good and bad in these decorative door frames is impossible to define; in a general way it lies rather in questions of proportion and of truth to the material than in any rules of what decoration may or may not be used. The frame, or architrave, as it is called in the classic styles, must not be so wide as to seem to overload the door and press it in, for a doorway, above all else, must never appear constrained. Nor must the frame seem attenuated and wire-drawn, though metal frames and trims naturally are thinner and simpler than those of wood. Occasionally, too, in masonry walls, a completely plain opening, without any decoration whatsoever, may be appropriate, strong, and beautiful. Hardly more than this can be said; it is for the reader to investigate door frames for himself, noticing always the proportions between frame and opening, and in the frame itself looking for a certain element of strength and quiet dignity, and, besides, for a subtle play of light and shade over the moldings and faces that act as transitions between the dark of the opening and the quietness of the wall.

In the second form of door decoration, the decoration does form a frame around the door, but this frame is not continuous, for the uprights and the lintel or arch above them are treated in different ways. For instance, the uprights may be decorated with pilasters or columns, and the lintel above treated like a little entablature. In Gothic church work the principal doorways are usually treated with columns, and the arch above them carved into bold moldings; this is but a variation of the same scheme. It was very popular in the early Renaissance in Italy, and in the United States in Colonial and early Republican times builders and architects used this scheme for front doors in a charmingly gracious way.

Often these two schemes of decoration are combined. That is, some treatment of columns and pilasters, with arch or entablature above, is placed around a well-marked and continuous frame that encloses the opening; the projection of this from the wall may be increased until a genuine little porch is produced, and this may be crowned with a gable or a pediment.

Even the richness resulting from this double decoration, however, did not satisfy certain splendor-loving peoples, for whom the door was the all-important feature of the exterior of a building. Consequently they made the doorway itself a mere center for an immensely rich piece of decoration, which often ran several feet on each side and the entire height of the building. Mohammedan nations seem to have done this first; it is almost universal with them. In certain of the Persian mosques, for instance, the door itself is set into an arched niche often forty or fifty feet high, flanked by slim minarets, and the whole is encrusted with colored tiles. In Constantinople many of the mosque courtyards are entered by gateways set into decorated niches running up the entire wall, and often still further importance is given to the composition by a dome crowning the whole. The grandeur of such an entrance set in a long stretch of simple wall is unmistakable, and the beauty of this accent and this contrast is exceedingly effective. Among all the Moorish influences

on Spanish architecture this method of door treatment is pre-
eminent. The Spaniards seem to have felt at once the impressive
charm of the great Moorish doors and set out to adapt it to their
own uses and their own forms. In this they succeeded to a remarkable degree; perhaps the most beautiful things in all Spanish buildings are the doorways and gates—masses of delicately frosted ornament framing the dark door and mounting tier on tier to the cornice
itself—set in a severe and unornamented cut-stone wall. (See Plate
XIII.)

These doorways offered a particularly fertile field to the architects
of the Baroque period in Spain—the so-called Churrigueresque—
when convolutions of every architectural form and complexity in
every line were the vogue. The designers piled form on form around
and above the opening; used reduplicated frame lines, broken in and
out with the most exuberant imagination; crowned the whole with
curved and scrolled and broken pediments. At their best these gateways were superb and exciting symphonies of light and shade, true
and effective climaxes to the façades they decorated. In Mexico and
in Central and South America generally, the Spanish Colonial
architects, priests, and builders outdid even the mother country in
the size and fantastic poetry of their great doors, as for instance in
La Santisima in the City of Mexico (Plate XIV) or the front of the
cathedral at Tasco. The missionaries carried this tradition with them
to the more distant, more primitive colonies, and one can see many
simpler and usually cruder examples in the doorways of the Spanish
missions of the southwest United States. The best example of great
beauty of design and unusual perfection of execution, which rivals
the best work in Mexico, is on the front of the mission of San José
de Aguayo, at San Antonio, Texas (Plate XIV); a cruder example is
the front of San Xavier del Bac at Tucson, Arizona.

In fact, the designers of the Baroque and Rococo periods everywhere delighted in the opportunity doorways offered them for
dynamic and dramatic compositions. The palaces by Fischer von
Erlach in Vienna and Prague use combinations of architectural
forms and sculpture with superb sensitiveness; the entrance to the
Zwinger Palace (now almost completely destroyed) in Dresden, by

Pöppelmann, was a fairy-like fantasy of curves, appropriate to the recreational purpose for which the palace was built.

The revolutionary changes both in structural methods and in taste which have been the basis for the development of contemporary architecture have necessarily changed doors and doorways, as they have modified other architectural forms. The great strength of steel and reinforced concrete makes the possible width of door openings almost unlimited, and there is a new impressiveness and welcoming quality in broad bands of metal and glass doors, suggesting the entrance of crowds of people. Broad sheltering slabs overhead not only give protection from the weather but also strikingly emphasize the horizontal quality. Richness is often provided by rich marble or tile veneers on each side, and bright metals in door frame and door give brilliant accents. Moreover, modern construction and materials allow the complete daylighting of halls or vestibules, so that they serve admirably as transitions from the outside to the interior. Transoms of plate glass, as well as side lights or transoms of glass tile, carved or plain, fill the spaces behind with light, as, for example, in the entrance halls of many of the Rockefeller Center buildings. Similarly the inviting beauty of the halls, vestibules, and stairways of many recent houses is made possible only by modern materials and modern construction.

Since windows and doors have grown similarly out of primitive holes, it is not strange to find their decorative treatment sometimes similar. But given the same two original schemes, arch and post-and-lintel, it is remarkable how the treatment of doors and windows grew apart; for, whereas the purpose of a door is to admit people, the purpose of a window is to admit light and air, and the shapes suitable to one are not necessarily suitable to the other.

In ancient Greece, where so much outdoor life was possible, windows were usually small and inconspicuous. But windows, some of considerable size, were much used by the Romans, especially in their town buildings and their country houses. The close-ranked shop, warehouse, and apartment buildings that characterized much Roman city building (see Plate XV), especially in Italy, made essential some means of furnishing light to the interiors; relatively large and regularly spaced window openings were the natural result. The more recent excavations in Rome, Ostia, Pompeii, and Herculaneum have revolutionized our conception of what ancient Roman towns were like; they show us several-storied structures of surprisingly modern aspect, with many large simple windows and frequent balconies. In the great basilicas, palaces, and public bath halls, large windows were also frequent and the system of clerestory lighting, in which central halls were lighted by great windows set high over the roofs of lower parts of the structure, was widely used. Basilica windows were usually simple rectangles, like those of apartment houses, but those of the baths and market halls, such as the so-called Mercato Traiani in the shopping center close to the Forum of Trajan at Rome, were arched openings under the vaults that covered the halls. At first these windows were probably closed by wooden shutters and curtains of cloth or leather; later, sheets of translucent or transparent gypsum or mica, set in wooden frames, were used and in the imperial period seem to have been the usual window material; but glass was also used as early as the middle of the first century of the Christian era. Pliny the Younger, in his letters, describes its use in the important windows of his Laurentian villa. Glass in metal frames probably filled the clerestories of at least the later baths and basilicas, and numerous fragments of glass windows have turned up in the excavations of Roman towns and Roman villas as far afield as Britain and Germany.

But the great era of window development came only with the Middle Ages and was bound up with the development of the Christian church. Windows in a classic temple had not been necessary, for the great sacrifices and public ceremonials were always out of doors. But Christianity demanded places of worship capable of receiving crowds of people, and a prime requirement of this new form of worship was light. Windows, therefore, were continually increased in size and number, till some of the later Gothic churches are scarcely more than walls of glass.

At first these windows may have been mere openings, unglazed. Later, as glass came to be more common, the windows were filled with glass, probably in very small pieces, joined in a pattern by little H-shaped lead bars. Such a window is never strong and can be made only in narrow widths, even when reinforced with iron bars. The whole development of Gothic architecture from the dark, heavy-walled Romanesque churches of southern France to the brilliance and airy lightness of King's College Chapel in Cambridge, England, or the cathedral of Carcassonne in France, was one long struggle to get much window area, much outside light, into a stone-vaulted church. (See Plate XV and Figure 15.)

France artistique

FIGURE 15. CATHEDRAL OF ST. NAZAIRE, CARCASSONNE, FRANCE

A Gothic building which has an almost complete wall of stained glass.

One of the early innovations in this struggle was the grouping of two or three long, narrow windows under one great arch. Later, a circular window was placed above these smaller windows to fill up the space—or lunette—under the arch. This arrangement was the origin of tracery; from here on it was but a step to the reduction of the wall between the grouped windows and the rose above them to a mere framework, and then the elaboration of this framework into the glory of the best Gothic tracery, as seen in the transepts of Notre

Dame in Paris or the west front of York Minster in England. In Germany, tracery was developed to an even greater extent, but without such consistent success, for the German love of the bizarre and the grotesque came finally to overbalance good taste; tracery was forced into weird and fanciful naturalistic forms, such as branching trees or the national eagle, and the novelty of these can in no way compensate for the loss of the dignity, the strength, and the simplicity innate in the more structural tracery of the French and English work.

Naturally the churches, the monuments of the community, enjoyed the luxury of glass to a large extent before its use came to be common in the house. Even in many comparatively recent English cottages in out-of-the-way villages one may see windows few in number and tiny in size, made so because glass was prohibitive in cost. But in towns and in the great houses, from the fifteenth century on, glass was used more and more extensively, until Francis Bacon, in the time of Queen Elizabeth, complained that some of the houses of his day were built of glass rather than of brick or stone, so that in them was neither shade in summer nor sufficient shelter in winter.

Much of the charm of these early windows lies in the fact that they were always glazed with small panes, separated by metal or wooden bars, which broke up the surface of the opening and prevented its looking like a black hole in the wall (see Figure 16). Today, when we can make large sheets of clear, unruffled glass, the problem of window design has changed. Where the wall is a supporting wall and the windows are comparatively small units, the same aesthetic necessity for breaking the window area and preventing the black-hole appearance of the opening may persist. But in more modern types of construction the window is no longer a mere hole in the wall; it is rather just a special part of the wall screen made transparent instead of opaque. Because of its integration with the wall, the glass in modern buildings is often brought out as close to the face of the walls as possible, and windows are grouped in long unified strips or banks. In the exquisite Daily Express Building in London, the impression is not of windows and wall but rather of a rich, glossy envelope surrounding and enclosing the building—some

PLATE XIII

Santa Sophia, Constantinople:
exterior

Escuelas Minores, Salamanca:
doorway

PLATE XIV

La Santisima,
Mexico City:
entrance

From *Spanish-Colonial Architecture in Mexico*

Author

San José de Aguayo,
San Antonio, Texas:
doorway

PLATE XV

Ernest Nash

View in the Forum
of Trajan, Rome

Carlisle Cathedral:
interior of north choir aisle

From *Architectural Illustrations
. . . of Carlisle Cathedral*

PLATE XVI

Santa Sophia,
Constantinople:
interior

Santa Maria
dei Miracoli,
Venice: interior

of the material opaque, some of it transparent. In such a building, or in a modern house where the whole side of a room may be of glass, the need for subdividing the glass area with bars, in order to "preserve the surface," does not exist, and the only things which dictate the pane sizes are the practical necessities of the material and its use—the questions of cost, easy replacement, and the need for opening a part or parts of the window for ventilation. Moreover, our new delight in wedding the outdoors to the interior makes it desirable to use glass in the largest and most unbroken areas possible. And, where there is a wonderful view of sea or highland or far-flung city streets, a large unbroken sheet of plate glass is the obvious window material; any sash bars or divisions would be an unforgivable intrusion. Thus the new developments in the manufacture of glass, as well as the development of beams and lintels that allow tremendously wide openings, form a superb opportunity for the architect to develop new and characteristic forms and to create with them a new and organic beauty.

FIGURE 16. HARVARD HOUSE, STRATFORD-ON-AVON, ENGLAND

The typical ranked windows, with small leaded panes, which characterize many Tudor buildings.

There still remains to be considered the last of these exterior structural necessities, in some respects the most fascinating of all, the chimney. Primitive man had to have a fire. At first the fires were probably outdoors; but farther to the north, where they were needed for heat as well as for cooking, men began to build fires inside their houses. Then came the necessity of letting out the smoke, which led to the building of chimneys. Chimneys are of comparatively recent

date in the history of mankind; primitive tribes are still content
with holes in the roof. In large portions of central Europe and in the
islands off the Scottish and Irish coasts, many modest houses are
chimneyless to this day; as one winds through the fascinating valleys
of Yugoslavia, for instance, one can see from the train windows
village after village apparently on fire, for every cottage has a wisp of
blue smoke curling out from the top of each deep-eaved gable—and
those openings are the cottage chimneys. One hates to imagine the
condition of the inmates of such a smoke-filled house; the chimneyless houses of the Orkneys are, significantly enough, called "black
houses," just as the primitive central hall of the earliest Roman
houses, equally chimneyless, was termed the "atrium," from *ater*,
black. Such a solution of the indoor fire could never satisfy more
sensitive or inventive peoples. The smoke rose; therefore over the
hearth men came to build a vertical chimney. It is not known when
chimneys were first used, but in the Middle Ages they became common and their artistic possibilities came to be recognized.

It was in the northern countries of Europe, as one might imagine,
that chimneys were most highly developed. To this day Italian
chimneys are tiny, unimportant features, made as low and unobtrusive as possible. Frenchmen and Englishmen, on the other
hand, demanded more fires than their southern neighbors, and it
was but natural to group all the flues from rooms in the same vertical
tier into one large chimney. The result was a mass entirely too large
to be neglected, and the artistic genius of the people welcomed the
opportunity thus furnished. Indeed, it seems to have been a particularly attractive problem, for chimneys exist in numberless forms;
often in buildings otherwise severe and simple there will be a little
touch of fantastic playfulness in the chimneys that cheers and
wonderfully warms the whole effect.

There are no rules for good and bad design in chimneys, save, of
course, the one rule that a chimney should look like a chimney.
There are certain Elizabethan houses, built when the classic orders
were just coming into fashion, in which the chimneys are little examples of the Doric order, each flue built as a separate column, and
the flues of each chimney grouped under a little entablature for a
cap. The result is amusing, but certainly not beautiful or satisfactory;

the roof of Burghley House (1570–1583), for instance, looks like a plateau covered with some great columnar building, roofless and ruined, and to discover that this group of columns is made up only of chimneys is a decided shock. Earlier and later than this period the English were more fortunate in their chimney design; they were immensely skillful in the use of brick and stone, twisting the chimney shafts, making them polygonal, varying the design all over the house so that in every shaft it was different, building them up from a solid base, and crowning them with a molded cap. Later, when they built their chimneys solid, they were equally successful, often emphasizing each flue with a little terra-cotta chimney pot above the cap and delicately paneling the sides of the whole. In France the art of chimney design was equally advanced during the Renaissance, but the French chimney was always more monumental and less informally charming than the English type. The French loved high stone chimneys, paneled in formal designs and topped by architrave, frieze, and cornice, so modified as to appear frankly what they are, chimney caps.

We city-dwelling Americans are losing our feeling for chimneys. With gas or electric ranges and steam heat, chimneys are almost a rarity in most of our cities; that is one reason for the bleakness of New York or Chicago roofs, when compared with the roofs of Paris or London or Strasbourg. There are no crowded chimney pots by thousands to make one dream of the cheerful fires below. With the reduction in number of chimneys we have diminished the smoke nuisance, but with it has gone a not unmeaning expression of human living. Somehow the vent pipes that now stud our roofs do not invite dreams; charm in them is hard to find. No, to us who dwell in cities the romance of chimneys is of another kind; it is the romance of industry, of towering slender columns seen over grey, busy harbors and inland industrial centers, belching their billowing smoke across an evening sky.

It is all the more important, therefore, that when we Americans build our homes in the country, whether summer houses or farmhouses, we should build them with adequate, well-placed, and well-detailed chimneys. We must remember the comfortable and dignified houses of our elders, with their massive brick chimneys and all the friendly intimacy and homeliness they suggest. We must not be satisfied with little, insufficient chimneys scattered willy-nilly over the roof; we must see to it that the house is so planned that its flues will group into massive and dignified chimneys that compose well with the whole design. Frank Lloyd Wright's houses show many examples of such superbly simple and beautifully composed chimneys.

These are the chief elements with which the architect deals in designing the exteriors of buildings. But in addition there are a number of subsidiary features that may add enormously to the whole effect, especially those which serve as a tie between the outside and inside of a building, or between the building and its site. These elements are steps, porches, balconies, loggias, piazzas, terraces, garden walls, railings, fences, and the like. Without them, how much poorer our architectural world would be! They serve a double purpose, expressive as well as formal. They express the relation of the building to the world around, the coming and going of people, and the quiet outdoor life where climate and weather permit; more than any other feature they somehow tell us that no building, no totally enclosed volume, is or can be entirely self-sufficient. And aesthetically and in terms of form they act as a unifying agent that makes any building not merely a closed aesthetic experience, like a book between covers, but part of a larger whole comprising not only site and community but the whole pageant of external nature.

Walls, roofs, doors, windows, chimneys, exterior appurtenances— it is from these simple elements that the designer, by careful treatment of the forms themselves and by their careful combination and composition, with the addition of a certain amount of decoration, evolves a whole to delight our eyes and to satisfy our minds. The simplicity of the list is the architect's limitation, but at the same time it accounts for the tremendous beauty of architecture when it is good. One of the great achievements of modern architecture lies in the fact that it has recognized and emphasized the function and nature of these simple elements, and out of them—untroubled by falsity or ornament—composed its masterpieces.

6

INTERIORS IN
ARCHITECTURE

IT HAS BEEN the custom of architectural historians to lay entirely too much stress on exterior architecture. One might almost
suppose from their writings that architecture was mainly the construction of a mere artistic shell, the kernel of which was of no importance. Half of those who are not interested in architecture base
their lack of interest on the fact that they think of architecture as
something dealing with luxurious and unessential external ornament
which concerns them and their interests but slightly. In reality, the
whole evolution of architecture proves the contrary; almost every
important development in it was produced not by any desire for mere
external grandeur, but because changing conditions had rendered
necessary new internal requirements, or because new improvements
in building skill and new types of construction had made new interior
forms natural and desirable. Egyptian architecture is largely a matter
of interior design, for the temple courts might almost be called interiors, and the hypostyle halls certainly are. The external grandeur
of Greek temples arose from the desire to give fitting expression to
the supreme glory that resided within. The greatest contribution of
Roman architecture to civilization—its great vaulted halls, and the
systematic, elaborate planning of its colossal structures—is a result
of the demand for impressive interiors. The Byzantine tradition of
great domes was the result of an attempt to produce a gorgeously
decorated, vaulted church, and the whole development of Gothic
architecture was a striving for the perfect church interior. It has been
the same throughout the ages, and those who think of architecture
as a matter chiefly of exteriors are considering only a small portion
of the whole great field.

In studying the structural materials at the architect's command, then, it is important to consider the internal as well as the external requirements of a building. There are great similarities between the two, but there are great differences as well; for the purpose of the exterior of a building is to protect the inside from the weather and from objectionable people, whereas the entire interior, having been so protected, must be so treated as to fulfill most perfectly its specific purposes.

The similarities in exterior and interior requirements lie chiefly in the absolute necessities which confront the architect, the differences mostly in their treatment. A greater freedom is allowable in the treatment of all interior features, for several reasons. In the first place, it is understood that the interior of a building is protected from the weather; this at once allows the architect great latitude in the interior material he uses and suggests a greater richness and delicacy of surface. In the second place, when one is inside a room, the whole scheme of a building usually is not evident, as it is to one outside; consequently each interior space can be handled at least partly as a separate individual unit, provided, of course, that its basic harmony with the whole is preserved. And, lastly, inside a building you generally have a closer view of all the architecture of the interior than one outside is likely to get of the exterior.

Perhaps the chief interior element with which the architect works, like the principal exterior element, is wall design; the greater freedom within, moreover, offers a further challenge to his skill and imagination. In interior bearing walls, which carry weight, expressiveness demands the same apparent strength inside the building as on the exterior. Thickness, weight, power; openings strongly arched or with deep and accented reveals—these are all appropriate. Stone or brick exposed frankly to view may help create this feeling. But in interior design there is always the possibility of greater richness, greater delicacy. Stone walls may be richly paneled or molded; stone or brickwork may show a richer and daintier texture than when it is used outside. Veneers of white or colored marble, or areas of rich tile, may be used to produce brilliantly varied effects, as in the marble wainscots of Santa Sophia in Istanbul (Plate XVI) or of Santa Maria dei Miracoli in Venice (Plate XVI), or in the tile linings of many of the rooms of the Alhambra. Mosaic, too, seems admirably fitted to enhance large structural forms in interiors, as, for instance, in St. Mark's in Venice or the tile mosaics of Goodhue's Nebraska capitol. Like the greater amount of mural painting, mosaic seems to demand a certain conventionality in treatment, a certain touch of flatness or unreality in color or drawing, in order to preserve the feeling of solidity and strength in the forms it decorates. Too much realism, too much breaking of the apparent surface of the wall or vault, tend to produce restlessness, sentimentality, and finally boredom.

But in many modern buildings interior partitions have little if any structural function. They are primarily division screens between different portions of a building. As such, their treatment can be more playful and the possible materials are almost unlimited. Plaster, wood, glass, metals, textiles—these are all appropriate in places for which each is suited. Colors may be infinitely varied; mirrors may flash back interesting reflections, break the sense of enclosure, or increase apparent sizes.

A new feeling for living, a new desire for space and for sun, and a new hatred of the idea of confinement have combined with the nonstructural character of most partitions today to produce a revolution in interior design, especially in houses. A house used to be an assemblage of boxlike, rectangular rooms. Now, the earlier box type of room is tending to disappear, giving way to interiors more open, more carefully organized, in which there is always the feeling of space beyond. Living rooms open broadly onto the garden or terrace with great unbroken windows, and are themselves sometimes L- or T-shaped, with special spaces for dining, reading, music, and so on, all combined to get the maximum openness (see Plate VII). Frequently, too, to break up the enclosing limitations of the box effect, the walls of a room may be painted in different colors. The furniture (often built in and stationary), the color of the walls, and the room shape are all treated as one organized space composition.

Modern wall treatments are legion. Wood paneling is still one of the most adaptable, because it is at bottom a structural form, founded on the qualities of the material itself. The richness of a

Louis XV boudoir, such as the Salon Ovale in the Hôtel Soubise, and the simple homeliness of a Colonial kitchen are examples of the extreme variety of effects that wood paneling can produce. But modern machinery and techniques have not limited the use of wood to panelings of the old type. Rotary-cut veneers and built-up laminated sheets now allow us to use great unbroken areas of wood, in which the beauty of the texture and the grain and color of the wood can be displayed to the best advantage. Smoothness, curved corners, suavity, and a lack of fussiness in details and moldings all result from this new type of wood usage.

Plastics too—chiefly sheets of synthetic chemical rosins—bring new opportunities for color to the modern architect. Never before has he been able to command such perfect surfaces, dull or shiny, of clear and beautiful permanent color or deep and lustrous black. Yet such is the conservatism of popular taste that the manufacturers have been forced to manufacture this beautiful material largely in imitative patterns—patterns imprinted with a texture resembling woven fabrics, or scored like tiles, or imitating (usually badly) the veinings of marble. It is not the imitation that seems so distressing as the obvious waste, the obvious blindness to the special beauty characteristic of the material itself.

And, lastly, there is the new beauty of new metal alloys that do not tarnish. Strips, extruded moldings, frankly expressed screw or bolt heads, or even in rare cases sheets and plates—all these are, as it were, new colors for the architect's palette, each a new opportunity and a new challenge. When, therefore, it comes to the choice of treatment for a wall, it is best to cast aside all thoughts of "style" or period, or theory or fad; to think only of what will be most suited to the purpose and the pocketbook, and of what will be most beautiful and possess the most lasting appeal, the most aesthetic repose.

If repose is a *sine qua non* in wall design, it is even more indispensable in the design of floors. The floor in the landing of the grand staircase of the Ducal Palace in Venice, for instance, is of black and white marble so designed that it seems, despite its real flatness, to be made of cubes set cornerwise—a myriad of points sticking into the air. Such a floor is an abomination; one is almost afraid to step on it for fear of hurting one's feet. In fact, any floor in which the appearance or sense of flatness is lost is a bad floor. This is true whatever the material. Mosaic designs realistically picturesque are bad; so also are loud-colored carpets or those in which the pattern is so pronounced that it seems to rise from the background. The charm of good Oriental rugs lies in the fact that in spite of the richness, even the gorgeousness, of the colors—sometimes mingled bright reds and blues and yellows and even whites—they are so interwoven and blended in the intricacies of the conventionalized design that the rug never seems to be anything except one flat plane. So, too, colored marble or tile floors are successful only when they have this appearance of being absolutely flat.

This, then, is the one criterion of floor design. Stone or brick, wood or marble, tile or carpet—this one requirement must be fulfilled. And just as it was in the desire to give himself a flat and dry surface to walk on that primitive man first smoothed his cave's earthen floor and later covered it with flat stones, or boards of wood, or skins or cloths, so this flatness that man has with such great effort perfectly attained he will not, even in appearance, forgo.

In buildings today two subsidiary requirements of floor design are common—ease of maintenance and insulating quality. The best floors are easy to clean and have high insulating value against both cold and noise. Terrazzo floors—broken marble chips in cement, polished—have great value in some parts of a building; they can be as rich in color as desired, and patterns made by inset metal strips can easily be made, but these floors are both noisy and cold and therefore manifestly unsuited to some sorts of interior. Cork block floors are warm, quiet, and rich in tonality, but they are difficult to maintain. Good hardwood floors are beautiful when rightly finished, and warmer and slightly less noisy than marble or terrazzo. Rubber and linoleum floors are warm and quiet and offer great opportunities for richness and variety in color, but they are relatively soft and furniture sometimes dents them. Various types of synthetic tile have been developed in the effort to combine all the possible virtues, but in many the color range is limited and the appearance drab, and some have a pervasive and unpleasant odor. The fact is—and in this respect floors resemble many other architectural materials—there is no one type of perfect modern floor. Each material is best for the areas it suits—that is about all one can say. And, like other modern materials, modern floor materials afford opportunities for the architect and challenge his sense of fitness and of beauty. With them he can give us as beautiful effects as those we admire in buildings of the past, provided he keeps in mind always the quality of the material with which he is working, the purpose of each floor area, and, above all, the dominant requirement of all floor design—repose and flatness.

But man needs not only walls around and a floor below; he needs, even more than these, a covering above. The next structural requirement of a building, therefore, corresponding to the roof on the outside, is the ceiling within. In some cases, as in certain churches and great halls that extend the full height of a building, the ceiling is merely the interior of the roof. If the roof is a sloping one of timber all the structural parts are exposed—the rafters, the under sides of the roof boards, the trusses that support the whole—and these may be treated so richly that the effect becomes not one of poverty but one of luxury. There is something tremendously impressive in such an "open-timbered" roof; the combination of the naked, all-apparent strength of the supports, with the richness of light and shade of their crisscrossing, complex yet systematic, in the shadows above, is well-nigh irresistible. Memories of Westminster Hall in London (Plate XVII) or the hall of Hampton Court Palace, of English Tudor churches, or of the rich colors of the San Miniato ceiling in Florence throng to the mind in confirmation, and churches and halls and libraries more and more throughout the country bear witness to its puissant charm. The Chapel of the Intercession in New York, by Cram, Goodhue & Fergusson, the great dining hall of Yale University in New Haven, and the simple and dignified Protestant Cathedral in Albany are but a few examples.

Something of the same charm of strength and complexity exists in a frank treatment of steel-framed roofs, particularly when combined with glass. The train concourse of the Pennsylvania Station in New York is a superlatively good example of the kind of thing which should be more common. The truth is, we are not used to steel, even yet. It has been the origin of so much engineering ugliness that one forgets it can be made a means of architectural beauty. Our aesthetic hatred of steel is a heritage from those Pre-Raphaelite days when steel and iron meant system and machinery, and machinery meant all that was evil. Now we are beginning to learn that machines need not necessarily destroy beauty; on the contrary, they can be used to create new and characteristic kinds of beauty. The same is true of steel and of concrete; both the webbed lightness of steel frames and the continuity and solidity of concrete can give us new types of interesting roofs.

Steel-framed roofs have been much simplified in recent years by the common use of welding; continuous members made from welded parts can now be used instead of the elaborate braced and riveted truss parts of earlier steel construction. The gain in simplicity, grace, and repose is often tremendous, and many direct and pleasant factory interiors (see Plate XVII) owe much of their quality to this change. Another type of steel-framed roof that is becoming common today is a sort of transitional type between arched and girder treatment; it is the so-called braced-frame type, in which girders and posts, welded or riveted together, form one continuous member from the ground or the foundation up, and across and down to the ground again. These frames are often given strong and graceful outlines, subtly curved, and interiors in which roofs are thus supported often combine the grace of the vault with the lightness of the truss and the simplicity of the girder. The interiors of several of the great power-houses of the Tennessee Valley Authority, which may be counted among the most beautiful of American buildings, are thus roofed (see Plate XX); the clean simplicity and accented structural quality of these roofs harmonize perfectly with the great shining cylinders of the turbine cases beneath them.

The ceilings we have considered so far have been merely the insides of roofs, but there is a larger number of buildings the ceilings of which are below the roofs and, to a large extent, separate from them. There are, besides, the ceilings that are the under sides of floors. There is one large class of ceilings in which the floor itself forms the ceiling and all the beams and girders which support the floor boards are exposed. In rooms of considerable size and height there is the same structural charm in a ceiling of this kind as there is in an open-timbered roof. In the Davanzati Palace in Florence there are several ceilings where two or three great girders span the room, with smaller beams closer together running from one girder to the next; almost without exception such ceilings are handsome. They have a sober dignity about them that neither the vault, grander or more graceful though it may be, nor the flat plaster ceiling can ever have. But they have their drawbacks, too. In the first place, anyone who has lived in an unceiled country cottage knows that such a ceiling is noisy; the drop of a pin on the floor above re-echoes as if it were a spike, the fall of a shoe is like an explosion. In addition, such rooms are cold and there is no space for running electric wires or pipes, so that it is small wonder that some sort of covering below the beams has come to be almost universal. In certain cases it is possible to combine the delight of one with the comfort of the other, by raising the finished floor above the structural floor, thus giving space between them, or by plastering directly under the small beams and letting the larger ones project below, or by putting the plaster at a level half way between the floor above and the bottom of the beams. Sometimes this effect is imitated by building false beams below the ceiling. That is not legitimate; at its worst it is an artistic insult, as when the speculative builder puts tiny sticks two inches square across a ten-foot apartment room, with the idea of producing "atmosphere." Better a thousand times the inoffensive simplicity of plain plaster than this.

The beamed ceiling was developed to a splendid perfection in the Renaissance. Gradually the Italians found that the simple method of the Davanzati ceilings could be varied. They made all the beams of the same depth and crossed them at right angles to each other, filling the spaces between with squares or rectangular panels, painted and molded. Often the under side—the soffit—of the beam was itself decorated, and sometimes the beams were so arranged as to give large panels in the center, decorated with huge "mural" paintings, with a frame of simpler, smaller pattern around. Then came the use of diagonal beams, and curved beams, until there was no limit to the variety of designs possible, with octagonal or square or oblong or star-shaped or oval panels. Such ceilings have a richness that is most effective in large rooms; since they developed frankly into decorations finally, one feels no qualm at seeing the projecting members used merely as a decoration and not at all as a support for the floor above. The color of the wood, the shadowed panel moldings, dull gold perhaps, and the paintings in the center—here is indeed an alphabet of decoration. Go to the New York Public Library and look at the ceiling of the main exhibition room; then go upstairs to the main reading room and look up. There is richness, there is strength, there is delicacy, there is warmth, there is dignity. No other type of ceiling gives just that effect of studied charm and rich simplicity.

Modern steel construction, using widely spaced floor beams fireproofed in concrete, with flat slabs between them, has brought the beamed ceiling again into common use. Since we have learned to insulate floors so that sounds will not easily carry through them, hung ceilings are no longer necessary as insulators; accordingly it is simpler to plaster direct on the under sides of the concrete slabs and beams. But this brings a new responsibility to the architect and to the engineer. When ceilings are plastered flat, the position of the hidden beams is aesthetically unimportant, and frequently the structural pattern of a building (the position of the steel frame members) and the plan pattern (the shape and size of the rooms) have nothing to do with each other. In buildings with the beams exposed, however, the two patterns must be organized into one, and the beam layout made such that its appearance in every room has aesthetic design as well as structural meaning. Buildings in reinforced concrete sometimes have deep beams, and these offer to the architect just as much opportunity for meaningful design and appropriate decoration as did the wooden beams and girders of the past —as the rich yet frankly expressed interiors of the Los Angeles Public Library will show.

Yet by far the commonest ceilings today are flat plastered ceilings. Because of the interest given to an interior by floor and wall, by furniture and fittings, many designers feel that the best possible ceiling treatment is the simplest, and that to call attention to a ceiling when all the rest is so "busy" is only to produce confusion. With the generally low ceiling heights that are typical of modern buildings this is in most cases true, but in large, high, monumental rooms some decorative treatment of the ceiling still seems desirable. As yet, however, the architects of today seem generally to fail in realizing this. Thus far, mural painting and delicate plaster relief have been considered the most appropriate ceiling treatments for such large interiors, though Frank Lloyd Wright has on occasions successfully used flat wooden strips in discreet geometrical patterns over plywood ceilings. Even the low ceilings of the simplest rooms often demand more thought than they receive, and other colors besides white or cream are frequently restful to the eyes and helpful to the atmosphere of the room.

Still another new ceiling treatment is most effective in many cases —the use of the ceiling, or part of it, as a source of artificial light. Indirect lighting of the older, cruder type, which made a ceiling blaze so dazzlingly as to become disturbing and even hypnotic, was often unpleasant and seldom architectural, in the sense of truly enhancing the building's effect. But, as we have come to learn the possibilities of controlling light, we have gradually transformed this crude earlier lighting effect. By using recessed, lighted channels, coffers, or dome-like recesses, we can pattern a ceiling most interestingly in light and dark, and we can control color and intensity as we wish. This method of ceiling decoration, which also serves to illuminate the room, is still in its infancy, but occasional banks, theaters, office-building lobbies, and the like are beginning to reveal its real potentialities for beauty. A good example is the Irving Trust Company bank interior on Forty-eighth Street at Rockefeller Plaza in New York.

Still more interesting than flat ceilings are those curved ceilings we know as vaults. The vault, in its simplest form, is merely a continuous arch, like a tunnel. This is the form in which it was first used —in the beginning for drains, and later, in countries where beams of stone or wood were hard to get, as a covering for buildings. The long, narrow halls of the great Assyrian and Babylonian palaces were undoubtedly ceiled with barrel vaults; but these vaults were built of such perishable sun-dried brick that they have all vanished, and only the great thick walls remain. This Mesopotamian tradition of vault building had an intermittent influence on the builders of western Asia, but it is entirely to the Romans that we moderns owe the origin of all European vaulting. The Romans soon appreciated the immense opportunity offered by the vault for roofing in a majestic way great unencumbered halls, and with their customary ingenuity and sound sense they developed to the limit this new method of building. Not satisfied with the plain barrel vault, they used with greater and greater skill all kinds of interesting vaults and domes and thus started that great tradition of vault building which has flowered so gloriously again and again all through Gothic and Renaissance and modern times.

The dome is another form of continuous arch. A barrel vault, as we have seen, is produced when an arch is continued over a line at right angles to its own span. Imagine a similar arch pivoted through its center and highest point and then spun around; the result would be a dome, a hemisphere on a circular base. This beautiful form has been spoken of before, and we need not particularize further here, for the same facts apply to the interior that apply to the exterior dome, and the resultant artistic effects of grandeur and strength and lightness are much the same. But it will be well to keep in mind that there are several classes of domes.

First, there is the Roman dome, as seen in the Pantheon at Rome (Plate XVIII). This dome is designed with the interior effect supreme in the designer's mind; the exterior of the Pantheon depends for its effect not on the dome but on the entrance portico, the doorway, and the great unbroken stretch of cylindrical wall. From near by the dome itself is completely invisible outside; it is only when one enters that superb building and sees the great dome rising from all sides above him to the "eye," the open space in the center, that he grasps the full effect of the splendid concave above, with its many coffers and its perfect relationship to the walls below.

The Byzantine architects, the next great dome builders, strove for a dome that would be equally impressive inside and out. They accomplished this by raising the dome high up on a series of smaller half domes and subsidiary vaults, so that from both inside and out there is a wonderful effect of height and spaciousness, dome building into dome, vault into vault, up to the crowning glory of the whole, the principal dome. In Santa Sophia this form of design reached early a perfect expression (Plate XVI); centuries later, when the Turks conquered Constantinople, they used that church as a model for their larger mosques, and the glory of their domes is second only to that of Santa Sophia itself.

The architects of the Renaissance aimed at still different effects. They sought for a dome proportionately lower than that of Santa Sophia and more like the dome of the Pantheon; yet because of the length of their churches it was necessary at the same time to have a high dome to give external effect. Consequently a dome of two or even three shells was developed, in which the interior dome was proportioned with sole reference to interior effect, and the exterior dome with sole reference to exterior effect. Between these two shells there was sometimes a third, built to carry the weight of the "lantern," the small, many-windowed cupola which took the place of the "eye" of the Roman dome. Such domes may be seen in St. Peter's in Rome, in St. Paul's in London, in the Panthéon and Les Invalides in Paris, and in many American state capitols.

There was another objection to the simple Roman dome besides its exterior smallness. It had the same fault as the barrel vault; it exerted a continuous, strong sidewise thrust, which had to be counteracted by a tremendously heavy wall. The Roman builders constantly strove for some method of roofing a large space that would avoid the necessity of this heavy wall, and soon arrived at the solution, the groined vault. The groined vault consists of two vaults intersecting each other at right angles. In other words, imagine a square room roofed with a barrel vault. Two opposite walls will have arched tops. Now let us take another vault of the same size and place it across the room at right angles to the first. If we then cut out all the superfluous matter, the result will be a groined vault; the four walls of the room will all have arched heads now, and the whole weight of the vault and all the thrust will be concentrated at the corners, at

PLATE XVII

Westminster Hall, London: interior

Vickers, Inc., Factory, Detroit, Michigan
The Austin Company, architects and engineers

PLATE XVIII

Pantheon, Rome: interior

PLATE XIX

From *Grandes Constructions*

Market Hall, Rheims: interior
M. Maigrot, architect

St. Antoninus Church,
Basel, Switzerland:
interior
Karl Moser, architect

From *Die Baukunst
der nuesten Zeit*

PLATE XX

Hedrich-Blessing; Museum of Modern

Recreation Hall,
Great Lakes Navy Train
Center, Chicago, Illinois:
interior
Skidmore, Owings & Merr
architects

Chickamauga Power House
TVA: interior
Roland Wank, architect

TVA

which points it is easy to build masses of masonry to counteract the thrust without making the whole wall thick. This form of vault gives a feeling of height and grandeur, and a pleasant play of light and shade over its varied surfaces, which the simple barrel vault could never produce. The Romans adopted this form of vault as their favorite, and their great public baths became impressive and tremendous palaces because of its use.

FIGURE 17. GOTHIC RIBBED VAULTING

The diagram at the left shows the ribs, built first as free-standing arches; that on the right shows the vault filling that is built upon them.

All through the Middle Ages the groined vault was the controlling form in architecture, and the development of Gothic architecture is primarily dependent on its requirements. But the Gothic architects had difficulty in raising heavy, continuous vaults like those of the Romans; they sought, therefore, for some means of lessening the amount of surface that had to be built at one time. Consequently they adopted the ribbed vault. In the true ribbed vault all the ribs were built first; each, being an arch, was self-supporting (see Figure 17). Then the framework was filled in with very light masonry, each space left between the ribs being built separately. Later, particularly in England, the architects grew so fond of the decorative effect of these ribs that they multiplied their number enormously, at first in a simple way as in the Lincoln Cathedral choir, and then, as they grew more skillful, into a complex network—called lierne vaulting— as in Gloucester Cathedral. But in this development the richness of the result came to be an end in itself, and the structural character of the ribs was lost, until at last, in the exquisite mazes of fan vaulting to be seen in the Henry the Seventh Chapel in Westminster or in

King's College Chapel in Cambridge, the intricate ribs are merely decorations carved on the stones of a vault as uniform and non-Gothic as the old Roman vaults themselves.

The Renaissance vault builders went back to Roman examples for their inspiration, but, particularly in France, the ribbed vaults of the Gothic builders had left an impress too strong to be forgotten. As a result the vaults of the Renaissance are much more free and varied than those of Roman days. The builders learned alike from Roman and Byzantine and Gothic sources and applied their knowledge with continually growing skill. From the Romans they took the groin, from the Byzantines the pendentive (Figure 18)—that simple method of supporting a dome over a square—and from the Gothic builders the rib. The result may be seen in the loggia of the Farnesina Villa or the Villa Madama in Rome, in the entrance hall of the Boston Public Library, in St. Peter's at Rome, and in St. Paul's in London.

Recent developments have brought a new renascence of vault forms. For a time, the ease with which large spaces could be roofed with wood or steel girders or trusses led to an almost complete abandonment of vaults; when the romantic longings of popular taste did force the architect to use the vault form, he built inside the rectangular space of the real structure a light framework of metal or wood lath, which was plastered and imitated the shapes of masonry vaulting. Often the plaster was scored with grooves to imitate stone joints and decorated with all the panoply of ribs and bosses that were developed in Gothic stone vaults—forms alien to the spirit of plaster. That was the great error of the Gothic Revival of the mid-nineteenth century, and its evil influence is with us still, for even today many churches still are built with such false "birdcage construction," with piers too thin, and with vaults the wiry ribs and false non-structural shapes of which betray them and show them to be palpably of plaster. At its best such a building can have only the questionable appeal of a fancy-dress ball. But modern structural ingenuity, which first made such falseness possible, has now made it unnecessary. It has given us modern tile vaults that are strong, light, and beautiful; it can provide them, moreover, with a surface which is acoustically absorbent and kills the echoes that are so disturbing in many stone-vaulted interiors. These tile vaults seem particularly well adapted to domical forms, and can be richly treated both in surface and in color, as in the National Academy of Science Building in Washington or the lobbies of the Nebraska state capitol (Plate V). New types of concrete vaults also are continually being developed; these are structurally sound and of daring lightness, which allows a freedom of design, a varying of vault shapes, the like of which Gothic architecture at its height never knew. Such concrete vaults have been more highly developed in Europe than in America and are the chief reason for the airy lightness of many great market halls as well as of the poetic and imaginative mystery of many German and Scandinavian churches. Essentially fluid and plastic, the concrete vaults fall simply into almost any pattern, from shallow segments like those of the French churches of the Perret brothers, or Moser's Basel church (Plate XIX), to the soaring parab-

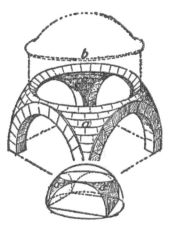

FIGURE 18. PENDENTIVES

This diagram explains how, by means of pendentives, domes may be built over square plans. Since the pendentives, when complete, are mutually self-supporting, the dome can be raised on a cylindrical wall or drum, without endangering the construction ("a a" are the pendentives, "b" is the dome built upon them).

olas more popular farther north. This parabola shape, functionally the most efficient, has introduced a new direct beauty into the world; like all new and lovely functional forms it has often been copied thoughtlessly in places where its use is meaningless. But when well used, as in the market hall at Rheims (Plate XIX) or the post office at Utrecht, it has an effortless soaring effect that is magnificent. In this country, too, recent years have seen great developments in the use of these thin-shelled concrete vaults, particularly in wartime factories, airplane hangars, and similar structures. Curved ceiling and roof forms and tall, airy interiors are new notes of variety in the architecture of today and wonderful opportunities for the creation of structural, organic beauty.

Somewhat similar in spirit to these new concrete vaults are certain types of wooden roof and ceiling forms that are vaultlike in structural nature as well as in appearance. One type, called "lamella construction," uses a thin, weblike network or frame of small wooden members following a shallow vault curve; on these the roof boarding is placed. Such a construction exerts thrust, like a vault, and is light and strong; with it wide spans can be efficiently roofed. Lamella construction has thus far been used chiefly for garages, rinks, and the like, but there is no reason why it should not be used as well for chapels or halls for more dignified purposes; the effect of its network frame is strong and beautiful.

Another type of curved wooden roof depends upon the use of "laminated" arches—great arches made by gluing together thin and easily shaped pieces of wood into one continuous form. Such wooden arches are light and strong; they are usually made continuous from floor to top and to floor again, like the braced frames in steel mentioned on page 131; for the sake of strength they are often parabolic in shape. This type of construction was frequent in certain types of wartime building—hangars, laboratories, camp halls—and its use permits beautifully graceful interiors, with strong rhythmical accents given by the laminated arches. Excellent examples can be seen in the recreation hall of the Great Lakes Navy Training Center near Chicago, by Skidmore, Owings & Merrill (Plate XX).

Thus it is true in vault building, as in other types of design, that contemporary architecture, which at first seemed to restrict the possible shape types of building and even to impoverish architectural tradition, has, as it has matured, done quite the reverse. It has developed quantities of new, expressive, and beautiful forms, all appropriate and honest. It has opened the door to new beauties true to our time. It is a challenge to the architect's imagination, not a limitation; all over the Western world, little by little, there are arising bridges, factories, halls, and churches that bring into our lives a new richness of aesthetic experience. It only remains for all of us to learn to accept these new forms, to become discriminating in our appraisal of them, to distinguish in them the bad and the good, so that we may aid the architects in the gradual evolution of a new architectural tradition.

Of the interior treatment of doors and windows, little need be said, for all that is true of their exterior treatment holds true of their treatment within, save that, as in the case of the wall, a greater freedom is allowable. And the present type of free and open planning gives great opportunities for this free treatment. With glass we can make functional divisions between areas and still preserve the wide, airy feeling of earlier undifferentiated spaces. We can lead light deep into the interior by means of glass. We can permit persons working, say, in a kitchen to command a wide view over children playing in a playroom or living room and still preserve quiet in the kitchen and keep cooking smells out of the rest of the house. With glass brick or tile we can get light and still preserve visual privacy. And glass now may be made with a microscopically thin mirror coating on one side, so that it is transparent in one direction but not in another. Thus windows and doors today, as never before in the history of architecture, have become opportunities for exciting and interesting interior effects.

There remains, then, but one more structural requirement to consider, that of the pier and the column. The pier is in essence merely a post, placed as an intermediate support where the width of a room is too great to be spanned by one beam or one vault, or placed so as to subdivide a large room into separate units that shall still be part of the whole. Gradually in their evolution the corners of square posts were cut off, to allow more ease of communication around the post and wider, more open views; later the whole post was rounded into a column. In the great temple halls of Egypt such columns were used by the hundred, giving an impression of tremendous mystery and size. In countries farther north, where wood was more abundant, the column was probably developed from a tree trunk used as a support. The round column has a grace that the square pier lacks; on the other hand, the pier has a strength and simplicity beyond that of the column. Each is good in its place, and some of the most impressive buildings in the world owe a great deal of their success to the careful use of both pier and column, each contributing its particular note to the beauty of the whole. For example, see the lovely cloisters of Santa Maria della Pace in Rome (Plate XXI). Note how the contrast of pier and column is used on the second story to suggest the pier and arch below; see, too, how exquisite is the balance and the rhythm of the whole.

The pier is such a simple element that little has been done to elaborate its form—save in such details as capital and base—except by Gothic and Romanesque architects. The Gothic architects were enthusiastic about structural expression, and, once given their ribbed vaults, it was but natural for them to wish to extend the feeling of the ribs down to the floor. This they did by making the pier very complex in plan, with a strongly marked projection under each rib. The accumulated richness of the vertical shadows on such a molded pier led them eventually to elaborate on this complex pier for its own sake, and to mold it richly without regard to the ribs above. Their successors in the Renaissance went back to the simple pier, breaking it only slightly with attached pilasters—as in the Santa Maria della Pace cloisters—or even treating it as a simple rectangular piece of masonry, unbroken.

In large modern buildings the piers one sees in the interior are but portions of great steel supports running continuously from top to bottom. For this reason it seems to many designers illogical to emphasize in the fireproof casing of these piers any strongly marked bases and capitals; better to let their stark naked length suggest their continuation below the floor and on above the ceiling (see Plate I). In smaller buildings, such as houses, when a skeleton construction with metal supports is used the problem is different, and various methods have been suggested to express them. In the lavish Tugendhat house, in Brünn, Czechoslovakia, as in the exhibition pavilion in the Barcelona Exposition (Plate XII), Mies Van der Rohe has merely surrounded the supports with slim casings of brilliant and glistening metal.

These, then, are the interior structural requirements that an architect must treat in his design; these are the usual indoor units of every building that he must make beautiful. Wall, roof, door, window, chimney, ceiling, vault, supports—these are the things he must supply. He must compose and arrange them in a beautiful form even before he thinks of the details. It is these necessary elements which those who wish to appreciate architecture must understand first and analyze first and appreciate first; for, though the greatest buildings are not only beautifully composed but beautifully detailed as well, detail is secondary, and no amount of refinement or exquisiteness in the treatment of minor elements, however lovely, can ever compensate for bad composition. The essentials of a building, the necessary parts, and their relations and arrangement must always be first in the minds alike of the architect and of the critic; only thus can great architecture be conceived and adequately appreciated.

7

THE DECORATIVE
MATERIAL OF
ARCHITECTURE

THE LAST two chapters have attempted to show how the structural necessities of a building may be made to serve an artistic end by careful composition and arrangement in accordance with the demands of function and of beauty. This use of structural elements, if rightly handled, will produce a beautiful building, and such a building may even have great and striking beauty because of its absolute simplicity. Yet a building so designed often fails to realize all the opportunities that architecture offers for enriching human life. There are other, more intimate, personal, and human types of beauty which architecture can also create. The greatest buildings not only are superbly composed and expressively designed but also have a manifest richness of content, a studied variety of surface, a careful handling of each smallest part, a sense that man's creative and imaginative power has played over them with loving care. In the largest sense of the word, they are as superbly decorated as they are magnificently composed. From the earliest times mankind has decorated those things which are useful, letting his imagination play over the forms he requires, until he makes of a necessity a thing of beauty as well.

This tradition of decoration, which has become almost a psychological necessity, does not lose its force when the necessary object is beautiful in itself; indeed, quite the reverse is the case, for the beauty innate in it furnishes the designer with a tremendous inspiration to start with and gives him the supreme opportunity to show his genius. This is true in architecture; always the purely necessary part of the building, the structure, however beautiful in itself, has been an invitation and an inspiration to the world's architects and has furnished them opportunities for creating beautiful works of a great art which forms, next to literature, the most perfect expression and the most vivid evidence of the world's life.

The part played by this decorative element in architecture is very large. To some critics, of whom Ruskin is the foremost, architecture is merely decoration, nothing more; they judge architecture merely by its ornament. This point of view is as one-sided as that of some engineers, who tend to think all architecture a waste of time and money, because they could build buildings equally strong more cheaply. To the great majority of men and women both extremes are equally absurd. To them a beautiful building has always meant a place in which to work or play or rest, as well as an aesthetic emotion, and a house has meant not only a roof above but beauty within and without as well.

Throughout architectural history the governing tastes as to what is good architectural decoration, how much enhancement of structural motifs is desirable, and what should be the basis of this enhancement have swung widely. Some peoples have loved more decoration, some less. Some have preferred purely abstract forms, some have demanded naturalism and representation. But wherever the architect has refined the shapes of a structural member with the idea of making it lovelier, wherever the craftsman has carefully carved stone or wood to bring out its nature or to give it a more human appeal, there architectural decoration, in its largest sense, is present. Yet in architecture this decoration, this enhancement, of whatever nature, is primarily upon members structurally necessary, and not a mere arbitrary contortion or breaking of the surface; if it has not the closest relationship to the nature of the building, its structure, and its materials, it is not architectural decoration at all.

It is true, therefore, that an adequate appreciation of good architecture can come only from a knowledge of both structural and artistic elements, from an appreciation of ornamentation as well as an appreciation of the building as a whole. This double knowledge is particularly necessary because in the greatest buildings of the world these two sides of architecture are inextricably combined, so that it is difficult to say just what is purely structural and what purely decorative.

Of course, the decorative material of architecture cannot be codified in any such simple manner as can the structural material. It is far too wide in scope. Forms of almost every conceivable nature have at some time been used to decorate a building; geometrical shapes, the world's flora and fauna, man, woman, child, and all the mythologies of the nations, the heavens above, and the earth beneath have been called upon to furnish decorative forms. Two great types of classification, however, are possible. One is the division of all decoration into *structural* and *applied* decoration; the other is its division into *non-representational* and *representational* decoration. The first classification is particularly important in dealing with the larger phases of the appreciation of decoration, the second in analyzing its many detailed forms.

Structural decoration, as its name implies, is that which results from the imaginative shaping of structurally necessary elements— posts, columns, buttresses, and the like. Applied decoration is that which is obviously added, like much sculpture, mosaic, or mural painting. When the Greek architect developed the bracketed column capital of Asia Minor into the Ionic capital with its graceful scrolls, when the Gothic designer molded arches and carved crocketed spirelets on buttresses, when the modern architect surrounds a steel column with a sheath of glittering metal like those in the Tugendhat house, or with a rich covering of marble that expresses the underlying shape, like those in the lobby of the International Building at Rockefeller Center (Plate I), he is producing structural decoration. When, on the other hand, the Egyptian carved pylon walls with ranked deities or conquering pharaohs, when the Greek sculptor filled the gable ends of his temples with magnificent figures of gods or heroes, or when the modern mural painter paints on a wall, the decoration is obviously applied.

Different architectural periods have held various notions with regard to which type of decoration is preferable. Architects today disagree on this subject; some prefer the starkest and simplest structure, with all decoration applied in the form of sculpture, mural paint-

ing, or planting; some, on the other hand, claim that only the enhancement of structural elements is true decoration and point to
Gothic architecture as confirmation. The Egyptians, many Moslem
cultures, many primitive peoples, and some modern designers have
preferred applied ornament. The Romanesque and Gothic architects, as well as the Chinese and Japanese builders, have generally
depended largely on structural decoration. The Greeks and Romans
and the Renaissance designers used both kinds, and in that respect
we today are following the classic tradition.

To tell the truth, under present conditions this differentiation between structural and applied decorations has little meaning; it may
further our understanding of historical development, but, although
it was a favorite battleground of nineteenth-century architectural
critics, it is of no help in telling us whether any given ornament is
good or bad, desirable or the reverse. Alberti defined architectural
beauty as that arrangement of parts so perfect that nothing can be
added, and nothing taken away, without damaging the total effect;
this criterion we might well apply in judging the decoration of the
buildings about us. If all seems necessary, organic, and harmonious
with the structure's purpose, construction, materials, and basic forms,
it is good. If, on the other hand, decorations are there for ostentatious
display alone, or if they fog the nature of the building and destroy its
clarity, they are bad. According to this point of view applied decoration may be as organic as structural ornament, and structural decoration may be as false as any applied enhancements could ever be.

The differentiation into representational and non-representational
decoration is not intended as a criterion of merit but merely as an aid
in the analysis of the whole vast field. It contains no implications as
to the history or origin of decorative forms. By non-representational
decoration is meant simply that which seems obviously not to seek
to depict any one thing, or any group of things, in the world around,
whatever its ultimate origin. By representational decoration is meant
that which depicts, naturalistically or conventionally, some natural
or recognizable object. Under the first head we shall include geometric forms and certain of those shapes which, though originally
developed from representations, have come to have a form almost

absolutely conventional and imaginary. The egg-and-dart motif, for example, which, though originally developed from the lotus, has come to have a well-known form almost entirely conventional, we shall class as non-representational. On the other hand, all those myriad forms of classic and Gothic art which, though unrecognizable as depicting some one plant or animal, are yet obviously and unmistakably plants and animals, like the anthemion, the acanthus, the gryphon, the sphinx, or the gargoyle, we shall class as representational.

The most important type of non-representational decoration—the molding—is at the same time one of the most important elements in architecture. The world "molding" is a broad term applied to any modulation of a surface, either projecting or receding, or both, such as would be described if a straight or curved profile—the section of the molding—were drawn along a surface in a given direction. In fact, many moldings are made in precisely this way; a knife is cut with an edge formed to the profile of the desired molding, and this knife, by means of a plane or a hammer, is driven through the material; what it leaves is the molding.

The origins of moldings lie chiefly in certain structural necessities of a building. Roof eaves project, and projecting beams or brackets, as well as the edges of gutters or the border of roofing materials, all suggest refined and beautiful treatments which have developed into molding types. Post and column design gave rise to flutings and reedings. Molded capitals and bases for columns were the result of what originally were structurally necessary elements to spread the load below and to furnish better support for the beams above. The fact that foundation walls are often thicker than the walls above made necessary some kind of treatment where the thickness changed; base moldings of many kinds were the result. Where two different materials came together, like stone and wood, or stone and metal, or glass and masonry, some kind of strip or member was often essential to cover the joint; a whole series of moldings developed from the necessity of such covering strips.

Moldings have decorated buildings for long ages. Their origin is manifold, due in some places to one cause, in others to something else. In Egypt, it has been suggested, moldings were developed from the early method of building with reeds and clay; several reeds were bound together into a cylinder to act as a framework around the top and corners of a hut, and thus formed a molding. In countries farther north, such as Lycia and Greece, moldings were derived from wooden forms, from several timbers placed together, and from the projection of tree trunks used as beams in the frame of the wooden roof. Whatever their origin may have been, moldings were appropriated universally and developed and refined and modified continually; they have been used with ever increasing freedom, so that the chief distinction and crowning beauty of many a building consists in its moldings and their perfection of form and placing.

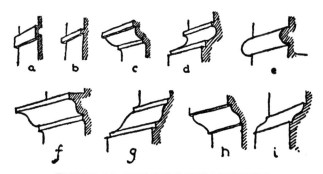

FIGURE 19. THE COMMON MOLDINGS

(a) Fascia. (b) Fillet. (c) Ovolo. (d) Scotia. (e) Torus. (f) Cyma recta, as cap. (g) Cyma recta, as base. (h) Cyma reversa, as cap. (i) Cyma reversa, as base.

Like any class of forms used again and again by mankind, moldings have little by little come to be grouped into different classes. Though the profiles that are possible are infinite in number, there are in nearly all of them certain easily recognized elements. These are briefly as follows (see Figure 19):

The fascia—a flat band projecting or receding from the face of the wall.

The fillet—a flat band narrower than the fascia.

The ovolo—a quarter round, convex.

The scotia—a concave curve of the same general cylindrical type, usually elliptical in section.

The torus, or bead—a semi-cylindrical mold, convex.

The cavetto—a quarter round, concave.

The cyma reversa—a complex curve, convex above and concave below. This is perhaps the most important molding of all.

The cyma recta—another complex curve, concave above and convex below.

It is surprising how much of the effect of good architecture depends on these few moldings and their proper combination and placing. The reason for this lies in the fact that their effect on the eye is that of long bands of modulated light and shade; for architecture is in general an art that deals primarily with light and shade, and only secondarily with color. It is not strange, therefore, that these long bands of light and shade and half light, incisive as they are, determine to a large extent the final success or failure of a building as well as its specific character.

Today, too, there is a structural basis for the best molding design. In fact, the present strong aesthetic trend toward simplicity, toward clarity of basic geometry rather than lavishness of ornament, has tended to restrict the use of moldings to those places where they are absolutely necessary, as around window and door frames, for cover strips, in hand rails, and the like; the tendency also, where they are used, has been to choose the simplest types, the profiles of which suggest the machines by which they are produced. Thus modern designers prefer simple fascias, fillets, toruses, beads, and ovolos to the more complex curves of the cyma type, and for rich effects will use continuous modulations of surface, like reedings or flutings, rather than any modeled or carved ornament. Yet even in the most modern buildings the final quality of beauty may be determined by the beauty and the fitness of these moldings—these metal frames around doors and windows, these subtle and definite members which separate material from material.

Thus moldings are an important factor, even when relatively small in amount. Take, for instance, an Egyptian entrance (Figure 20). Note how its cornice, that great sweeping cavetto, with its broad shadow and the light, narrow shade of the torus below, sets perfectly the note of the simple, massive dignity of the whole. Then, for contrast, look at a late fifteenth-century Italian tomb, chiseled with a delicacy like that of silverware, and note its crowning cornice —a group of different moldings, topped with a delicate cyma recta— each molding carved till it sparkles (Plate XXII).

FIGURE 20. TEMPLE GATEWAY, KARNAK, EGYPT

One of the most radical changes in the conception of buildings which the twentieth century has brought has been a change from thinking of a building as "mass"—that is, basically something solid —to thinking of it as the envelope, the enclosing cover, of a "volume." This has necessarily changed our attitude toward moldings, and tended to reduce their number and complexity. A mass can be carved and modulated, like sculpture, but a thin box tends to take the simple shapes made by unbroken planes. Yet even in the most advanced modern building moldings are sometimes necessary. If a building has an overhanging roof of any kind, the eaves form a sort of molding. Wherever two different materials come together, some sort of covering of the joint is necessary, and this may take the form of a molding. These modern moldings will vary in profile, and therefore in light and shade, according to their materials and their uses.

Of all the categories of moldings in past centuries, the most important is that comprised within the "classic" tradition—that is, the tradition which began in the works of ancient Greece, continued down through the Roman world, and through it into the Renaissance. This is a tradition of molding design especially important to us because, of all the molding systems, it is the simplest to understand. In classic moldings there is frequently the same triple nature that characterizes so many classic architectural features—like the base, shaft, and capital of a column; the architrave, frieze, and cornice of an entablature; and so on. In the cornice, for instance—in classic buildings usually the most important molding group—there are three main portions: a crown molding, called the cymatium, often a cyma recta; below this the corona, a broad projecting shelf which casts a deep shadow over the wall below it and shows a flat band as its front edge; and, finally, under the corona and supporting it at its juncture with the wall, a molding or group of moldings called the bed mold (Figure 21).

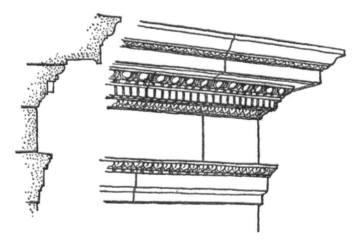

FIGURE 21. A TYPICAL CLASSICAL CORNICE

At the top, the molded cymatium (the gutter member). Below this, the undecorated band of the corona. Underneath and supporting all, a triple bed mold.

Now, in cornice design, as in the base, shaft, and capital of classic columns, this triple character is no accident, for the design of good cornices is rooted both in needs and in construction. In fact, one might make the broad generalization that all those architectural forms which have lived, which have entered the great onrushing stream of architectural tradition, have been living forms precisely because their origin is so closely bound up with function and structure. This is true of the classic cornice.

Essentially, and as it was handled in the beginning, a cornice is merely the highly developed treatment of the eaves of a sloping roof. The roof slope projects beyond the line of the wall or the beams of a porch in order to keep rain away from the wall or out of the porch. In order to keep the water from the roof from dripping off in a continuous band at the outer elge of this projection, a gutter is necessary; this collects the water and directs it to a few well-placed spouts, where it can be run off as desired. We must, accordingly, take care of the roof projection and the gutter. The top member of a cornice, the so-called cymatium, was originally the front of the gutter, and in much Colonial architecture it still preserves its original function. The middle member, the flat band of the corona, in wooden cornices is a board across the ends of the projecting roof rafters; in masonry cornices it is the front edge of the projecting stone course that holds up the gutter on its outer edge. The third and lowest member, the bed mold, in wooden cornices is a development of the moldings which close the joint between vertical wall and projecting eaves; in masonry construction it consists of the decorated outer edges of a course, or courses, of stone which project slightly from the wall line and thus help to support the corona above. The bed mold is essentially, then, a corbeling or bracketing member.

One can follow this structural basis in many types of cornice design. The Greek Doric cornice shows evidence of a gradual development from wood construction, through wood sheathed with terra cotta, and finally into marble (see Figure 22). In the Corinthian cornice the bed mold becomes large and complex, with actual projecting scrolled brackets, or modillions. Dentil courses are probably distant reminiscences in stone of the earlier ends of closely spaced wooden crossbeams, and much of the carved decoration on classic moldings is an interpretation in relief of earlier flat decoration painted on wood or terra cotta. Many types of cornice have gone through similar developments. In China and Japan, for instance, an early system of supporting the roof eaves by simple curved wooden brackets was gradually elaborated into the almost bewildering complexity of the great polychromed bracketed cornices of the Sung and later dynasties.

In the usual classic cornice, the cymatium, or crown mold, is usually a cyma recta, because this molding has the most delicate profile, and because the lights and shades and half lights are so gracefully modulated on its ever changing surface. The corona, its flat band catching the light, runs straight and strong around the whole building, binding it together like a fillet. Below this, in its shadows, are the playing half lights on the bed mold, which relieve the darkness and give strength and support to the whole cornice, so that it may form, with its many bands of differing value, a crown to the building or element it decorates (see Plate XXI).

In playing with this idea the classic designers devised many variations. They elaborated the bed mold, made it double or triple, or inserted a row of dentils, the flat, narrow blocks of which gave a pleasing accented note. In Roman times modillions or scrolled brackets were added under the corona, producing the Corinthian cornice, a form that produces the richest and most complex light and shade of any of the various classes of cornice. The Romans ap-

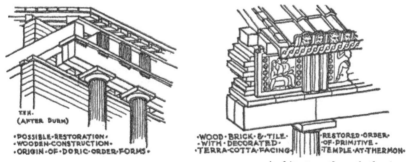

·POSSIBLE·RESTORATION· ·WOODEN·CONSTRUCTION· ·ORIGIN·OF·DORIC·ORDER·FORMS·   ·WOOD·BRICK·&·TILE· ·WITH·DECORATED· ·TERRA·COTTA·FACING·   ·RESTORED·ORDER· ·OF·PRIMITIVE· ·TEMPLE·AT·THERMON·

Architecture through the Ages

FIGURE 22. DEVELOPMENT OF THE GREEK DORIC ENTABLATURE

At the left, a conjectural restoration of the wooden construction system which gave rise to the Doric entablature. At the right, a later stage, from a temple at Thermon, in which terra-cotta revetments decorate the cornice and the frieze.

preciated early, too, the value of contrast in molding design—of alternating square and round, and convex and concave; the value, for instance, of a narrow, flat band or fillet between two curved moldings—and they became expert in using all the possible combinations of these square or flat and receding or projecting curves.

During the centuries, say, from 1200 to 1550, when Gothic was the prevailing architecture in all the European countries save Italy, new uses for moldings gave a fresh impetus to molding design. The earlier Romanesque methods of building had begun this development, particularly in the use of the stepped arch. A stepped arch is a combination of concentric arch rings, one within and behind another; a section through them would be a series of steps. It was the simplest thing in the world to round the corners of the successive projecting concentric arch rings, and once this was done the door was open to a thousand further complications and modifications. The whole development of medieval moldings is as intimately connected with the development of these arch forms and sections as that of classic moldings is with the development of the horizontal cornice.

The Gothic molding designer recognized no rules. Gothic molding profiles are infinite in variety. In general, however, they may be easily differentiated from classic moldings by the small use made of the fillet or, in fact, of any flat members at all, and also by the use of deeply cut, receding members, which give very dark shadow lines. "Quirking," that is, the bringing of the top or bottom of a molding strongly and suddenly out or in, to give emphasis, is here the rule rather than the exception. In addition, the Gothic architect liked to combine all sorts of moldings, projecting and receding, into one band, much wider and more complex in light and shade than any the classic architect would have permitted; indeed, no small part of that air of impressive and complex mystery which is so characteristic of a Gothic church comes from precisely the complexity of surface of these elaborate moldings, with their lack of flat surfaces.

This omission of fillets, with its resulting roundness and softness of effect, sometimes became almost a fault. In English "Decorated Gothic," which is the style of the choirs of Ely and Lincoln (Plate XXIII), the arch molds became mere series of almost meaningless curves, this one projecting and the next receding; though there is a certain mysterious charm in the continuous changing light and shade of such a molding, the trained eye feels the need of some flat surface on which to rest. Between the cornice of the Erechtheum at Athens and the arches and piers of an English Decorated Gothic church there is much the same difference as there is between a dialogue of Plato and a medieval romance.

During the Renaissance, classic moldings inevitably came back into use along with the rest of the classic forms. But there was a difference. The eye of the architect had been too long trained in the freedom and subtleties of the Gothic molds to be entirely satisfied with the Roman or the Greek forms; it is therefore in the moldings of the Renaissance, particularly those of early date, where the greatest differences may be seen between Renaissance work and the earlier buildings of the Greeks and Romans. Thus, in the tomb mentioned earlier, there are a hundred subtleties and peculiarities of molding profile for which it is impossible to find an exact precedent in ancient buildings.

Gothic architecture struck off the shackles of the molding designer, but it remained for the Renaissance to instill personality into molding design, and this quality it has retained ever since. All the most successful architects have been very careful with moldings; if one could look into the office of a great architect when a building is being detailed and see with what loving care every molding is studied and restudied, by itself and in relation to its surroundings, by means of drawings and models, until the right section is arrived at to give the proper band of light and shade, he would realize more clearly why a good building—the Boston Public Library, for instance—is more pleasing than a bad one. One may realize that an apartment house door is ugly, but he probably does not realize that it is too big and flaring and soft in design, or that the moldings around the door are big where they should be small, and small where they should be big. If he did understand this, it is certain that when he came to build for himself he would see to it that he had his house designed, and designed well, by an architect, and not merely thrown together by an underpaid builder's draftsman.

There are some moldings which do not depend for their effect upon their profile alone, for the surface itself is broken up by intricate carving. From earliest times the decorative instinct of man was never entirely satisfied with the plain curved surface of a molding. Throughout the long course of Egyptain art the one important molding, the great cavetto cornice, was painted in brilliant colors which varied the monotony of the long, simple shadow. The Greeks, even in primitive times, seem to have painted almost all their moldings, and as their skill grew they came at last to carve the moldings in patterns similar to those they had painted before. To them we owe the egg and dart, that most common of moldings, and the water leaf, as well as the successful use of dentils—small rectangular blocks, placed close together—which give, with their alternating light faces and deep shadowed clefts, such life and variety to a cornice. To the decoration of their moldings the Greeks applied the same subtlety, the same insight, the same delicate refinement of taste, and the same beauty of workmanship which they applied to their sculpture. Working as they did with such mental tools, they stumbled almost immediately upon the prime principle of molding decoration; they discovered that the most beautiful decorated moldings were those in which the very form of the decoration expressed and emphasized the profile of the molding (Figure 23).

FIGURE 23. THE MOST COMMON DECORATED MOLDINGS

(a) Greek egg and dart. (b) Roman egg and dart. (c) Greek water leaf. (d) Roman water leaf.

The egg-and-dart motif is one of the most universally admired decorations of classic moldings, because it illustrates this principle so perfectly. It is a form devised to decorate the ovolo, the convex quarter round; even the most cursory glance shows how every accented line emphasizes this convex curve. The sides of the egg are of this shape, and they are emphasized strongly by a frame. The egg itself has a pleasing roundness that emphasizes the roundness of the molding, and the straight darts between the eggs serve merely to accentuate the roundness on either side. It is this absolute correspondence between the shape of the molding and the shape of its decoration, coupled with the exquisite rhythm of accented and unaccented, of wide and narrow, of lights and darks, which has made this egg-and-dart molding so generally appreciated.

The water leaf is another example of a similar correspondence. The water-leaf motif is applied to a cyma reversa molding, and every line in it is a line of double curvature that recalls the double curve of the profile. Consequently, next to the egg-and-dart, the water-leaf molding has been the most popular of all classic moldings. At the dawn of the Renaissance in Italy, it was these two moldings which took fastest hold of the imagination of the fifteenth-century sculptors and architects, and tomb and altar piece and door and cornice were embellished with them.

This principle of the correspondence of profile with decoration is not limited to the architecture of Greece, Rome, and the Renaissance; it is universal, for to try to decorate an object which has a peculiar and accented surface, like a molding, with a form that neglects and contradicts the shape of this surface is manifestly illogical. In Gothic architecture the principle is somewhat hidden by the Gothic artist's love for naturalistic representation, but in the best Gothic work one will find the shape of the molding always carefully considered and subtly expressed in the design of its decoration. It is only a sign of decadence in the florid Gothic of Germany or Spain that the pure form of the molding is forgotten, and naturalistic exuberance runs riot, forming moldings into twigs and branches, hiding forced and uncouth forms under a gorgeous luxuriance of intricate carving.

The design of moldings today is conditioned by two things—by the prevailing desire for simplicity noted earlier, and by the fact that the great majority of moldings are now run out by machines. Stone moldings are cut by grinding wheels of the proper profile, and wood moldings by running thin strips through planing machines; those of metal are largely drawn, or extruded, through apertures which control the section. All these techniques have one quality in common—the exact continuity of the product. Machine-made moldings, therefore, are not fitted for carved decoration, or for sudden breaks or chamfer stops which require hand-finishing; ideally they should be continuous for their entire length, with profiles bold, simple, and lacking in easily damaged edges and corners, and with richness given by continuous groovings or raisings of the general surface as in flutings or reedings. With such forms just as effective results can be obtained in the buildings of our own time as were produced in the past; in addition, if we accept the limitations in design imposed by function and by techniques of production and if we design imaginatively in accordance with these requirements, we shall produce a beauty necessarily harmonious with our industry and our life.

The study of moldings is full of fascination. Their myriad delicacies of form and the subtle play of light on their changing surfaces may be a continual delight. And it is not necessary to go far afield to begin the study. In one's own home there are undoubtedly many moldings: door trims, picture frames, table tops, bookcase cornices. Begin with these, running your thumb over them; follow their curves, watch them under different lights. You will soon learn to notice slight differences, to find that some of them please and others leave you cold, to see that some are coarse and others delicate and refined. That is true appreciation. It is only when moldings are studied with relation to their position, however, that their importance and significance can be grasped. A molding may be good in one place and bad in another, coarse in one position and refined in another. It will be worth while, then, to summarize briefly the principal uses of the molding, and to show what bearing they have upon its design.

In many buildings the most important moldings form the cornice. A cornice originally served two purposes: one was to decorate the edge of a projecting roof, as we have already noted; the other was to serve as a coping, or protective covering, for the top of a wall. Later, because of the decorative value of its broad shadow, the cornice was used purely as decoration, without practical use; as a decoration, too, it was often extravagantly misused. Take, for example, the greater number of cheap apartment houses and business blocks built between 1880 and 1910 in the United States. Almost all of them have garish, over-decorated cornices, stamped out of sheet metal, cut off sharply at the ends, and glued willy-nilly to the building as obvious excrescences. Sometimes they are painted stone grey and sanded, in a hopeless attempt to make them look like stone. Is it strange that a reaction against all this has set in?

As city buildings have grown higher, we have come to realize that classic cornices at their summits are absurd, taking light and sun away from the upper windows and increasing the shadow in the streets; moreover, placed as they are, high in the air, their effect is almost nil. They are the results of pure "paper architecture"—things that look well on a drawing but are meaningless in reality. And with the increasing use of flat roofs for all kinds of buildings, where the upper part of a wall has become a parapet, the necessity for a cornice treatment has disappeared; this fact, together with our growing dislike of unnecessary frills in architecture, has made buildings without cornices almost the general rule. Such cornices as we do still use are likely to be either the frank expression of the eaves of a sloping roof or the decorative elaboration of a projecting, water-shedding hood or shelf over a door or porch. We might say that wherever a cornice seems an integral and necessary part of the building it is good; elsewhere, the sheer unbroken sweep of wall cut off simply with a coping at the top seems more logical and more lovely.

It is difficult to dogmatize about cornice design beyond the widest generalities. Lighter, more delicate moldings, like the cavetto and the cyma recta, seem appropriate at the top, with stronger and heavier moldings below; usually, too, it seems advantageous to have one strongly marked flat face carrying strongly through to bind the whole together, like the corona of a classic cornice. And generally it seems appropriate for the cornices formed by the eaves of a roof of gentle slope to have considerable projection, as in many of the earlier houses of Frank Lloyd Wright, whereas those used with steep roofs should be of the smallest possible projection. The châteaux of the Loire valley, nearly all of them dating from the time of Francis I, owe a great deal of the beauty of their cornices to this relation; the cornices are kept extremely flat because the roofs above are so steep, and interest is given by elaborate decoration of the nearly flat surfaces, where bold projecting moldings and a deep shadow would have cut the building in two and destroyed the connection between walls and roof, instead of emphasizing it, as do these lovely flat cornices with their rich carved decoration (Figure 24).

Moldings are also important at the base of a building or of a wall, inside or outside, to mitigate the harshness of the angle between wall and ground or wall and floor, as well as to cover the joint between the two different materials of floor and wall. Any building looks stronger if it has an adequate base. On the exterior, as we have noted, base moldings indicate or express the projection of the foundation beyond

FIGURE 24. CORNICE FROM THE WING OF FRAN-
CIS I, CHÂTEAU OF BLOIS

Rich surface decoration takes the place of bold projection.

the wall above it. As such, in many buildings the base is a necessary feature and serves also to relate the building to the ground; its strong horizontal line, drawn across the building near its apparent bottom, is, as it were, a sort of reduplication of the level line of the earth itself. Frank Lloyd Wright has used such strong simple bases on many of his houses with delightful effect. But in large modern city buildings the case is different. These are usually supported on isolated piers or columns, and their foundations are far below the grade. The wall line usually coincides with the legal building line, and only the slightest projections beyond this are permitted. An accented base, therefore, on an average city steel-framed structure is as false and unreal as anything one can imagine, and the attempt to imitate in such buildings the strong projections suitable to bearing-wall structures in wide and open sites is bound to produce only confusion in the design. Yet even in these modern city buildings, with their screen walls rising sheer from the pavement, some differentiation near the ground is often necessary and appropriate. Many materials suitable for exterior screen walls above the grade are not fitted for the excessive water and dampness and the hard wear which the lower parts of a wall receive; at the grade line, and for some distance above it, only the hardest and most impermeable materials will do. Thus, frequently, where walls above are of limestone or tile or marble, close to the grade they will be of granite, and this change of material gives a decorative line around the building which serves the same aesthetic function as a projecting and molded base.

It follows from the very position of base molds that they should be strong in effect, not weak and indecisive. A weak base is almost worse than none. Often in brickwork the base consists merely of one or two small projections, unmolded, sometimes further accented by a row of bricks on edge—a solution that is entirely satisfactory because so absolutely in harmony with the material. But in stone buildings there is a much greater flexibility of treatment, the only requirement being apparent strength and adequate size. A common molding for this use is the cyma recta upside down, for in this position it is as strong and sturdy as it is light and graceful in the cornice. There is something about the cyma reversa that makes it too abrupt for a base; it lacks just that touch of horizontality which makes the cyma recta so successful. In wooden buildings the structural problem is different, for the masonry foundation wall usually recedes from the face of the shingle or clapboards, instead of projecting, and in this case the wall covering is merely given a little curve out at the bottom, with a simple molding below; somehow this simple base, or water table, always seems ample for the building above it.

Perhaps the most common use of moldings is as frames; door trims, window trims, and paneling are a few of the many places where they are so used. As a general rule moldings used as frames must be more delicate and flatter than those in cornices or bases, for moldings that are too large cast such a heavy shadow that they cut off the opening or panel with too great a distinctness. The change in the design of picture frames obvious at any exhibition of modern paintings, from the heavily molded and modeled gilded frames of seventy years ago to the simple bands of projecting or receding faces common today, reveals our growing appreciation of this fact. It is one of the chief faults of Victorian architecture, both in this country and in England, that all its trim moldings are monstrously heavy, full of bold curves and deep cuts, piled one on another, till they become forbidding rather than decorative.

Door and window trim exists for a purpose; it is not a mere frame decoration. As we have noted, one of the common uses of moldings has been to cover joints between different materials, and this is the prime purpose of door and window trims. The frames here are usually of wood or metal, but the wall surfaces in which they occur are frequently of plaster or stone or brick. Some sort of cover over the joint between the two materials is an absolute necessity, and "trim" is the result. In the criticism and appreciation of door and window trim this basic structural fact must always be kept in mind. Good trim is generally of three sorts: flat, or with one main molding of delicate section on the outside and flat faces diminishing in width within, or so molded as to produce one easy and delicate sweep from outside to inside. And no frame, no matter what its scheme or use, must ever be so large as to overbalance the space framed, or so heavy in projection as to appear to be an excrescence instead of a decoration of the surface on which it is placed.

In many modern buildings the use of metal for door frames and window sash has profoundly altered the basis of molding design. Steel door frames often use the trim as an integral part of the frame, and through structural necessities the trim naturally is much narrower than the traditional wood trim. The qualities of steel, too, are manifestly different from those of wood or stone; steel is suited to simple flat faces or to quiet, suave, convex curves, and not at all to the sharp edges and tiny delicate moldings of the best wood trim. Where steel window sash are used, no trim or decorative frames whatsoever are necessary. Yet how often does the irrational conservatism of our taste force the recalcitrant steel into expensive and difficult shapes in order to surround our doors with classic architraves and our windows with useless trim!

The case of panel molds is different. Here the molding is often an integral and necessary part of the design, and its size and projections are, to a certain extent, already determined. Then, too, its size is usually so small that any complicated system of molding is impossible. The same rule that governs the design of trim, however, governs panel molds; this, coupled with considerations of general delicacy and beauty of profile and shadow, forms the only criterion of good and bad design in panel molds.

In masonry walls openings or niches are often framed with decorative systems of moldings analogous to the trim. These systems are termed architraves; many of the most beautiful doorways of the world owe a large part of their beauty to architraves. And, if flatness and apparent unity are necessary in interior door frames, how much more so are they in monumental architraves! For there is a playfulness allowable in wood or plaster which in dignified stone would appear frivolous and out of place.

Some there may be who will object to this rule for frame design and point triumphantly to a superb Gothic gateway as an example of a heavy series of moldings used successfully as a frame—the doorway of Notre Dame, for instance. The basis for this objection is more apparent than real, for in good Gothic the moldings never project far in front of the wall; they are cut on the thickness of the wall itself, revealing its depth and giving mystery and charm to the door within. In reality, these myriad moldings are a frame only incidentally; primarily they are an expression of the powerful arch that supports the great wall or gable above. Exactly the same is true of the intricate moldings on the nave arch of a Gothic church; they are less a frame than an expression of the arch idea itself. Notice in them how strong and virile are the lights and shadows and how the arch line is repeated over and over again in lines of light and dark (Plate XXIII).

The last main use of the molding is its use as a "string course," that is, in horizontal bands across a building between base and cornice. The string course may be used to express floor levels, or it may be used merely decoratively to cut the building into pleasing vertical relationships. There is often one above the first or second floor, to make the bottom stories count as a base, and one near the top of the building to form with the cornice an adequate crown; the shaft between is usually unbroken. String courses, like all good moldings, often have a structural basis and in design always reveal certain practical requirements in their use. For instance, where a building has many windows close together and at the same level, it may be desirable to connect their projecting sills and thus form a continuous string course. Where such bands are used to express story heights, their position obviously is determined by the position of the floor beams, and the like. In the profiling of good string courses one can always see revealed a recognition of the fact that moisture is the great enemy of all walls, and that any projection from a wall face which would interrupt the free drainage of water must be designed to throw the water away from the wall. The upper edges of such string courses, like those of window and door sills, must be sloped, so that water will run off them; on the under side of the projection, too, there should be a hollow groove, or "drip," so that water running down the face of the string course will not run back to the wall but will drip clear. Good cornices, Gothic buttress offsets, and similar elements show an analogous use of drips.

String courses themselves are of comparatively little importance; it is by their position that they gain significance. In general, in small buildings they are to be avoided, and in large ones to be used with restraint. Our love today for simple, unbroken geometric surfaces has much reduced their use. Of the profiles of the string course there is little more to be said; a hundred different buildings may require a hundred different profiles, and the effect produced is the sole test of their excellence. They ought never to conflict with the cornice, or seem to cut the building into too distinct parts; beyond that, the architect's only limitation is the proportion and the style of the rest of the building.

No attempt has been made in this chapter to give an absolutely complete list of the use of moldings, or to treat of them exhaustively.

Such a treatment would be beyond the scope of this work; it would demand a book in itself. The foregoing discussion is offered merely as a suggestive outline, to point out certain salient features of molding design, so that the reader may start out for himself to study moldings and thus lay the foundations for a clearer and truer personal appreciation.

There are, of course, other kinds of non-representational ornament, but there is not much that need be said of them. There is the whole field of geometric ornament, the use of squares, ellipses, checkerboards, and frets, either in bands or over broad fields. Another kind of ornament to which reference must be made, because of its sincerity, its beauty, and its gradually growing use, is that produced by the richness and beauty of different materials, such as brick and tile, or brick of different colors, or brick and stone, or wood and marble and metal. This is an old practice and one of ever growing importance today, when science and industry have given us such a magnificently varied palette of materials with which to work. We find it employed on Tudor houses in England, in the form of lozenge-shaped patterns produced by the insertion of dark and light bricks in certain places; the pattern is usually charmingly irregular, wandering naïvely over a gable end, then dying away, or changing abruptly where the width of the brickwork made it difficult to make the pattern come out straight. There is an especially good example of this treatment on the front of Hampton Court Palace, near London.

Roman and Byzantine architects loved this type of decoration resulting from the use of rich materials. Like the strong and simple veneered lower walls around the interior of the Pantheon at Rome, the richly veined grey marble veneers of the interior of St. Mark's at Venice show the magnificent effect of this form of decoration. The bandings of Siena Cathedral form a more staccato but still effective note, and today we are growingly skillful in producing this sincere and honest type of lavish decorative beauty that results from the free use of lovely materials.

There is still another type of architectural decoration which is of tremendous importance today—living plants. Again and again the concept of a modern building is bound up with their use. In times

not so long ago, the surroundings of a building might be city sidewalks or a country garden, but the relationships between the building and any planting that might surround it were often accidental
and at the mercy of the whims of owners, landscape designers, or
nursery salesmen. Mounds of absurd and inharmonious "foundation planting" were the frequent result and served only to hide the
building and prevent any true relationship between it and its site.
Today this is not so. Living greenery is often interwoven with the
design of the building itself, be it in the city or in the country. Roof
gardens, planting along copings, carefully placed greenery around
porches and doors, vines arranged not to hide but to enhance—these
all become part of a good building's actual architectural design, as
truly a part of its ornament as were the carved acanthus leaves and
garlands of earlier eclectic work. The green of growing plants which
bank the stairs of the Museum of Modern Art in New York is no
decorator's afterthought; it is integral with the architectural design.
And this is but one of many examples. In fact, one of the great
achievements of contemporary architecture is this realization of
the possible beauty of living plants as architectural ornament—the
substitution, as it were, of the reality for the representation.

Of all kinds of ornament, however, it is the ornament of representation which has the strongest grip on human sensibilities and
touches with the greatest poignancy the depths of artistic appreciation. Ever since our ancestors painted buffaloes and mammoths on
their cave walls or carved them on bones, mankind has delighted in
pictures. Almost every child draws pictures of the things that appeal
to him most: engines, and boats, and motor cars, and airplanes, and
houses, and people; however deeply buried by later training and
daily tasks, in most of us this picture-making instinct lives always.
It is this same picture-making instinct applied to architecture which
produces representational ornament and makes us warm to a beautifully carved flower frieze more readily than to a Greek fret.

From earliest times this picture-making instinct has been bound
up inextricably with the religious instinct. The savage often endows
his pictures with a magic life and a deep symbolism, and traces of
this feeling linger yet. That is why Ruskin laid such stress on

representational ornament, looking at it with a religious earnestness. Ornament to him was more than decoration; it was a form of worship, almost sacramental. Its appeal was as much moral as aesthetic, and from this attitude of his he developed his queerly colored views of architecture and his queerly warped theories of ornament. All praise to him for the serious and reverent nature of his criticism! A great deal more of that spirit in our American design would give us better, freer, more beautiful buildings. And yet appreciation of Ruskin's earnestness and sincerity must not blind us to the errors of his one-sided viewpoint; nor need we follow him in every detail. We may rest assured that the lovely fall and the swaying curves of a piece of hung drapery are as properly decorative as the similar curves in a twining vine; the beauty of the ornament lies primarily in line, and balance, and light and shade, and not in subject.

But to deny that subject matter has anything to do with the effect of ornament is as illogical as to go to the other extreme with Ruskin. The Egyptians felt an awe and a thrill at their painted lotus that is foreign to us; but the medieval peasant's pleasure at seeing his native plants carved on his church door we might have, if we would. Yet modern methods of building and the intensive specialization of each step, not only in the actual construction work but also in the architect's office and designing room, are so totally different from any conditions that ever existed before the twentieth century that the whole problem of architectural ornament has been altered. Its production, design, and even its presence on a modern building are all subjects for controversy.

One school of modern thought, of which the late Eric Gill, the English sculptor, is perhaps the best spokesman (in his *Beauty Looks After Herself*), argues that any ornament at all is an anachronism on modern buildings. Ornament in the past, this group argues, has been a natural, lyric expression produced sympathetically by skillful individual craftsmen. Today this is impossible; what we get is mechanical copies (hewn with a pneumatic chisel) of plaster casts of clay models, themselves mechanical copies of an architect's detail drawing. Nowhere in this process is honest individual expres-

PLATE XXI

Alinari

Santa Maria della Pace,
Rome: cloister
Donato Bramante, architect

Riccardi-Medici Palace,
Florence
Michelozzo Michelozzi, architect

Ware Library

PLATE XXII

Tomb of Count Hugo, the Badia, near Florence. Mino da Fiesole, architect

PLATE XXIII

Amiens Cathedral: interior

Ware Library

Ware Library

Lincoln Cathedral: interior

PLATE XXIV

Chartres Cathedral: transept porch

sion possible, and the result is bound to be dead; it is no longer a creation of beauty, but only an expression of ostentatious wealth at so much per foot. Moreover, these critics say, our modern world can be honestly expressed not in this economically wasteful expenditure but rather in a building's size, mass design, clear unbroken planes, and even starkness. Lastly, they say, modern building materials, if frankly and beautifully used, give little scope for ornament.

Such a view, sound though its foundations may be, neglects many facts of human psychology. In the first place, it demands an aristocratic austerity of taste as foreign to reality as is the sentimental love of copies that such critics deplore. Then, too, there are still many classes of building—tombs, monuments, occasional houses, and some civic structures—in which economic logic is only a secondary consideration. And there are still large masses of people, and many artists, who rebel against the coldness and impersonality of pure undecorated expression of function. The human need that made the Greeks decorate cups and vases still exists, despite all the changes in economic conditions and means of manufacture.

The answer to the problem of modern decoration, then, seems to lie in finding a modern type of ornament fitted to our present life rather than in a defeatist surrender to stark bareness. And the possibilities of such a form of decoration are still numerous. First of all, there is the great class of ornament resulting from the qualities of manufactured material imaginatively used—the sheen of metal, the bright transparency of glass, the rich color of tile, the brilliance of sheets of plastic, or combinations of these. Second, there is the creative decoration of the actual structural materials, like that of the precast concrete blocks of some of Frank Lloyd Wright's California houses—the forms and repetitions of which are exquisitely expressive of the way the whole was made. Third, there is the suave and continuous modulation of surfaces—in bands, channelings, or reedings, which are easy for machines to produce—where the very perfection of the profile and of the execution are the result of machine manufacture. And, fourth, most important of all, there is the decorative use of true sculpture and mural painting.

It is in this last form of decoration that we are most backward today, for we generally use sculpture and painting, if at all, without understanding their true functions and in ways that are unsuited to modern conditions. We tend to make use of them merely as permanent museum pieces rather than as integral parts of the artistic conception as a whole; they are frequently afterthoughts and look it. Naturally architectural sculpture or painting for modern buildings will be as different from Greek and Gothic sculpture and painting as our buildings are different from Greek and Gothic structures. To achieve a real integration, sculptors and painters and architects all need a new vision, a new unity of outlook and training, and their co-operation must begin in the early stages of the design of any project. The rich, schooled beauty of the Nebraska state capitol, of which B. G. Goodhue was the architect, Lee Lawrie the sculptor, and Hildreth Méière the mural painter, shows that such co-operation is possible even in twentieth-century America, and the use— not always successful—of much sculpture, mural painting, and mosaic in the buildings of Rockefeller Center, in New York, is significant of a growing movement in American architectural taste.

Historic ornament, nevertheless, has a tremendously important place in the understanding of architecture, not only because of its important relation to the work of this day, but also because of its inherent importance in the monuments of its own times. Of Egyptian, Babylonian, and Persian ornament little need be said, for, interesting as they are, and beautiful in their own place, their symbolism is so important that it is impossible to begin to understand them without at least some knowledge of the mythology on which they are based, and that is beyond the scope of this book. Egyptian ornament is interesting from two standpoints: the use of decorative conventionalizations of the sacred lotus, and the use of color.

Forms, to the Egyptians as to all primitive peoples, are fluid and susceptible of infinite change, provided certain formulae are observed. Thus the lotus was changed into a thousand forms—into capitals for columns, into ornaments for all kinds of furniture, into decorative spots to be formed into rosettes or bands or all-over patterns. Thus the human figure was gradually conventionalized from the fine naturalism used under the earlier dynasties, and the size of the figures was determined not by reality or the demands of perspective but by the symbolical importance of the figures represented. A king filled a whole temple front, whereas his slave was scarce two stones high. But these Egyptian figures were always grouped in serried ranks and combined, big and little, with hieroglyphic inscriptions, into a whole that was beautiful, well composed, and carefully executed. The Egyptian, for all his symbolism, was always an artist; the magnificence of his buildings in their ruin bears eloquent witness to the fact that his symbolism and his aesthetic creativeness walked always hand in hand.

This decorative ability, this innate feeling for beauty, is equally evidenced by the color decoration of the Egyptian buildings. We, who live in the quiet, cloudy north, can never realize the absolute necessity for color in the architecture of the sun-steeped south. The blaze of tropic day on stone or stucco demands color to mitigate its dazzle, and color the Egyptians were lavish with—blues and greens, browns and reds, and a very little yellow and white, for in the use of color the Egyptian was as conventional as in his use of form. The color, whether outdoors or in, was always in flat masses, so that the solidity of the decorated surface was never lost. Therein lies the lesson to us; if we wish to produce that decorative greatness, that quietness, that solidity, that air of ever living strength, there is but one way to do it—to make our ornament, whatever it is, pictorial or otherwise, primarily decorative; to keep it always an integral part of the surface to which it is applied.

Chinese architecture shows an even bolder use of color; perhaps nowhere in the world are magnificence of form and color so combined as in such a group as the Forbidden City in Peking (Peiping). Below, foundation and enclosing walls stuccoed and stained a rich soft red that fades into all kinds of varied sienna shades; white marble balustrades; rich oxblood red columns, with grille work between in green or red, picked out with the gilt of hinges, handles, and braces; beams and bracketed cornices chiefly in pure cobalt and emerald green, accented and patterned with white, darker blues and greens, and sometimes touches of red and gold; crowning all, sweeping roofs with decorated hips and ridges, all in shiny yellow porcelain tile—

this all makes for a visual experience of stunning richness and power. Even Chinese houses and house gateways frequently depend for their effect as much on color as on form.

Chinese decoration, however, has had little direct influence on the architecture of Europe, whereas that of Egypt is of the greatest historical importance, and the development of Egyptian concepts by later peoples was decisive. Decoratively skillful as the Egyptians were, their ideas of composition and design were purely elementary. It was only with the Greeks that we see the beginning of a real grasp of the value of line. It is true, they built largely on Egyptian origins, but one thing which with the Egyptians was a mere incident became for the Greeks the foundation of their system. This was the S curve, "the curve of beauty," as Hogarth called it. There is something particularly fascinating about its continually changing curvature, which, once discovered and applied, can never be forgotten. The Greeks used this to the full and along with it discovered the value of gradually changing the curvature in every line they used. There is scarcely a Greek vase, or a Greek molding, or a Greek ornament that has any circular curves at all; every curve is subtle, starting nearly a straight line, becoming more and more curved throughout its length, and ending with the sharpest curve of all. This wonderful mastery of curved lines was combined with a delicacy of feeling and a perfection of execution unparalleled to this day.

It is also to the Greeks that we owe several forms that have been father to a tremendous tradition: the conventionalized acanthus leaf, the anthemion, and the combination of these forms with a branching scroll. The acanthus leaf especially—at first spiky and flat, but later rounded and deeply cut—with its serrated edges and strongly modeled surface, forms a motif admirably suited for almost any decorative purpose, as its long history proves (Plate XXV).

Probably, however, it is for their skill in using the human figure decoratively that the Greeks are best known. A thousand people know the Parthenon frieze where one knows the anthemion. In this field they were supreme; no such flat conventionalizations as those used by the Egyptians pleased these truth-seeking, beauty-loving people; their figures must be real, they must be as perfect in truth

and beauty as their carvers could make them. Obviously it is much
more difficult to use naturalistic figures in a decorative way than it
is to use flat and conventionalized figures; but the difficulty was not
too great for the Greeks, because they were always pressing on toward
an ever growing ideal. Nearly all the early oriental peoples were
conservative, priest-ruled, and superstitious, and their ornamental
forms developed naturally into standardized sacred types, with
which they were satisfied. A thousand years produced less change in
the art of Egypt than a hundred in Greece or Rome, because in Egypt
the hieratic ideal had been attained at the start. In Greece, however, the ideal was never attained. Their philosophy was an eager, passionate, unceasing attempt to get at the facts of nature and of life, an
attempt that grew and broadened as the years passed, always searching, searching, and never attaining; in the same way their art was a
continual and eager development, ever pressing on to ideals never
attained, because, as the art developed, so did the ideal. Always
striving after new beauty, never satisfied, even in its decadence trying for new forms of splendor never before achieved—therein lies the
secret of Greek greatness.

There was something of the same eager idealism, though of a
more homely kind, in the Romans who followed the Greeks as
leaders of the world. They realized the beauty of Greek art, but, if
anyone is tempted to say it satisfied them, let him study a little some
of the myriad fragments of Roman friezes that remain to us. They
are unsurpassed. To be sure, they use the acanthus—a Greek form—
and perhaps the branching scroll, also a Greek form. But there is
about them a luxuriousness of light and shade, a forceful modeling,
a saving naturalism, that is new (Plate XXV). True, the Romans
could never carve a Parthenon frieze or the Phidian fragments, but,
on buildings of the great scale the Romans loved, it was an impossi-
bility to use figure sculpture as the Greeks had used it. Sixty feet of
perfectly sculptured figures are wonderful; three hundred feet would
be monotony. That the Romans had a decorative theory different
from that of the Greeks is no argument against it, and the ornament
of the medieval and modern world owes infinitely more to the
Romans than to the Greeks. In particular, the Romans were the first

people to use naturalistic foliage extensively as ornament, and the first people to appreciate the value of varied relief in carved ornament. The relief in all Roman ornament is in some places high and bold, in others almost dying into the background; the resulting light and shade, though perhaps less precise than in Greek relief, have a life and variety which the Greek never knew.

The Byzantine artists had still another decorative idea; their moldings were flattened and often soft and coarse in profile, and their relief is flat and hard. Nevertheless Santa Sophia in Constantinople is gorgeous in decorative effect (see Plate XVI). The Byzantine covered large surfaces with patterns of extreme intricacy, and for such use too interesting a relief had to be avoided. Of Romanesque carving it is not necessary to speak, for all that is good in it either is similar in spirit to Roman or Byzantine models or else was developed to a far higher level in the ornament of the Gothic period.

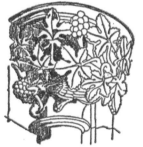

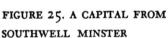

FIGURE 25. A CAPITAL FROM SOUTHWELL MINSTER

FIGURE 26. FRENCH GOTHIC CAPITALS

English Gothic capitals are often dominantly naturalistic, French Gothic capitals dominantly structural with conventionalized foliage.

This Gothic ornament has already been treated at some length, and it will therefore not be necessary to add much more concerning it. Suffice it to say that in Gothic ornament we get the lovely flowering of the whole Gothic spirit—its delight in good craftsmanship, its slow-growing but insistent individualism, its naïve sincerity, even its reverent mysticism. At times it suffers from a lack of the classical grasp of line. This is particularly true of English Gothic; the capital illustrated has, for instance, a somewhat bulbous silhouette, and the wreathed effect contradicts absolutely the supporting function which the best capitals express (Figure 25). But, however many flaws we may pick with details of line, no fault can be found with this capital as an interesting and sincere interpretation of the ever fascinating, ever delightful outside world.

French Gothic ornament is often as beautifully structural as the English is beautifully naturalistic (Figure 26). This is particularly true of figure sculpture, which according to many critics is the most successful architectural sculpture in the world. French Gothic decorative figures are always strong, upright, structural; always, too, the best are beautiful in themselves, with well-modeled heads and masterly drapery. Conventionalization in these figures never goes so far as to make them bad sculpture though good architecture; like all the best ornament, they are both good in themselves and good in their place (Plate XXIV).

The development of Renaissance ornament is the story of the gradual struggle of classical ideas, the classical feeling for line and relief, to a new ascendancy. But the Gothic influence never completely died. Renaissance ornament, particularly in France and England, was never completely like the ornament of Greece and Rome, because the Middle Ages had left an indelible influence on men's minds. There is no classic prototype for the heavy garlands of very real fruit and flowers that the English architects of the eighteenth century loved so well. There is certainly no classic prototype for the "strap" ornament and the curved shields and curved cartouches so popular in the early Renaissance of France, and even more in Germany, for it is only in periods of artistic decadence that rigid copying is indulged in. Then, too, the whole development of Renaissance art was influenced by the great individualism of the times, the new humanism. Particularly in Italy, each artist had his own peculiar style; the history of the art is the history of successive men of genius, from the time when Brunelleschi reared the Pazzi Chapel, and Desiderio da Settignano and Mino da Fiesole put up their lovely tombs and altar pieces, to the time when Michelangelo, by the very force of his misunderstood tremendousness, ushered in all the good and bad of the Baroque, until all Italian art thundered in stucco splendor and plaster profundity to its wild and riotous decay.

With respect to post-Renaissance ornament, there are three or four influences it may be necessary to mention. First, there are the French "periods"—known chiefly by the names of the reigning kings, Louis Quatorze, Quinze, and Seize, and the Empire period— and the corresponding trends in the ornament of other countries. In all these, for the first time, the artist seems consciously to seek his ends in an abstract way, unrelated to the past. In them, for the first time, the artist seems self-conscious; though there is a loss of naïve charm, there is a corresponding gain in abstract skill.

There is system in the art of these periods, too. They are illustrative of the continual conflict of two contrasting ideals, the restrained and "classic," and the free, unrestrained, and often erratic "romantic." In the so-called Louis Quatorze and Louis Quinze styles, although exteriors are severely classic, the lighter, freer style had full sway in interior design and resulted in that combination of sweeping, graceful curves and gilt and white and light colors that all of us know too well but too often know only from modern caricatures that are out of place and misunderstood. Could we see a real interior in the style at its best, furnished in perfect tone, and peopled with the joyous costumes of the day, we should appreciate more its strength, its grace, its wonderful grasp of abstract line, the perfection of its curves. Later came the inevitable reaction, expressed in the restraint of Louis Seize and the work of the Adam brothers in England, and then in the severity of the Empire—periods losing more and more the talent for creative ornament in itself and for itself. This tendency developed finally into the long and dreary monotony of eclecticism, from which we have scarcely yet emerged.

Even more important for us is the reaction against this nineteenth-century eclecticism—a reaction which, in the last years of the century, produced an almost world-wide explosion of originality known variously as *art nouveau, Jugend-styl,* the "craftsman" movement, and so on. It was characterized by a definite, self-conscious, and eager revolt against the use of any traditional forms whatsoever. Its actual historical background in the craftsmanship movement of

William Morris and the Pre-Raphaelites, as well as in a new aware-ness of the beauties of oriental, especially Japanese, art, is less im-portant than its aim—the creation of a new beauty for a new and changed civilization. Its immediate architectural results were not often impressive, for it was too purely a personal revolt, and in its emphasis on individual craftsmanship it was as much a denial of the machine basis of the modern world as were the styles it sought to supplant, so that today its products often look strangely outmoded and gauche.

Yet its eventual results were astounding. Its honest creative passion started great architectural movements—in France, Germany, Aus-tria, England, Holland, and the United States—that are still alive. Most significant of all, it utterly destroyed that deadening sense of dependence on the past which nearly a century of eclecticism had produced. Now, in this twentieth century, mankind is at last free of all that. Now, at last, true understanding and appreciation of the great achievements of the past bring with them no longer the desire merely to copy but rather a knowledge of why past ages produced what they produced, and hence a greater desire to create for ourselves today. Now at last the architect and the artist are free, and for that freedom much of the credit must go to the brave revolt of the early followers of the *art nouveau*.

8

DECORATION AND
STRUCTURE

L ET US ADMIT at the outset that the question of modern ornament for a modern building is still a controversial subject. Let
us admit that much modern ornament is silly, sentimental,
and stupid. Let us admit that many of the most beautiful modern
buildings have little if any ornament as such. Nevertheless, in any
broad appreciation of architecture, the question of ornament is still
important; ornament exists on many buildings, and in the buildings
of many cultures and many periods it is an important element in
design. Moreover, as has been noted, it seems probable that as we
achieve mastery over the machine and its products and realize its
possibilities, we shall again achieve a creative and appropriate ornament. It seems worth while, therefore, to examine further the
aesthetic problem of ornament, whatever its style or subject. Ornament can be judged in two ways: first, as a thing in itself; and, second
and more important, in relation to the building it adorns.

Ornament as a thing by itself should be beautiful. This ought to
be self-evident; for ornament is by its very interest the element of a
building on which the eye dwells longest, and on which its attention
becomes at last fixed. In a way, therefore, ornament is a sort of climax. At a distance the whole of a building is seen as a mass, even
perhaps as a silhouette; as one approaches, interesting details begin
to show themselves—doors, windows, columns—but when one is
close to a large building even these may be overlooked, and the eye
will dwell on what is immediately before one—a widening door,
the swelling curve of a base mold, a piece of decorative sculpture, or
the soft texture of varied brick. And it is an interesting fact that the
larger the building the more this is true, the more the effect of the
thing as a whole is lost on a close view, and therefore the more the

eye seeks for interest in what it can see. Yet in every case the integrity of the whole must be preserved, so that the experience of the *detail* will harmonize with the experience of the whole.

Ornament, then, from its very function—which is to beautify—must be beautiful. Consequently it must follow all the demands of beauty which have been enumerated earlier: unity, balance, rhythm, climax, grace, harmony, and so forth. Criticism of ornament as an entity by itself consists, therefore, in the application of these criteria. But that is not all. The demands enumerated in Chapter 4 are demands of pure form, and most ornament is more than this. Architecture is pure form based on good structural sense, and ornament is pure form based on a just and sincere spirit; for with ornament, and the idea of representation, there has entered a new element. This element is the direct appeal of the representation to our personal imagination and our individual memories—that is, the emotional effect of that complex of emotions, sensations, and associations which the forceful representation of anything, beautiful or unbeautiful, produces in us.

Of course architecture, too, has a certain amount of this element; a Gothic church produces a very definite, direct emotional effect in us; so may a building of any other period. In a Doric column we see Athens, before a Corinthian colonnade we are in Rome, in a Louis XIV room there rises before us the picture of that pompous silk-clad court. But this associative value of architecture appeals at its fullest only to a mind well trained, keenly alert, and stocked with such a store of the past as education alone can give; it is both more intellectual and more sentimental than the direct emotion one feels in good ornament.

Ornament is democratic; a good representation of their brother men strikes a chord and sets it thrilling in those to whom Athens is unknown and Rome only a vague word. It follows, then, that the subject matter represented is important to the effect of good ornament, and more important than most of our present-day architects realize. In the foregoing chapter one aspect of this question has already been discussed—the analysis of various types of decorative elements. But there are other aspects besides this on which it is necessary to make our minds clear, and it is these with which this chapter must deal. Chapter 7 was concerned with material; the present chapter will deal with artistic theory.

Representational ornament, whatever its subject, must first of all be *suitable*. It must have a subject fitted for the material out of which it is made, appropriate to the medium in which it is made, and harmonious with its place on the building and with the building's purpose.

The fact that ornament must have a subject suitable to its material is not so strange as it may at first seem. Consider for a moment the qualities of granite and bronze. Granite is hard to cut, heavy, with a coarse and interesting texture. Bronze is metal poured molten into a mold; this mold has itself been cast from a model prepared in clay or wax, soft, easily worked, and capable of the most delicate variations and modulations of surface. Bronze has a glossy, shiny surface when it is finished and reflects a changing light from every slightest curve. Is it strange that what would be a fit subject for one of these materials should be ridiculous in the other?

True, human figures could be represented in either, but not figures designed in the same way or treated in the same manner. The granite figure might be a tremendous Colossus, with simple angular features and draperies falling in simple, severe lines. It should be posed strong and upright, or seated with enormous dignity and repose, with an age-long quality in the posture like the age-long character of the material, as in the seated figures on the façade of the Egyptian cave temple at Abu Simbel. The bronze figure may be dressed in intricate folds, or nude; it may dart hither and thither at the artist's fancy, or be in a posture of swift motion like the St. Gaudens Diana which once topped the tower of the old Madison Square Garden, and yet there is something in the ductile quality of the material that makes the representation seem perfectly appropriate.

Or consider the effect of different plants fashioned in different materials. For instance, the English in the seventeenth century loved to decorate their great iron gates with a conventionalized vine with delicate, twisting lines, thin curling leaves, and tiny tendrils curving in spirals. Can this sort of ornament be imagined carved in granite?

The very grain of the stone would be coarser than the tendrils; in the play of light over its granular, multicolored surface the delicate shadows would be lost, and the whole seem weak and pointless. A branch of white oak, on the other hand, with its strong leaves and its hard, round acorns, could be carved in granite more effectively than cast or wrought in metal.

It is a universal rule, in fact, that the harder and more durable the material of the ornament, the severer and more dignified must be the object represented. In general, the sequence from the hardest and most durable to the softest seems to run in some such fashion as this: First, granite, diorite, and similar hard stones, suitable for severe, somewhat conventionalized figures and for plants with large units and hard, strongly marked lines. Next, marble, though here there is a tremendous variety of textures and surfaces, suitable to a great number of different subjects; it must be noted, however, that any marble with strongly marked color and veining is even less fitted for delicate ornament than granite. Next, limestone, the ordinary white stone of our American buildings. This, like marble, is an extremely variable material, and comes midway in the scale; it is thus perhaps the most widely adaptable. Next, Caen stone, very soft, easily cut, and therefore suitable for all sorts of naturalistic ornament; yet, since it will not stand up in some cold climates, its architectural use on exteriors is severely limited. Then wood, again a rich and varied material, especially suitable for subjects in low relief, but also, if the subject is naturalistic, for high relief. And even with wood there is as great a variety of hardness, color, and texture as in marble, so that the good sculptor or carver will necessarily vary both subject and treatment according to the quality of the specific wood with which he is dealing. Last, the metals, in which such a freedom of line and subject and such a riotous play of fancy are permitted as no other material allows.

This list is merely an approximation of the range of materials and their possibilities, but it is significant and it is based on truth; since there are so many cases in our modern work where the different qualities of different materials have been forgotten, it has seemed necessary to include it. We are always tempted to try to do two things at once; love for rich materials and rich ornament has often led us to forget the simple demands of good design. Let the reader take this to heart, and look at the ornament around him with this in mind; the sense of the necessary fitness of ornament and material in good architecture will soon make itself felt.

It is here that excessive craft skill often leads the designer astray. With modern tools and that extraordinary technical ability which modern specialization of work has often produced, one can literally carve or model almost anything in any material. The merely clever artisan or designer has often wished, as it were, to show off how great is his command over his art; he delights in the impossible and evolves merely the inappropriate—that which despite its elaboration is basically ineffective. Eclectic architecture in the latter half of the nineteenth century and the first two decades of the twentieth was particularly at fault in this respect. The system under which ornament was produced—a system, described earlier (page 168), of mechanical copies of mechanical copies—effectually prevented true craftsmanship from working. The client wished to display his wealth, the architect his knowledge of past styles, the modeler his cleverness, and the carver his ability; at the mercy of all these types of ostentation and self-display, appropriateness and creativeness fled away. Is it strange that so much architectural ornament in eclectic buildings is hard, cold, spiritless, even vulgar?

Ornament must be suitable to the medium in which it is executed and to the technique that produced it. This is a simpler and more obvious truth than suitability to material; almost every person realizes at once that there are things one can paint which would be absurd in sculpture. Painters know, too, the obvious difference in subject and treatment suggested by different techniques—fresco, oil, water color, pastel. But the designers of eclectic ornament, like many of the sculptors of the period, forgot there were equally radical differences in the various techniques of both sculpture and ornament —that modeling and carving were two entirely different things. In modeling one adds bit to bit; he can work over the whole indefinitely, smoothing, roughening, rubbing out and starting over again. In carving, on the contrary, one cuts off, and when once a piece is cut off it is gone forever. Modeled ornament (bronze, clay, terra cotta) is therefore basically different from carved ornament in stone; different kinds of beauty and interest are developed by the two different systems. Yet how frequently on eclectic buildings one sees terra cotta pretending to be stone; how often one notes exactly the same ornaments, handled in exactly the same way, in metal (the result of a modeling technique) and wood (which is carved). This insensitiveness to material and technique is one of the causes of the violent reaction of sensitive designers of today against any ornament.

There have been other periods in architecture which had little sensitiveness to material and technique. The Baroque designers, for instance, seemed to care little whether they were working in stone or plaster, painting or relief. They even made almost a game of deception, painting moldings and shields and garlands as though carved in relief—and these all so skillfully executed as to appear at first almost "real." Yet there is a profound difference in this respect between the Baroque designers and those of the recent past. The Baroque mural painter, with his painted architecture, knew he was deceiving. He counted on the general effect; he even seems to have made the observer's final discovery of the trickery a part of the effect he was seeking. And in larger matters of ornament the Baroque architects were creating primarily an exciting, new, amazingly creative visual drama, full of stress, conflicts, dramatic alternations of line and shade. They used either stone or stucco for figures with little change in approach, to be sure; but they never deliberately strove to copy accurately in stucco the figures or ornaments developed by earlier cultures for other materials, and even in their painted architecture there is usually a kind of fantasy, a patent dramatic and pictorial unreality, which tells the sensitive observer at once that what he is looking at is a dream, a picture, rather than actual columns and arches. When Pozzo, for instance, covered the vault of Il Gésu in Rome (Plate XXVI) with an extraordinary panoply of pedestals, balustrades, twisted columns, and figures, all laid out carefully according to the rules of aerial perspective so as to obliterate completely the architectural forms of the vault, he knew full well that no spectator would be really deceived and couple the painted

architecture above with the actual, simpler, true architecture below
it. He was merely symbolizing to the best of his enormous ability the
drama of the fact that above the church was Heaven, and all about
were the swirling forms of the Heavenly Host. Today, of course, we
neither could nor would want to do the same kind of thing, but it
makes eclectic *non-creative* insensitiveness to material and technique
no better by pointing to the Baroque *creative* insensitiveness as a
precedent.

And, finally, the subject of the ornament must be appropriate to
the purposes of the building which it decorates. Here again eclectic
designers were found lacking. There seems to have been a spiritual
blindness in that period, to make them carve exactly the same things
on churches that they did on theaters or railroad stations. Think of
the added life and zest our achitecture would have if always the
modeler and architect had fixed ineradicably in their minds the
purpose of the building for which they were designing ornament.
It may be right to carve or paint plant forms almost anywhere, for
the world of green nature seems always at home; but the moment
the human element enters in we must be careful—and this human
element ought to enter in a great deal more than it does. Surely we
missed something in our architecture when we decorated the frieze of
villa, courthouse, theater, and church with the skulls and sacrificial
ribbons of the Roman temple.

It is at this point that the subject of sculpture and painting as
applied to buildings inevitably arises. We may say, in fact, that the
greatest ornament a building can have—and perhaps the greatest
unused source of ornament today—is great sculpture and great mural
painting, conceived integrally with the building in purpose, in material, and in style. The buildings of today are particularly suited
to the use of such forms of decoration; their simple planes, their clear
surfaces, their sharp and concentrated accents at door or porch all
seem ideally designed for it. Little by little we are becoming aware
of this, as great architects have always been. When during the great
depression of the thirties the problem of the relief of artists arose and
the Federal Art Project was formed, a goodly portion of its activity
went toward furnishing sculpture and mural painting for public

buildings and low-cost housing groups; an accompanying art project also was set up in the Treasury Department to see that new governmental buildings had their quota. For the first time in the United States, a regulation was put in force setting aside a definite percentage of each building's cost for sculpture or painting or both. This marked almost a revolution in taste, and its definite, official recognition of the need for sculpture and painting in architecture was epoch-making.

The results have been amazing. In town after town over vast areas of the country, people have seen painting and sculpture for the first time put to actual, social, public use. Popular interest was tremendous; even the controversies which arose over the subject matter of some of the murals indicated a lively consciousness that they were more than mere "pictures." Post offices, courthouses, schools, and official office buildings in Washington and elsewhere took on new vitality, became a truer and more definite part of people's lives, and achieved a new meaning and value because of their sculpture and painting. More important still, this whole enterprise has given rise to a widespread realization that mere building is not enough, and that the greatest and most human decoration a building can have is that which the sculptor and the painter can give.

Artistically the result of all this effort was less impressive; much good and much bad work was produced, and some work by even the most noted of artists seemed weak and vapid in its place on a building wall. The reasons for this variation in merit are not hard to find. It is not merely that the greater number of our sculptors and painters had had little opportunity to create architecturally, and that many were so inexperienced in working on buildings that they could not read an architectural drawing. It is not merely that subject matter, in some cases extraneous to the purpose of the building, often obsessed the artists, or that even the juries judging competitions for this architectural decoration sometimes judged sculpture as though it were individual garden pieces, and painting as though it were easel painting. All these things were doubtless true in one case or another, but the real cause of the frequent artistic disappointment lay deeper; it lay in the fact that in practically all these buildings the sculpture and mural painting were a pure afterthought. The wonder of it is, under such conditions, not that so much is ineffective, but that so much is living, exciting, and beautiful.

In the future, let us hope, things will be different. Architect, painter, and sculptor will collaborate almost from the inception of a project, as the late Bertram Goodhue collaborated with Lee Lawrie and Hildreth Méière in the Nebraska state capitol. Then sculptors and painters will have opportunities they never had under the old Federal Art programs; they will learn to appreciate the new and different and difficult problems inherent in architectural design and will paint and carve and model true architectural decorations, just as architects will come to appreciate the special design problems—of lighting and of distance from the eye, for instance—which face the sculptor and the painter. Then the beginnings we have made so far will seem crude indeed, and buildings will gain a new humanity. It is significant that in the Soviet Union sculpture and painting are deemed essential in public work; the theorists there consider this the surest way to indicate that the buildings exist for people, and not people for the buildings. And anyone who has watched children playing around the carved animals in the playgrounds of Queensborough Houses, for instance, must agree. It is tragic that this decoration of housing groups was seen in this country not as a worthy and important end in itself but merely as a by-product of a program for the relief of starving artists. Let us hope that in the future our public buildings and our schools and our residence groups will be gay and alive with sculpture and painting as free and right as those happy children who sing everlastingly from the famous Cantoria of Luca della Robbia in Florence (Plate XXV).

Our ancestors have seen and appreciated the value of living, relevant ornament and have produced it. There is no inability in us; our sculptors have the skill, our architects are awaiting the chance. There is only one thing lacking—the desire; for one must remember that what the mass of people want, that they get. It is only because the person who is building does not know what he wants that the architect is usually compelled to exert such complete sway over the building. Let us hope, then, that the day may come when the great majority of people will come to appreciate the value of this live, human ornament and demand it; for then our American architecture will blossom into new beauty, and our common life will contain a new element of richness and joy.

There is one great class of ornament that is needful to mention in any discussion of the criticism of ornament, because probably more has been written with regard to its merits and demerits than with regard to those of any other class. This consists in the decorative use of elements originally structural. Myriad examples will occur to one immediately: columns, niches, gables, arches, domes—like the exterior shells of the Renaissance domes, such as St. Paul's in London —and the like. The column and the forms closely related to it, the pilaster and engaged column, are perhaps the most obvious. Originally the column was a purely structural member, where a support was necessary. Later, columns and colonnades were used merely decoratively, because there is nothing else that has the restful rhythm and strong grace of the colonnade. Of course in some places the colonnade has a true function as a real porch, as in the Capitol at Washington, which has so often been cited before. But even in this case there is more colonnade than the actual demands would require; the decorative reason for the colonnade is really more important than the structural reason. And when we get examples of a colonnade like that of the Louvre in Paris or of the State Education Building in Albany, the porch idea is practically non-existent; the colonnade is frankly decorative, and it is as decoration wholly that it must be judged.

The Romans began another decorative use of the column. They used engaged columns, that is, columns partly built into a wall, in conjunction with arches. This combination is seen especially in their theaters and amphitheaters like the Colosseum, but it was used on other buildings as well—on the basilicas, for instance, and the tabularium, the Roman governmental building, which rose high above the forum on the Capitoline Hill. This combination of arch and column or pilaster was extensively used all through the Renaissance period; naves of churches, palace fronts, and cloisters all were treated with it from time to time. The Vendramini Palace is a great example. During the Renaissance the Italians began to use columns and pilasters—"orders" as they are called—in still another way, closely allied; that is, they decorated a plain, unbroken wall with engaged columns or pilasters, one, two, or three stories high.

There has been a world of abuse flung at this decorative use of the orders. Critic after critic has assailed it as non-structural, insincere; critic after critic has pointed out that these applied orders contradict the whole feeling of the wall and claimed that they are a base practice of a decadent and hypocritical civilization—a practice which has poisoned our architectural taste and directed us away from the true virtues exemplified in the Gothic. This charge, so often repeated, has been defied consistently by the architects of many periods. It seems necessary, therefore, to look somewhat closely into the merits of this criticism and see what are the real facts in the controversy.

The validity of either opinion seems to lie in the point of view. If we are willing to accept the viewpoint of the adverse critics, we arrive inevitably at their conclusions; similarly, if we accept the architect's point of view, we shall understand his use of these "insincere" decorations. The crux of the matter seems to be that the critics who have so denounced this decorative use of structural members have too much intellectualized the art of architecture. They have deified the virtue of sincerity and applied it with a strictness entirely unwarranted. It is true that columns are in essence supporting members, and that to use them as decorations is to ignore this original function. But, on the other hand, the column is a very beautiful object in itself, aside from its function as a support. Its strong, vertical lines, with its decorated cap and base, are an architectural note that is unique, that can be obtained in no other way. Why, then, if the purpose of architecture is to create beautiful buildings, should the architect not use this uniquely beautiful motif solely because of its beauty? Moreover, these column or pilaster forms symbolize support; they often produce an apparent, if not an actual, strength.

Let us look for a moment at one of the most criticized uses of the orders—their combination with the arch, as in the Colosseum (Plate II). The beautiful rhythm of this building has already been analyzed, and nothing that critics can say can destroy that; the wonderful, stately rhythm of the building is a reality. Here, although the arches really do the supporting of the wall and the columns are a mere decoration, note how the vertical lines of the columns *express* support, how they seem to make still stronger the strength of the arcaded wall. Similarly, the deep shadowed entablatures over the columns express the story heights, and tie the whole enormous circuit of columns and arches together. Now architecture is an art that appeals to the sight first and foremost; it is therefore the things one sees, and their expressions, that are in fact more aesthetically real than the actual construction of the building. It seems logical, then, to conclude that whatever has an expression proper to its position is good architecture, provided it is beautiful; consequently the columns and entablatures of the Colosseum are good architecture, because in effect and expression they merely accentuate the actual supporting nature of the piers and the actual division into stories.

A somewhat similar method must be employed in judging the use of colonnades. One must use common sense; where common sense tells one that the colonnade is not an actual contradiction of or detriment to the needs of the building, and his aesthetic sense tells him it is pleasing as well, he may accept it as good architecture. The colonnade of the Louvre in Paris is such an example. The majestic ranks of coupled columns set on the strong basement, and broken just sufficiently by the corner pavilions and the central pediment, are manifestly pleasing; strong and graceful, this colonnade forms a fitting ornament to the square on which it faces. Nor does it offend structurally, for, although it is not a necessary porch and has little actual relation to the building behind, the spacing of the windows gives it an apparent relation, and the building itself is not of a character to demand any marked structural expression. Equally satisfactory is the impressive colonnade of the New York Post Office, already described.

But colonnades can be detrimental. The New York State Education Building in Albany has probably the largest permanent colonnade in this country; it is also one of the greatest architectural monstrosities of the twentieth century. In the first place, situated as it is on a comparatively narrow avenue with a steep slope, there is no such opportunity for getting the effect as a whole as there is in the case of the Louvre colonnade, and therefore no such reason for sacrificing the structure of the building to decorative effect. And the building itself, a great office and administration building, would seem to demand a treatment expressive of its official and educational purpose— a purpose that would apparently indicate many windows, floods of light and air, and in addition a monumental and inviting entrance to typify the democracy of the state. In the building as it exists the strong projection of the colonnade throws a deep shadow over the wall behind, and the main entrance is marked only by an insignificant flight of steps, so that windows and entrance alike are lost in the dark. Every possible expression of the building's purpose is concealed; the one thing prominent is a regiment of enormous columns, close to the ground at one end, and at the other mounted on a high basement because of the slope of the ground. Here the sacrifice of structural expression has been complete, and in the colonnade itself, with its over-ornamented, crowded Corinthianesque capitals and the heavy, boxlike entablatures above, there is no supreme touch of beauty or dignity to compensate. Here, then, ornamental use of structural features has gone too far; here is a building where love of grandeur and exterior effect have led to insincerity and manifest absurdity and ugliness.

From this discussion, it would therefore appear that in the criticism of the decorative use of structural architectural members there can be both good and bad. We must neither entirely condemn nor entirely commend; each example must be judged on its own merits. Pierced Gothic gables over pointed arches with no roof behind, colonnades, and engaged columns or pilasters are not of themselves either right or wrong. If there is no absolute structural contradiction entailed by their use, if they are not an absolute obstacle to the proper use of the building, one may excuse them and, if they are beautiful and fulfill a true aesthetic function, accept them as good architecture. If, on the other hand, their use seems actually to veil and contradict the purpose of the building, or to fulfill no imperative artistic de-

mand, then one is at liberty to condemn them for their patent insincerity and as an architectural blunder.

In artistic judgments of all kinds, approval does not necessarily
mean license to imitate or copy. The early medieval travelers to
Rome admired much that they saw, but when they came to build
at home they built Romanesque, not Roman, architecture. Some
things we admire we are incapable of reproducing. None but a
Chinese, for example, could paint a true traditional Chinese landscape; we can admire Beethoven and still not be able to be Beetho-
vens. Other admirable artistic products are so alien to our culture, our
needs, and our ways of work as to make attempted copying absurd.
And each phase of historical development, in architecture as in other
things, is marked by certain controlling patterns of thought and taste.
At any period, the greatest artistic work is produced by those who are
most sensitive to this "spirit of the times," who feel it so intensely
that they become prophetic of future developments—"ahead of their
times." And nowhere must we keep these facts more acutely and
vividly present in our thoughts than in the judgment of architecture
and architectural ornament of the past and of the present.

This is the case in the problem of the ornamental use of structural
elements. Some periods in architecture have delighted in this; some
have been shocked by it. Today, the entire trend of architectural
thinking and architectural design seems to be against it. We have set
ourselves a high and noble ideal—perhaps too high for complete
achievement—an ideal not unrelated to the scientific thinking of the
time. It is the theory that the greatest architectural beauty for us lies
in complete functional honesty, that there shall be on any building
no unit, no decoration, which is not precisely what it pretends to be
—no unit but what actually does the work it seems to be doing—
and that there shall be no unit merely for the sake of "prettifying"
the structure. When, therefore, we admire the engaged columns of
the Colosseum, or the pilasters of the cloister of Santa Maria della
Pace, or the pierced gables of Rouen, we must realize that their language is not our language, their special values not the ones we should
imitate or emulate in our buildings. Only by being true to the ideals

of today can we produce an architecture by which today will be proud to be known.

In these few pages devoted to the decorative use of structural members, the reader has already been brought face to face with another great fact in the criticism of ornament, which must be elaborated further—the relation of ornament to the building it decorates. In some ways this relation is a more important fact in the evaluation of ornament than the criticism of ornament by itself and for itself; for many a great building has some ornament that is far from perfect, and even the loveliest ornament cannot redeem a building if this ornament is badly placed or manifestly unsuitable. We must therefore determine what are the relationships between a building and its ornament which produce good architecture.

The most obvious relationship between building and ornament is probably that of quantity. As one walks through any city, the difference between buildings in the amount of ornament used may be the first thing that strikes him. He will notice that some buildings have a great deal of ornament, and others very little; at first he will see no relationship between the amount of ornament and the merit of the building. Some buildings almost covered with ornament may be good, and some with an equal amount bad; some of the plain, unornamented buildings may seem bald and uninteresting, and some may be instinct with sturdy beauty.

And in various periods there have been great differences in the amount of architectural ornament; severity and lavishness have alternated. In Austria, Adolf Loos, one of the most challenging of the earlier protagonists of a revolutionary architecture for our times, correlated ornament with primitivism or decadence—the more ornament, the less culture, he said. Savages like rich ornament; they even tatoo and scarify themselves to produce it. Late Roman architecture is profuse in ornament, and so is decadent late Gothic work. Disgusted with the glitter and lavish ornament so loved in the Vienna of Franz Josef, Loos saw in it only an evidence of disease and dissolution and for the present and future demanded an architecture starkly stripped of non-essentials. We may not wish to go so far as Loos, we may feel with Frank Lloyd Wright that an organic ornament is possible and right today; yet no one can fail to notice the profound revolution in taste with regard to ornament which has characterized the last twenty years. We prefer the minimum of ornament today. Indeed, it is difficult for many of us to look at a highly ornamented building with any sympathy or understanding whatsoever; much architectural ornament, where it is not absurd, seems merely quaint, merely old-fashioned. And in this reaction we may be doing the building a real injustice.

For there is great latitude in the amount of ornament that is good on a building. There is no general rule for determining this amount, any more than there is a general rule for determining the proper number of adjectives in a novel. Ornament is one of the most individual and personal things about a building, and in it all the personality of its designer enters freely. Some men are born with baroque minds, and some are born with the artistic restraint of the Puritan. It does not behoove anyone to call names, to claim the baseness of the one nature or the perfection of the other; there is beauty alike in abandon and in restraint.

Nor does there seem to be any inevitable connection between the amount of ornament and the purpose of the building. At first thought it might appear that a theater should be more ornamented than a church; that in general, the gayer and lighter the purpose of a building, the greater the amount of ornament that might be permitted. But even this simple statement will not bear close analysis or universal application, for the character of a building is determined by the general scheme of its composition and by the kind, not the amount, of its decoration. Some architects are such masters of the subtle emotional values of pure shape and form that the amount of ornament becomes a secondary matter; one architect can make a gay theater front of one broad entrance and one dancing figure, like the front of the Folies Bergères in Paris; yet there are solemn and impressive churches in the most florid Spanish Baroque. In the amount of ornament suitable to a building there is no one rule, and in criticism of the amount there is only one criterion and that of the vaguest —the amount should seem neither too great nor too small. Particularly, the ornament must not seem too great; better every time the under-ornamented than the over-ornamented building. Restraint is as valuable in ornament as in any other field of endeavor; in any building that gives the impression that the designer has put into it every scrap of ornament his brain could conceive, there is inevitably a quality of ostentation and vulgarity. Dignity lies always in quietness, and quietness in restraint.

This must always be kept in mind in judging the amount of ornament on a building. Some architects seem to have thought that by the intricate play of light and shade over surfaces luxuriantly ornamented they could blind one's eyes to the poverty of imagination behind the whole design. They did not realize that the difficulty of designing good ornament increases directly with the amount, and that the only way to keep a much ornamented building from vulgarity and ostentation is by the most careful consideration of the ornament itself, with regard to its absolute fitness and absolute unity.

If the amount, the quantity, of ornament, therefore, is comparatively unimportant in judging architecture, the placing of ornament becomes just so much more important. One reason over-ornamented buildings are likely to be ineffective is because the great amount of the ornament prevents some one climax spot from giving accent and interest. On the placing of ornament depends a great deal of its merit or failure.

Ornament should, first of all, be placed where the composition of the masses of the building demands it. The value and necessity of this use of ornament in the consideration of balance has been pointed out. Ornament may be equally necessary in establishing rhythm, or harmony, or climax. The true architect, as soon as the general scheme of his building is determined, will realize at a glance where the composition calls for ornament, whether as a door frame, an enriched porch, a grille, or a piece of sculpture. The perfect placing of ornament not only enhances the value of the ornament but also adds to the effectiveness of the whole building.

In large buildings the placing of the ornament becomes all the more important. In lavish buildings built at great cost, in which it is desirable to emphasize the note of dignified magnificence, many decorative notes may be used, provided always that they are never so placed as to seem to weaken the structure or fog the clarity of the basic conception. But in less formal buildings and buildings in the design of which the element of economy inevitably enters to a great degree—by far the largest class of buildings that surround us—ornament becomes a luxury and must therefore be used with all the greater care and restraint in order to produce the desired effect in the most economical and efficient manner. This can be done only by concentrating decoration in a few places, especially around the main entrance door and where an interior climax occurs. This method of design by concentration was carried to the greatest lengths in Spain, where we find again and again great stretches of simple wall, capped either with a bold painted wooden cornice or an open loggia and decorated with one great crust of intricate detail mounting around and above the door. The best of the Colonial houses were fine examples of the same concentration; in them a frequent general scheme comprised a simple, undecorated wall of brick or stone, with a delicate cornice to crown it and a beautifully detailed door in the middle. The simplicity of the wall gives the doorway an attractive prominence.

This ancient tradition of concentrated ornament, never entirely dead among us, has been strengthened during the last few decades because of the demands of economy in construction—a precept we have been all too slow to heed, for in this case it teaches a sane artistic truth. The fact is that a building where ornament is concentrated at one or two places is more effective than a building in which the same amount of ornament is scattered over the whole structure. Widely distributed ornament is often without effect. In the Parkchester housing group, for instance, the scattered terra-cotta sculptured figures that are peppered over walls and corners have but a fraction of the effect given by the two groups at the entrance to the main court of Harlem River Houses.

The kind of ornament that a building demands has already been considered along with its necessary suitability for the purpose of the building and to the material in which it is executed. It only remains, then, to speak of the size of the ornament. The size of ornament is important, because it is this that plays a large part in one's unconscious realization of a building's length or height. The size of the ornament is one of the architect's surest means of giving "scale" to the building.

The great front of St. Peter's at Rome is a monumental example of false scale set by the size of the ornamented parts (Plate XXVII). In the first place, it is decorated by a range of gigantic pilasters and engaged columns, each as high as a building itself. This order is capped by a correspondingly enormous entablature, on top of which is a balustrade at least seven feet high. All the windows and niches of the front are of similarly gargantuan proportions, and the statues are colossal. Now a balustrade is normally used as a railing, as we have noted earlier, and as such its height is rarely over four and a half feet; the eye also is accustomed to windows and niches of moderate size, and to statues so used that are only slightly larger than life. The result of the enlargement of all these forms on the front of St. Peter's can be seen at once; it dwarfs it tremendously, and the enormous size of the whole shrinks to apparently modest dimensions. One cannot believe that the balustrade is larger than the usual balustrade and that the statues are over twenty feet high; consequently he can have no conception of the true size of the great building in front of him. The first view of the front of St. Peter's is almost always a disappointment, and it is a great shock to see a crowd pour out of the doors; the people look like ants, not men. It is a shock, too, to see, high up on the front, a little bell, apparently the size of a locomotive bell, begin to swing, and to hear proceeding from it tones deep and low, like the tones of "Big Ben." It is only after repeated visits that the true size and greatness of the building begin to dawn on one slowly. An equally forceful example of false scale is the front of the Grand Central Station in New York; the great stone group on the top, with its thirty-foot figures, destroys at once the effect of size that the building should have. Both are examples of having the scheme of composition and of decoration suitable for a comparatively small building adapted for a large building by simply increasing every part proportionately— a scheme, in this case necessarily imperfect, which leads to false judgments.

The first rule for the size of ornament, then, is that ornament on any building should be so proportioned as to make the building appear its true size. This can be accomplished by keeping architectural forms such as balustrades and the like as nearly as possible to those sizes which are normal and usual, and by never unduly changing the size of representational ornament from the true size of the object represented.

There is a second rule that governs the size of ornament which sometimes modifies the strict application of the first rule. This can be stated somewhat in these words: the size should be consistent with the distance of the ornament from the eye. That is, ornament near the level of the eye ought to be smaller and more delicate than ornament far above it. This is another rule ignored in St. Peter's, for all the front has ornament of a similar size and one walks through doorways with the same gigantic type of moldings used a hundred feet in the air.

Common sense should tell us much about the size of ornament. If we are spending money on the decorative embellishment of a building, it is only common sense to have this decoration placed where it will "count," where it can be enjoyed by the passer-by. Here again the eclectic designer was often at fault; "paper architecture" —the illusion of the architectural drawing—led him astray. A band of ornament at the top of a skyscraper looked pretty on a drawing, hence the architect put it in, never realizing that it would be invisible to one passing in the street, and that from a distance, where the entire mass of the building could be seen, its richness would be entirely lost. Designers today have begun to learn this elementary fact. When Wright, for instance, sets a superb natural stone on the steps of Taliesin West, he has placed this magnificent piece of natural sculpture where one can approach it, walk around it, touch it, savor to his heart's desire its beauty of form, color, texture (Frontispiece). And the architects of Rockefeller Center similarly have concentrated their decorative richness close to the ground. As true architectural sculpture comes more and more into use, this true artistic economy will come increasingly into play; as architects and sculptors and painters come to collaborate with greater sympathy, we may rest assured that the sculpture and the painting will not be an almost complete visual waste, like so much of the routine ornament of the past that was placed where it could never be seen.

A greater freedom of scale treatment is possible in interior detail. Take, for example, the reliefs on the outside of the choir screen of Notre Dame in Paris—charming compositions with figures about three or four feet high that make a wonderfully decorative band around the aisles that encircle the choir. They do not offend the sense of scale, for, although they are very much under life size, they are just on the level of the eye, carefully worked out in every detail, and frankly miniatures. That is the secret of using naturalistic ornament at a size smaller than reality—it must be frankly a miniature; there must be no pretense about it, for pretense is insincere, and insincerity is bad art. This is perhaps the reason that near the eye things smaller than reality are so much more successful, as a rule, than those that are larger; for it is easier to make a miniature than an enlargement. At the entrance of St. Peter's there are some cherubs holding a holy-water vessel which are good examples of this; they are close to the eye, and they are carved cleverly with a masterly truth to child form. Yet in size they resemble everything else in that church. They are gigantic, seven feet high perhaps, and somehow their size seems an insult and fills one with a sort of unconscious stubborn anger, a desire to shout, "No, I'm not so small as you make me out to be, you overgrown and Rabelaisian infants"—a sentiment hardly religious. These cherubs are bad ornament and worse art, because of their patent theatrical insincerity.

In analyzing and criticizing ornament, then, one must study it from the following points of view: First, it must be beautiful in itself. Second, it must be suitable—to the purpose of the building it adorns, to the material in which it is executed, and to the artistic medium. Third, if it consists of structural members used for a decorative purpose, there must be some sufficient aesthetic demand for them, and they must not actually contradict the structure of the building, or detract from its actual usefulness. Fourth, ornament must be correct in amount, sufficient to give the desired richness consistent with the building's design, but not so great as to give any appearance of vulgar ostentation. Fifth, ornament should be placed where it will give the maximum of effect in the composition of the building. And, sixth, it should be of a size consistent with the size and design of the building and also with its distance from the eye. Moreover, in examining ornament from any of these viewpoints, we must always keep in mind that great demand of all true art: sincerity along with common sense.

Ornament is so large a subject and has implications so broad that it really demands a book in itself. Not only is it at the foundation of many of the arts besides architecture, but in architecture it is the factor that enjoys the most universal appreciation and excites the most universal interest, because it appeals most directly to the human need for decoration which is at the basis of all the arts. Yet, because of this very fact, we must be careful never to over-emphasize the importance of the purely decorative. Great architecture often uses nobly designed and appropriate ornament, but great architecture can exist without any pure ornament at all. However keen the interest ornament arouses in us, we must always remember that architectural ornament exists only for the enhancement of a building as a whole, and that works of true architecture are never mere frames for the support and display of decoration of any kind.

9

THE MEANING
OF STYLE

ONE OF THE many sides of architecture mentioned in the first chapter needs more discussion at this point. Up to the present we have been concerned to a large extent with the material side of architecture. Architecture has been considered as a matter of form, both aesthetic and practical, but it is one of the great values of architecture that it is more than this. It has a spiritual and intellectual message for us as well as a practical usefulness and the power of aesthetic stimulation. For behind the forms which architecture uses, and behind the plans which it adopts to solve the needs of the people whose art it is, there lies a meaning that is deeply bound up with the whole history of mankind. And it is this meaning which must be considered here.

Architecture is a key to history when this side of it is rightly appreciated and understood. Every quality of the builder is as truly mirrored in his building as every quality of a writer is expressed in his poem or play or story. Indeed, architecture is often even more relentlessly expressive than literature; for the architect's building is always the product of at least two personalities, that of the architect and that of the owner of the building, and oftentimes it is the product of a great many more—it may be the expression of a collective personality, of a guild, of a state, of a religion.

Moreover, the whole art of architecture, as the third chapter sought to show, is absolutely dependent on planning, and planning in turn is dependent on the practical needs of the people for whom and by whom the architecture is produced. Architecture, then, is always the result in any one period of two main ideas: the needs of the people, and the idea of beauty prevalent at that period. These two ideas are bound together by a common desire or purpose—the desire

PLATE XXV

Ornament from the Erechtheum,
Athens

Panel from the Ara Pacis Augustae

Cantoria, from the Cathedral, Florence
Luca della Robbia, architect

PLATE XXVI

DELINEATIO PICTURE IN FORNICE TEMPLI
S. IGNATII

Quod pictum ornat Roma hoc splendit in pre
Non uno incedit, pinxit et una manus

From *Perspectiva Pictorum*

Il Gésu, Rome: vault decoration by Pozzo

to create a useful and beautiful building—and are mutually interdependent.

It should thus be evident that architecture is one of the most complete expressions of life there is. Poetry and music and theology give us an expression of the ideals of beauty and goodness prevailing in the times that produced them, and political and economic history tell us much of the practical conditions of existence then current; but in architecture alone can we find an art which by its own character, and because of its very nature, expresses both great sides of existence and mirrors both the wealth and the dreams of humanity.

This is a fact which most people unconsciously appreciate. They begin when they are children to think of the Middle Ages in terms of castles and turrets, as well as of knights and men-at-arms. Later, as they grow older, they think of cathedrals, because in these buildings, more than in any other work of the time, the spirit of the thirteenth century flourished complete. The Gothic cathedral is fascinating because its style is what it is, and its style is the direct result of the life of that far-off time.

Style in architecture is merely a manner of building that is different from some other manner of building. It includes in its scope not only ornament but methods of construction and planning as well. The so-called "styles" of architecture can be so designated only by limiting the meaning of the word "style"; they signify merely convenient heads under which we can classify buildings, first according to date and nation, and second according to the forms originated at those dates and by those nations. One speaks of the "grand style" in architecture, meaning a large way of conceiving and ornamenting buildings; but one may speak with equal propriety of the Roman style, or the Gothic style, meaning either the style of Roman or Gothic buildings or the style of modern buildings which use analogous forms.

The style of today, in architecture, is not yet fixed; the whole problem of how we should build is still the center of violent controversy between the protagonists of the International Style, like Gropius and Le Corbusier, who would base architectural form on machine production and a stripped and stark functionalism, and others, like Wright, who look for a freer kind of creative design, less bound by doctrinaire dogmas. Yet this very confusion of aims is characteristic of our culture and reveals our mental, social, and economic bewilderment more relentlessly than it is revealed anywhere else. A civilization which in less than forty years has produced two world wars, mass production, slums, world-wide air traffic, advertising on the grand scale, tariff wars, international arms cartels, communism, fascism, Hitler's sentimental medievalism, the failure of the League of Nations and now the foundation of the United Nations of which so much is hoped, the extraordinary progress of Soviet Russia, housing developments, relativity, technological unemployment, cheap motor cars, the economics of plenty, tremendous philanthropies, the atomic bomb, *Ulysses* (Joyce), Lenin, Gorky, Romain Rolland, Liebknecht, Gandhi, and Franklin Roosevelt—such a civilization could have no other architectural expression but one resulting from befuddlement. Many a man, harassed by changes too rapid, contradictions too disconcerting, and strains too severe, seeks refuge either in a predilection for the architecture of a past that seems to him quieter and more harmonious than ours today, or else in a new heaven, equally unrealistic, created like a mathematical theorem out of thin air, all complete and hard and closed.

Yet even in the confused buildings of the recent past there is a "style"—here in America even an "American style." That is, there has grown up inevitably, in response to steel construction and the demands for space our culture brought, a certain large way of building and certain large categories of form. A single visit to any large city should prove this at once. Let the reader select any two large office buildings or apartment houses built in the eclectic manner, each in a different historical "style" from the other. All the detail on the two buildings is different: one, like the New York Life Insurance Building, may have the pointed arches, the delicate tracery, the crockets and finials of flamboyant French Gothic, and the other, like New York's Savoy Plaza Hotel, the stately columns and entablatures and round arches of Rome. Yet, if one could see them from a mile or two away these two buildings would look alike in every general respect. Both would appear as rectangular boxlike masses, with small and unimportant roofs, and with some sort of decoration near the top and also near the bottom. In between all would be a surface of wall emplaided with tiny windows set close together.

Anyone who has seen the silhouette of New York or Chicago, or Pittsburgh, or San Francisco, will appreciate the truth of this. All the buildings are similar in general line and effect; all show the same earmarks of need and structure. In their basic geometry, in their height, and in the size and number of their windows the effect of their steel construction is revealed; the spirit of modern America breathes through them. They are unique, those silhouettes of our American cities—as different from the silhouette of London, or Rome, or Paris, or Constantinople as our life is different from the lives in those great capitals—and it is our architects who have made them so. This unique outline in all its strength and daring, and its occasional awkwardness, is one sign of the fact that these city buildings have evolved out of our needs.

Let us acknowledge the American character of it all up to this point; but let us realize that this is not enough for us. This halfway modernity, this eclectic confusion, is no longer the true expression of the times. As our age comes to maturity it demands a mature, direct architecture, as characteristic in detail as in conception. As we look back over architectural history, we must recognize the fact that the Greeks built in one way and the Romans in another, the peoples of medieval Europe in still another, and so on, not only as regards planning and composition and outline and mass but also as regards detail and ornament. Each period of each nation seems to have had its own alphabet of decorative material, its own unique feeling for architectural ornament—all harmonious with the construction current at the time, and with the cultural ideals of the period. We, on the other hand, developed no important new decorative forms in the eclectic period, and critics often consider this a sign of some strange lack of creative ability on the part of architects at that time, as well as of artistic insensibility on the part of the majority of the public.

This lack of creativeness in detail—one of the hallmarks of the architectural style prevalent up to the First World War—is itself relentlessly expressive. What could be more characteristic of the whole confusion of the early twentieth century, with its outworn traditional laws, education, religious beliefs, and economic system, its struggle to keep abreast of the sudden rush of new inventions, new needs, and new opportunities, than these thirty-story buildings with their parades of Corinthian columns or Gothic arches?—what more typical than the wealthy suburbanite who can live only behind Norman towers or English half-timber?

Yet even before the First World War the foundations of other, better, more logical architectural achievements were being laid. Seeds sown long before in the nineteenth century—in the rationalism of Schinkel and Labrouste, in the criticism of Ruskin, in the largely conceived and creative freedom of H. H. Richardson, in the rebellion of Louis Sullivan against the slavish classicism of his time —were at last coming to flower, all over the world. The *art nouveau* was a symptom, but in spite of its vagaries it was important because it began to accustom people to forms not based on prior styles; it wakened their curiosity and their desire for more experiments, more creation. In this country Louis Sullivan, in the great office buildings he designed in Chicago, Buffalo (Plate XXVIII), and St. Louis, revealed that a new beauty and new forms would result if one believed, as he did, that "form follows function." In Holland, Berlage created in the Amsterdam Bourse a building fresh and strong, characteristically Dutch, but free of historical forms. In Vienna, with an idealism somewhat like Sullivan's, Otto Wagner was applying these standards in a manner typically Viennese and baroque, but at the same time letting into the stuffiness of *fin de siècle* architecture the fresh air of logical thinking and exuberant creation, and thus assisting the birth of that great wave of creative design, of liberation, which swept over central Europe and produced the free creations of Hoffmann and the mighty factories of Behrens. In Scandinavia, a new freshness appeared within the general frame of the current classicism. In England, Mackintosh, Lutyens, and the younger Scott were feeling for new and more modern building forms.

The movement was slower in the United States. Frank Lloyd Wright, to be sure, was building his lovely, low, imaginative houses in the Middle West; yet even he found his first wide architectural recognition among certain architects in Europe, becoming to many of them another source of inspiration while he was still comparatively unknown in the United States except in his own city. To understand the reason for this we must turn to a brief consideration of the history of architecture; we must consider not the fully developed climax points of architectural history when styles were in full flower but the causes and influences behind the developments that led to the various styles of the past.

In this consideration we may well omit the early oriental styles which soon were petrified by civilizations dominated by priesthoods whose traditional beliefs admitted of little genuine progress. In Greece, on the other hand, there was no such static rule of tradition; the Greeks, as has been noted earlier, were always striving after an unattainable and ever growing ideal of beauty, an ideal that grew as rapidly as did their powers of achievement. Furthermore, since Greek history is well known and widely understood, it is not difficult to trace the development of the Greek styles and to discover the causes that produced them. For instance, it is definitely known, having been proved beyond a doubt by contemporary inscriptions, that in the earliest days of Greek civilization, days before the time when the tribes who formed the historical Greek nation had reached their final homes, the entire eastern Mediterranean was inhabited by peoples living in close commercial and cultural relations. Even at that early date colonies from the Greek Islands had settled in the rich country of Egypt, and that great nation of sailors—the Phoenicians —was driving a thriving trade between one country and another.

It is not strange, therefore, to find that the art of this early time had many common, international characteristics and motifs. We find identically the same patterns of scrolls and rosettes in Crete that we find in Egypt. We find the lotus of Egypt and the palmette, or palm leaf, of Assyria in every country, sometimes modified and oftentimes used in a way which shows that the origin was forgotten or unknown. We even find that the Assyrian palmette and the Egyptian lotus may have been two variations of one and the same elementary branching form.

And the differences between the styles of the different nations are
equally easy to explain. They are due, first, to differing religious and
social ideals of life; second, to climate; third, to material; and,
fourth, to construction. In the autochthonous art of the Greek Islands there was no attempt at making an original national style;
these early Greeks of pre-Hellenic days merely built as their needs
required and their materials suggested. For their decorative details

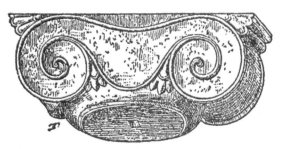

FIGURE 27. AN EARLY CYPRIOTE IONIC CAPITAL

they borrowed right and left. They used every motif that seemed to
them beautiful, whatever its origin; then, because they were more
skillful at making pictures than most of their neighbors, and because they enjoyed doing it, they added to the borrowed forms certain natural forms which they loved: fishes—particularly the octopus
—bees, and great long-horned cattle.

When the Hellenes—the people we know as Greeks—came to
Greece and settled it, either peacefully or by conquest, they gradually
absorbed a good deal of the aboriginal art. They themselves were
people of a different origin, perhaps of a different race; they came
from the dim north, a people whose birth is lost in the fog of the
past. In the goodly peninsula they came to inhabit they found an
art, a civilization, more highly developed than their own, and this
they did not scruple to adopt wherever it fitted their needs; nor did
they scruple to modify it to suit their own traditions. The result of
this amalgam of native and foreign influences can be seen not only
in early Greek architecture but in Greek mythology and literature as
well. The many loves of Zeus are but idealized stories of the gradual
combination and marriage of the pure Hellenic religion with all the
old local religions; in architecture the Doric order, though theories

concerning its origin are at best hypothetical, seems to have been compounded of analogous Hellenic and aboriginal traditions. Certain it is that there are resemblances quite as strong between the Greek Doric capitals and entablatures and those used by the prehistoric peoples before them as are the differences between the column shafts of the two peoples.

But Greek architecture is more than the Doric order. The Greeks developed the Ionic and Corinthian orders as well, though both seem to have been non-Greek in origin. That these were not developed to any very great extent on the soil of the Greek peninsula itself until comparatively late times, whereas the Doric was used alone and had no rival for two hundred years, is because of the fact that during those years the Greeks of the peninsula were a young people occupied in settling their own problems, and always confronted by the fear

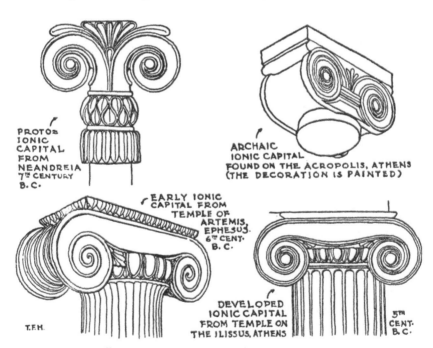

PROTO-
IONIC
CAPITAL
FROM
NEANDREIA
7ᵀᴴ CENTURY
B. C.

ARCHAIC
IONIC CAPITAL
FOUND ON THE ACROPOLIS, ATHENS
(THE DECORATION IS PAINTED)

EARLY IONIC
CAPITAL FROM
TEMPLE OF
ARTEMIS,
EPHESUS.
6ᵀᴴ CENT·
B. C·

DEVELOPED
IONIC CAPITAL
FROM TEMPLE ON
THE ILISSUS, ATHENS

5ᵀᴴ
CENT·
B. C·

T.F.H.

FIGURE 28. DEVELOPMENT OF THE GREEK IONIC CAPITAL
(*Architecture through the Ages*)

Various steps in the change from a pure bracket or bolster type capital to the refined scrolls of the developed examples.

of unknown peoples, unknown nations—the *Barbaroi*. The Greeks in Asia, on the contrary, were eager enough to seize upon and develop eastern art motifs. No fear of losing the national characteristics of their art restrained them from adopting and developing for their own use the Ionic capital (Figures 27 and 28)—now universally recognized as of earlier Asiatic origin—or the dentils of Lydia, or from recombining the lotus and palm-leaf forms into new elements of beauty. For the Greeks were eager always, as is truly said in the Book of the Acts, "either to tell or to hear some new thing," and equally eager to adopt whatever pleased them and develop it in their own way.

Greek architecture, then, which is held up as a purely national style, sincere and worthy of our emulation, is seen on analysis to be a development of motifs coming from many non-Greek sources, along with a few Greek motifs, all combined and used in harmony with Greek life, Greek materials, Greek religion, and that overmastering artistic idealism which has made Greek art what it is. The Greek never hesitated to take the result of other peoples' developments; he borrowed in his religion, he borrowed in his philosophy, he borrowed in his art. He modified what he borrowed not because of any dogmatic desire to make his art a national art, but because he could always make his borrowed motifs more beautiful by modification.

The history of Roman architecture reveals the same underlying method of development. The Romans came in contact with Greek civilization early in their career because of the Greek colonies in Italy and Sicily and by means of Greek commerce, which flourished at that time, as the quantities of Greek vases and imitations of them that are found in Italy testify. Furthermore, like the Hellenes, the Romans were a people who in their first few hundred years as a nation were occupied with their own affairs, with wars, and with social and political development. Even in their earlier history, however, the Romans were builders, and long before their final architectural evolution they had acquired no small skill in building as a whole, in arch making, and in the efficient use of their native materials. And the Romans were an art-loving people, keenly sensitive to beauty. The rapidity with which they assimilated Greek forms, after years of provincialism, bears witness to that.

Consequently, when at last internal peace and growing wealth brought them the opportunity to develop their fine arts, they turned for inspiration to the most beautiful buildings they knew— the Greek buildings—and adopted for their own use the Greek forms they were wise enough to love. These they combined with their own forms and the closely allied Etruscan forms and out of this combination, by means of their building skill, evolved their own wonderful Roman architecture, with all its magnificent qualities of bigness and large conception and careful planning and rich orna- ment, a combination of qualities before unknown.

This is not the place to go far into criticism of the much misunder- stood Roman architecture. Causes and methods of development alone concern us here. That the result—Roman imperial architec- ture—was a strong and virile art, intensely expressive of every side of that wonderful empire, is universally admitted. Critics who too strongly attack Roman taste and Roman buildings are not—most of them—architects; they are mere followers in the tradition of attack on everything connected with the Roman Empire—a tradition started by a Roman himself, that supreme Tory and reactionary, Tacitus.

One additional example of a more recent development of archi- tectural style will suffice. When Charles VII and later Louis XII and Francis I made their ill-fated expeditions into Italy to lay claim to the thrones of Naples and Milan, though they brought back no spoils of material conquest, they did bring with them into France a tremendous and enthusiastic admiration for the artistic products of the early Italian Renaissance, which was just in the first flush of its exuberant beauty. Brantôme comments frequently on the French court's admiration of Italian manners, Italian culture, and Italian cities. They brought back, too, Italian artisans whose work was eagerly welcomed by the French courtiers. But unlike Greece and Rome, when this new and beautiful art came to their notice, the French already had a magnificent and live and growing national

architecture of their own. The flamboyant Gothic of fifteenth-
century France was too dear to French hearts to yield to a new style
at once, too deeply filled with the French spirit to be deserted for a
foreign art without a struggle.

And yet the grace and loveliness of the newly discovered Italian
decorative work appealed irresistibly to these French courtiers, and
particularly to Francis I. His political aspirations in Italy may have
had something to do with his enthusiasm for Italian things; besides,
an Italian city at this period was a far more orderly and civilized place
than the usual French city, and the Italian Renaissance palaces far
richer and more comfortable than the contemporary French châteaux. Whatever the cause—political or social or aesthetic, and
probably it was a combination of the three—Francis I at once set
about building in the new popular Renaissance style. He imported
large numbers of Italian artists and treated them royally, and
naturally enough his admirers and courtiers strove to imitate him
as far as they were able.

Of course no absolute reproduction of Italian models was possible.
In the first place, the great guild of native stonecutters and master
builders, all bred in the tradition of flamboyant Gothic, was all-
powerful, and it was but slowly that they came to know well and use
correctly the Renaissance detail; it was years, too, before they came
to adopt the style in anything beyond detail—years during which the
whole spirit of humanism and individualism, of which Renaissance
architecture was but one expression, was making great strides in
France. France has always been a rapidly changing country, given to
idealistic enthusiasms, and in the years from the death of Louis XI
to the time of Henry IV it grew rapidly in homogeneity, in national
spirit, and in international trade and liberal culture. Had this change
not taken place, the Renaissance in architecture would doubtless
have been but a momentary florescence, a mere fad, to die with
French political aspirations in Italy, and the French would have
continued for years and centuries longer to build according to the
Gothic traditions of their building guilds.

But French growth did not allow this. The international communication of ideas was increasing rapidly, travel was becoming

more common, and humanistic culture was more and more spreading over Europe, bringing with it a tremendous admiration for
classic accomplishment; so that the delicate and lovely mixture of
classic and Gothic elements which is the style of Francis I, an architecture full of the charm peculiar to all transitional styles, like the
charm of spring in April, gave way not to a recrudescence of Gothic
but to a fuller appreciation of classic forms and a firmer touch and
finer skill in their use. Even with the growing use of classical forms,
however, there was in general but little approach to those forms of
Italian architecture which were the first inspiration of the French
Renaissance. Climatic requirements are the most important reason
for this—the necessity in cloudy France for large windows and
steep roofs. Even the imported Italian architects realized this.
Sebastiano Serlio, in his unpublished book on domestic architecture
(known only in manuscript), always gives two versions of his first,
simpler designs—one "in the Italian manner," and one "in the
manner of France." Those in the latter vein all have the large
windows and the high roofs and developed chimneys which the
climate required. And in his more elaborate designs for French
buildings it is the true French character that shines through the
classic pilasters and entablatures. Serlio was too true an architect to
attempt to make French buildings look like Italian Renaissance
palaces; he designed freely in accordance with French needs, French
traditions, and the French climate. In addition to these considerations, however, there was a certain constitutional gaiety and exuberance of spirit in the French people which found in cold classicism
but an imperfect expression.

It was the result of all these tendencies which made French
Renaissance architecture the strongly national style it is. There is
always a frank use of large windows; there is often a steep and well-
developed roof; there is always the same expression of intellectual
classicism and of exuberant unrestraint as well. French architecture
of the seventeenth century was a national style not because the
French did not copy for fear of denationalizing their art, but because their artists were true to their ideals, adopting what they
thought beautiful, but building always in conformity with their

conditions, their materials, and their environment (see Plate XXVII).

An analysis of the development of any other historical "style" will reveal the same influences at work. It will reveal, for instance, Romanesque growing out of Roman and Byzantine architecture, and Gothic out of Romanesque, seldom through sudden revolution, seldom through impetuous striving for originality, but always through the honest efforts of the architects and builders in each period to build as best they could under the different conditions of skill and the different social make-up of their own civilization. In every case the architects have copied past forms and foreign forms as well as they could, when these forms seemed beautiful; in every case, nevertheless, architectural styles grew up inevitably national, inevitably expressive of the contemporary life.

Any true understanding of the development of American architecture must be based on a similar analysis of the conditions which have influenced the broad stream of American historical tradition. First of all, we must realize the extreme variety in the background of the early white settlers of the country: Pilgrims and Puritans in New England; Dutch traders in the Hudson Valley; French Huguenots scattered here and there in New York, on the Delaware, in South Carolina; the aristocracy of the South and of the Hudson River manors; the merchants and craftsmen of the port towns; the French in Canada, the coast of the Gulf of Mexico, and the Mississippi Valley; the Spanish in Florida and the Southwest. We must realize, too, that at the outset the country was only a loosely integrated federation of separate states, bedeviled by local and sectional cross-purposes, and that the development out of all these differing strains, under the conditions existing, was political rather than cultural. There were bound to be great architectural differences between the various parts of the country for cultural reasons, then, as well as because of differences of climate. Variety, perhaps even unsureness of aim, was almost inevitable in design.

Moreover, in their new American homes the early settlers, coming as they did from countries with highly developed architectures of their own, attempted at first to build in the ways they had known in

Europe or Mexico. Only slowly did they come to realize the profound differences of climate, materials, and conditions which perforce imposed upon them the necessity of changes, sometimes radical, in building forms and types. The growth of Colonial architecture— English Colonial in the East, Spanish Colonial in the West, French Colonial in the North and through the center—was slow, halting, and experimental, as continuing touch with the mother countries brought to these shores the contemporary European architectural fashions, and as growing self-sufficiency and increasing skill in meeting local conditions with the materials at hand brought local architectural mastery. Thus the developed Colonial architectures of the United States—English, French, Spanish—became entirely different from the architectures of the home countries. Yet in each the national roots are recognizable, and in each there is a more or less belated reflection of European style development.

The American Revolution brought with it a vigorous new surge of national consciousness, a new impetus to architectural independence. And it occurred just before a time of radical change in European architecture as well as in the European political atmosphere. The final break-up of the old aristocratic Baroque and Rococo architectural tradition at the end of the eighteenth century was swift and decisive, and a new world in Europe as in America sought a new architecture. Both continents found it in new inspirations from the architectures of the ancient classic world, and the influence of the buildings of the Greeks and the Romans which the new science of archaeology was making better known became supreme. Of course America lay under this influence as well as Europe; again and again the architects of the young Republic expressed their indebtedness to that fecund source, but almost as unanimously they called for a creative use of this new knowledge, a new architecture for a new republic. Copying was far from their minds, save in details, and even these they often modified. Like Jefferson, they saw in the Colonial work which had preceded them only an outworn mode, either barnlike and undistinguished, or tricked out with all the gewgaws of Baroque ornament that a culture then already dead or dying had produced. Thus over the underlying tradition of Colonial work—essentially Renaissance and Baroque—was laid a new layer of classicism, a quieter, more monumental classicism based on the inspiration of Greece and Rome.

Jefferson, to be sure, in his reaction against Colonial architecture, turned to the work of Palladio for guidance; but his own home, Monticello, the Virginia state capitol at Richmond which he designed, and his master work the University of Virginia all show with what freedom he used this inspiration. The work of the architects who followed him—Latrobe, Mills, Strickland, Town, Davis, Rogers, and a host of others—was even more free and creative.

It was during this period of the classic revivals, too, that the first great flowering of art in America occurred. Popular interest was great; there was hardly one of the hundreds of little local periodicals which expressed the cultural vividness of the time that did not have its articles on architecture and painting. In painting it was the period of Inman, Trumbull, and Morse; in architecture it was that of Latrobe, Strickland, Mills, Isaiah Rogers, Ithiel Town, and Alexander Jackson Davis. And it was a period of excellent, conscientious building; these architects, though they used Greek or Roman detail, realized full well that the purpose of architecture was building, not pretty details. The rugged construction they used and the imagination and creative power that went into it are evidenced by the great obelisk in honor of Washington in the national capital and the stone-vaulted basements and fireproof construction of the New York Sub-Treasury, as well as by the simple strength of many New England, New York, and Ohio farmhouses. These architects of the Greek Revival never forgot they were building American buildings for an American climate and for American people; they never attempted to construct for Athens or for Rome. Thus at its very beginning the architecture of this country was given a strong foundation of creative classicism, and all over the country this Greek-inspired architecture seemed the usual—not the exotic—thing to build. It is little wonder, then, that this doubly based classical tradition has colored much American architecture ever since.

Later, of course, other world-wide aesthetic movements had their

American expression. The Gothic Revival produced some lovely churches, interesting public buildings, charming cottages and larger houses, but in some of its work a dangerous tendency appeared—a tendency to over-emphasize *effect* at the sacrifice of structure, to accept the shadow for the substance. Many Gothic Revival churches, even the finest like Trinity in New York, had elaborate vaults, pretending to be stone, of plaster on wood lath. The Gothic Revival architects had even less sense of the integrity of materials than did the Greek Revival architects and added much to the tradition of the purely pictorial conception of architecture that reached its first climax in the gimcrackery of a great deal of the building of the Civil War period, and its second in the classic skyscrapers of the early twentieth century.

The twenty years from 1855 to 1875 were years of confusion, money-grubbing, and shameless greed. Planning—the orderly, efficient, and effective arrangement of interior spaces—almost ceased to exist. Slums grew by leaps and bounds. Older men, trained in the earlier and sounder tradition, protested in vain and grew more and more aloof and bitter. The diaries and manuscript notes of Alexander Jackson Davis, in the Metropolitan Museum of Art, the New York Historical Society, and the Avery Library, Columbia University, are filled with his sound and mordant criticisms of the falsity of much of the architectural work of the period, his sketchbooks full of interesting notes as to how sound construction could produce new versions of Gothic, as it had of classic, design. Occasional critical articles, especially those during the sixties in the *New York Weekly*, protested in vain against the superficiality and tawdriness of the architecture of the time. Minard Lafever, Ranlett, and others had tried to develop a simple, straightforward type of house design— called the "bracketed style"—but all in vain; the flood of meretricious and picturesque "effects" in architecture swept well-nigh over the entire land and destroyed almost completely the sound earlier tradition.

One marked feature of American life in the era after the War between the States was a tremendous increase in foreign travel by the well-to-do. This was accompanied in the 1870's and 80's by a widespread revulsion in sensitive people against the crass vulgarity, the greed, and the political corruption rampant in post–Civil War America—a revulsion that bore fruit in the writings of Henry Adams and Henry James, and in the turning of art scholars and critics like Charles Eliot Norton to European art as the only art worth consideration. Ruskin was worshiped, Italian art had its votaries here, the palaces of Venice and the churches of Rome were well known to hordes of traveling Americans. And all this occurred when native architectural skill in the United States was at its lowest ebb and ostentation frequently passed for beauty.

In 1876, the Centennial Exposition in Philadelphia brought suddenly before the American people the most luxurious, the most beautiful, the most expensive products of European artists and craftsmen, which the makers of such things in America could not then hope to emulate. The American exhibits were outstanding in tools, agricultural implements, things of necessity and use; in articles of luxury they were hopelessly outclassed. The Centennial Exposition started a new awakening of popular taste; a new sensitiveness to the looks of things was born. Yet, in these circumstances, how could this taste be satisfied except by turning to Europe and the past? It inevitably brought in the doctrine of eclecticism in its train, the doctrine that the beauty of the past and of distant places is ours, if we want it; that we can pick and choose and adapt and copy as we will—a bit of the Renaissance here, of the Gothic there; here the colonnades of ancient Rome, and there the vaults of Constantinople. We are heirs of all the past, this doctrine held; the United States arose from many European sources, and there is therefore no European country whose architectural forms are alien to us.

Yet style is more than details, as we have already seen. And all through the bewildering changes of American taste certain deeper tendencies again and again appear. During the so-called Greek Revival period there was an unparalleled experimentation in house plans, for instance, as the old four-square Colonial house with its four rooms to a floor gradually gave way to houses of T or L shape, or houses with off-center halls, or one-storied rambling designs. And this experimentation, this refusal in house planning to be bound by

PLATE XXVII

Alinari

St. Peter's, Rome: exterior
Carlo Maderna, architect

From *Châteaux et manoirs de France*

Château Maisons
François Mansart, architect

PLATE XXVIII

Guaranty Building, Buffalo, New York. Louis H. Sullivan, architect

any precedent, went on undiminished throughout the nineteenth century and well into the twentieth. Somewhat similarly, in all the periods of American architecture from the 1820's down, there was a desire to do things in neat, simple, sharply definite ways, to treat windows as plain openings, to simplify wall surfaces wherever possible, to work for clear, unbroken, and undecorated planes. And there was likewise a great study of local materials, and a search for new and expressive ways of using them, culminating structurally in the development of "balloon frame" construction, and aesthetically in many charming summer cottages along the eastern coast and in the mountains. It is these basic tendencies which have played over all our borrowed or imported "styles" and made our expressions of them national in spirit. May they not, then, be considered the strongest elements in our American tradition? Are they not truly the American tradition? If this is so, then it follows, of course, that Louis Sullivan and Frank Lloyd Wright and a host of younger architects have been the great recent exponents of an American tradition, and that the creative architecture of today has been more traditional, in the truest sense of the term, than the Colonialisms and the pseudo-historical borrowings which so universally preceded it.

Eclecticism, however, was not limited to the United States. It was a world-wide expression of a culture swamped by the changes resulting from the rise of industrialism—the rapid growth of cities, the rise of a new class of wealthy owners with no tradition behind them, speculation, a growing imperialism. Trade was king, profits the one criterion of success. And the official teaching of the architectural schools aided eclecticism; these sought in the lingering fragments of classic tradition a guide through the confusion, a barrier against complete disintegration in architecture. They tried to find in scholarship—or a broad knowledge of past architecture—a rule of taste for present conditions. Yet beyond this inculcating of superficial taste they did generally achieve one great benefit: they kept alive the tradition of good planning. It is because of this that many eclectic buildings command our admiration still, for their riot of perhaps inappropriate borrowed decoration clothes a whole structure well planned, direct and impressive, efficient for its use, and full of interesting interior space arrangements. And this architectural academic tradition was basically international, taking its chief leadership from the French École des Beaux Arts in Paris, which more than any other school in the later part of the nineteenth century preserved something of the vitality of earlier days.

The effect of this internationalism on our American art can readily be realized. It made our artists, and especially our architects, eager to welcome inspiration from any quarter. In other words, just at the period when the awakening artistic taste of America was groping vaguely for beauty, Europe with all its stores of art treasures, new and old, modern and ancient, lay especially open to Americans; European art schools welcomed American students, and European resorts welcomed American tourists. Naturally, therefore, it was from Europe that the American architects of the time drew their inspiration—from the thermae of Rome, the palaces of Florence and Venice, the châteaux and cathedrals of France, the abbeys and manors and country villages of England. In drawing inspiration from these channels, and in adopting forms developed in Europe, our architects were only doing what it was inevitable they should do; they were merely following the same methods that the architects of all the greatest ages have followed. Beauty is the architect's goal, and beauty is a quality that knows neither race nor nation. The Cretan copied the Egyptian, the Hellene copied the Cretan, the Roman copied the Greek, the Renaissance copied the Roman, the modern architect copies them all—so ran the eclectic credo.

Yet the attitude of easy-going eclecticism contained within itself the seeds of its own death. The more brilliant architects found them-selves—almost in spite of themselves—departing more and more from past categories; the more thoughtful could not help seeing that the new building programs and the new constructional techniques produced forms often little suited to classic or Gothic dress—either the basic "true" forms (the real architecture) had to give way, or else the traditional historical ornament. Naturally this development occurred in industrial buildings first, and some of the magnificent groups of factories of the time could not help showing that another approach was possible. In Germany and Holland the inspiration of the Viennese Wagner and the Dutch Berlage grew by leaps and bounds. Behrens, in his factories for the German General Electric Company, the German Embassy at St. Petersburg (Leningrad), and other work; Van de Velde, in the lovely, flowing-lined theater of the Cologne Exposition of 1913; Hoffmann, in the Austrian Building at the same exposition and in the Stoclet house in Brussels; and Gropius, in the model factory of 1913 at Cologne—all these architects showed how new forms, creative and lovely, might flow from a frank acceptance of steel and concrete and stucco and glass. In America, though progress was slower because of the depth and reality of the American classic tradition, more and more the daring yet quiet loveliness of Frank Lloyd Wright's houses came to have admirers, and architects like Goodhue began to reach out toward a more creative type of design.

Moreover, in the years immediately preceding the First World War, the artistic world of America was thrown into violent controversy by the gradual infiltration of the works of the revolutionary painters of Europe; in this movement the famous Armory Show of 1913 with its display of all the "fauves"—Picasso, Matisse, Duchamp-Villon, Picabia, and so on—marks an epoch. America came to see that the whole basis of its academic art needed examination and revaluation. A great flood of fresh air had been let in; many sensitive people breathed it deeply, with a feeling of relief, of liberation, of gladness that new creation was still possible.

In architecture, the results were felt slowly—at first merely as a freer and freer eclecticism. Historical consistency of style yielded to artistic consistency, and new combinations of old motifs appeared more and more frequently. In the smaller domestic work, where as yet the full impact of changed conditions had not been felt, the results were often valid and lovely; it was almost as if new types of "Georgian" and "Spanish" were growing before us (nine-tenths just plain house and one-tenth "Georgian" or "Spanish" as the case might be), not by virtue of a solemn copying of book details, but often merely in the most general sort of way. Similarly, in cities, apartment houses were being built which more and more tended toward simplicity and directness.

Yet it was not until the 1920's that there was any full acceptance of the necessity and desirability of new types of architecture, or any realization of the extraordinary opportunity that glass, bright metal, and light, strong construction gave the architect; when that realization did come, it came largely as a reflection of European movements, and was in danger of becoming just another "style" to copy. And, as a "style," it was accepted first in furniture and interior decoration. The cause was the Paris Exposition des Arts Decoratifs, in 1925, which in architecture as well as in the decorative arts presented a clean break with the past, a searching for something new. It was a rather superficial searching, often flippant and ill considered, with not a little trace of the old almost forgotten *art nouveau*. It was this exposition which, logically enough, gave rise to that style known as "modernistic" (pseudo-modern); "modernistic" furniture, bric-a-brac, and gewgaws now became the delight as well as the curse of the department stores.

Meanwhile other tendencies were developing and becoming clarified. In Germany, particularly under the influence of Eric Mendelsohn and in considerable municipal housing that was being carried on under various architects like Bruno Taut and Ernst May (see Plate XXIX), there was coming into being a great mass of attractive buildings, soundly and freely designed, often entirely without applied ornament of any kind, and depending for their effect on subtle proportion or on sharp and interesting contrasts of vertical and horizontal lines. In Hamburg and the surrounding country, Hoeger and others were creating a new type of brick architecture. The Perret brothers in France were creating vital new expressions of reinforced concrete, as in the famous church at Raincy. Everywhere in Europe, it seemed, the ferment of new creativeness was at work.

In this ferment a group was developing, with members in Germany, France, and Holland, who looked at this new creativeness and found it wanting. To them it seemed futile and superficial, the mere dressing of a corpse in new clothes. Architecture, they reasoned, is

basically structure; a fit architecture for today must not only use
modern structural methods but must also develop its every line
logically and inevitably from these new methods. A modern building must show its structure even more directly than the Gothic
buildings showed theirs; its every beauty must be conditioned by
modern structural methods (steel and reinforced concrete) and
modern materials (veneered woods, glass, metal, and plastics).
Moreover, since the walls in a modern building are mere screens,
they must look like screens. As a corollary, buildings should no
longer appear like weighty masses, but like enclosed space. They are
built for their interiors—that is, the space they enclose—and therefore must appear as that space with its enclosures. Monumentality
and any type of axial symmetry are inconsistent with this ideal, these
architects felt. Sloped roofs express past and gone techniques;
therefore every building must have a flat roof. This type of thinking
was carried to great extremes and became sometimes rigid and
dogmatic, but the ideal behind it was essentially noble—the search
for an absolute truth, no matter what renunciations it brought. The
group's most important members were Gropius and Taut in Germany, Oud in Holland, and Le Corbusier (Charles Édouard Jean-
neret) in France; the style of architecture they created was called
the "International Style" (see Plate XXIX).

In the United States, too, a local style was developing during
these years, especially for large commercial and public buildings. Its
foundation was no such logical and even doctrinaire examination of
modern life, but the old, deep-laid classical tradition of the country
plus a desire for a newer creativeness in its expression. It reached its
first great achievement in the later works of B. G. Goodhue—the
Nebraska state capitol (Plate V) and the Los Angeles Public
Library. In both, the basic ideal of the design is the serene, balanced
monumentality of the classic tradition; but in neither building is
there any parade of Greek or Roman detail—whatever ornament is
used is architectural sculpture or painting. This tendency toward an
abstracted, refined, and monumental type of building without detail
from the past has become increasingly common. It can be seen in
Cret's Folger Library in Washington, in the Seattle Art Museum by

Bebb and Gould, and in much of Holabird and Root's public and commercial work in Chicago and the Middle West. In a simpler way a similar ideal is expressed in the quiet country houses of Delano and Aldrich in the East, and in some of the best work of Frank Lloyd Wright.

To all this the supporters of the International Style are volubly hostile. To them it is all halfway, transitional, ill thought out, untrue both to modern materials and to modern life. Architectural criticism for several years recently dealt chiefly with the controversy between these ardent defenders of the flat roofs, smooth surfaces, strip windows, pipe railings, and thin metal stiltlike supports—the language of the International Style created by Gropius and Le Corbusier —and others, equally desirous of a new architecture characteristic of our new times, who can see only limitation and stagnation in the rigid austerity of the International Style.

Of late years this controversy has quieted. Growing control of artistic media and growing skill in the use of new materials have brought greater and greater freedom into the designs of the more rigidly doctrinaire architects. Little by little the same developments have inevitably reflected themselves in the work of the freer designers, like Wright, who have come to adopt naturally many of the most unconventional of architectural forms—thin metal columns, unbroken sheets of glass, projecting cantilevered slabs, and so on.

And into the work of both schools has come a new controlling ideal which has inevitably tended to unify their efforts—a new realization that architecture exists for *people*, and not for theoretical exposition; that the first duty of a building is to be *human*—not only to act as an efficient frame for the physical activities of people but also to give them delight, to feed their emotions as well as to aid and rest their muscles. A new freedom and variety have thus entered the broad stream of contemporary architecture.

Along with this new humanism in design there has come a new sensitiveness to local conditions, to local climates and local materials, and even to local traditions. Good architects of all schools today increasingly design with the truest consideration of all the conditions of a program—human, climatic, local. The necessity for shielding windows from hot summer sun and letting in the low sun of cold winter days has brought all sorts of new window hood shelters; the free use of porches and terraces has given a growing variety of outline and a closer adaptation to site; and the use and placing of windows or glass doors in accordance with the needs of view, sun, and privacy—rather than as a display of a new material or a revelation of some abstruse theory of screen-wall design—have given increased variety to exterior design. All these factors, and many more, tend to break up the earlier rigidities. The contemporary building of today may be as free, as creative, and as personal as that of any past period and still be in harmony with the industry, the life, and the materials of today.

If this, then, has been the history of recent architectural development, especially in the United States, many puzzles in the history of popular taste in architecture become clear. In the strong classic foundations of earlier American architecture lies the reason for the obstinate persistence of classic forms, for their wide popular appeal, for the enthusiasm with which the Chicago Exposition of 1893 and the San Francisco Exposition of 1915 were welcomed. In the variety of American backgrounds lies the reason for some of the confusions of American eclecticism. The turning to Europe for artistic inspiration on the part of Charles Eliot Norton and his followers was an important factor in blinding us to the richness of our own tradition and the possibilities of a native art. And in the separation of architecture as external design from engineering as pure construction— a separation which both industrial specialization and eclecticism of taste helped to produce—lay one of the reasons why the average American grew eventually bored with, or at least indifferent to, the whole rich field of architecture. Eclecticism died hard here, because of the technical excellence of many eclectic designers and the excellent planning of many eclectic buildings, and because in vast stretches of the newer parts of the country eclecticism was the chief characteristic of all the "good" architecture—of the most expensive and impressive buildings—which people knew. But at last, today, eclecticism as a living force in American architecture is dead; it lives on only in the work of cheap real-estate subdivisions, and as an occasional sentimental hangover like the Jefferson Memorial in Washington. Creative work today, and beautiful architecture today, are of a different type. The TVA buildings, Rockefeller Center, the Museum of Modern Art, the Crow Island School at Winnetka, many beautiful Pacific Coast houses and a growing number in the Middle West and the East—these form our true modern architecture, harmonious with the best elements in the contemporary world.

In any case one may rest assured that style is but a means, and that beauty is the end in quest. Let our architects, then, and our laymen too, stop all their futile arguments about style, about the International Style, or about the good old traditions, or the Roman, or the Gothic; for the truest way to an honest and an inspiring architecture is through a sincere attempt to gain beauty in a simple way. The architect who designs carefully and thoughtfully, taking care to fulfill every smallest demand made by his problem in the most beautiful way at his command, is doing more to make American architecture a glorious expression of national life than could generations of theorizing critics.

10

ARCHITECTURE
AND THE
COMMUNITY

THE LAST half century has dinned one great lesson into the ears of mankind, a lesson man must learn, however reluctantly, or perish. It is the lesson of brotherliness, a recognition that all men are part of one great unit—the unit of all mankind —and that everything we do as individuals affects others in infinite ways, as everything others do affects us. The First World War proved that international conflicts between a few countries affected all countries. The great boom of the twenties was international; the great depression that followed in the thirties inevitably brought need and suffering to all men everywhere, whatever their individual worth or their individual efforts may have been. One small trade group strikes in one factory—it matters not what the merits of the case may be—and in a short time a whole industry is crippled and factories by the score are forced to close. The individual saves, is thrifty, "buys" a house (that is, he makes a down payment on it); a local slump in business occurs, and he is jobless through no fault of his own—good-bye house and all that he has put into it. Not one of us but is at the mercy of the actions of his fellow men, and of a system; conversely, there is not one of us whose every action has not its social effect on thousands of others.

After the depression came the Second World War, not unrelated to it; under the stress of danger men learned everywhere to work together for common ends as they never had worked before. And then, as a climax in this lesson, came the atomic bomb, and the lives of every one of us and of our children are at the mercy of what may be done with this new power. We must unite; we must understand that we are all parts of a single world, whatever our race, our color, or our language; we must develop a true community of feeling everywhere or we perish and civilization crashes.

Fortunately, little by little this lesson is being learned. The individual is growing less and less satisfied with considering merely the things that concern him alone. More and more he is coming consciously to feel himself a part of the fascinating and complex tissue of life; he is beginning to appreciate that his life is so closely bound up with the lives of his fellows, and their lives knit by such a multiplicity of ties to his, that he must settle all really important questions not by their effect on himself alone but by their effect on the total life of the community. The medieval or Renaissance moralist began with the individual soul and worked from that to the ideal community; the modern starts with the ideal community and works back to the individual soul.

This new attitude has furnished the world with an entirely new set of criteria by which to judge not only personal conduct but also the religion and the arts of the present day. This judgment is going on continuously and with a ruthless earnestness, and architecture must stand or fall in accordance with it. By any such criterion, much eclectic architecture must stand condemned, for, in ostentatious country palaces for the wealthy, in vast commercial buildings built solely for private profit, in some exhibitionistic educational buildings erected to cast glamor on a great fortune, one can see only the workings of an outgrown and selfish individualism; the architects of such works often appear as mere panderers to the false culture of a power-greedy plutocracy.

But fortunately this is not the whole story. It is true that there are certain architects who may be so judged and so condemned; but the art itself is greater than any of those who practice it, and the great majority of American architects are more truly alive to the social bearing of their profession, and its unique social value, than are many of their critics.

Architecture, in fact, is the greatest and most real of all the arts, precisely because it has a unique social opportunity, because it can, and at its best does, have tremendous social value. And this is necessarily so because of the very nature of the art itself—because of its dual nature, its double basis in practical needs and aesthetic ideals. Every real change in economic or sociological thinking, every major alteration in living conditions, will inevitably react on both these factors, and through them on architecture. This is particularly true when the change is one so deep in its penetration into the very heart of life, and so wide in its scope, as the present development of community responsibility, which must affect everything one does or thinks—a change that has produced socialism and settlement houses, model suburbs and public playgrounds. The socialized conscience inevitably has produced new ideals of housing, of sanitation, of factory arrangement, and of city planning, and all these have a direct effect on the art of architecture, because they present new problems in the buildings the architect is called on to design, and because they alter many of the basic conceptions under which he works.

In the Renaissance and Baroque periods, architects worked chiefly for wealthy and aristocratic individual patrons—for kings, princes, dukes, bankers, powerful cardinals and bishops. During much of the nineteenth century this remained partly true, and even many early twentieth-century architects retained the basic viewpoint established under this system of individual patronage. But gradually, as the basis of life broadened, as democratic ideals became more common, as business became more closely organized, this condition changed. Great corporations began to replace individuals as the patrons of architects. Governmental bodies and authorities began to control more and more construction. Architecture began to deal less and less with palace residences in town and country, more and more with buildings for commerce and industry (office buildings, shops, factories), with governmental buildings (post offices, courthouses, city halls), and with buildings for groups rather than for individuals, or structures erected for the social usefulness of an entire community (apartment houses, community centers, schools). The result has been perhaps a certain loss of individual prerogative on the part of architects, but it has brought in return a needed discipline, a sanity, and a closer and closer touch with the people as a whole. It has brought before architects a host of new and challenging problems.

In the main, modern architects appreciate and welcome these new problems. It is not on them that the blame must be laid for the slow realization of the social ideal in modern buildings. They are alert to the changing needs of the public; they do, as a class, study carefully and long the basic requirements of all sorts of new building types and investigate the implications of new city planning conceptions, long before the buildings are ever built or the conceptions realized. But, unlike the painter or sculptor or writer, the architect needs more than his own thought and his own skill in order to create. The architect's mission is not fulfilled by dreams, or noble aspirations, or even a concrete knowledge of what is desirable and possible; it is fulfilled only by actual buildings, constructed and in use. And to embody the ideas he has developed requires a large amount of money. To build requires individuals—people who are ready to appreciate the merits of new plans and to pay for them—or else governmental agencies sufficiently alert to the need to give broad financial support. So long as speculative builders and real-estate operators are content to build cheap and ill-designed structures because there is great profit in this evil trade, just so long, no matter how hard the architect thinks about new ideals and how perfect are the solutions his brain devises for the new problems, will the social ideal in architecture be thwarted and our cities remain chaotic, unbeautiful, depressing monuments of an inexcusable avarice. Good design costs money; high ideals must be paid for by society or by individuals; and until people are educated beyond the wild and thoughtless rush for abnormal dividends at any cost of beauty and health, it is futile to hope for great improvements. Failure to produce beautiful, healthful, and efficient towns and cities must be laid not at the doors of architects but at the doors of greed, lack of educated imagination, and appalling public apathy.

It is significant in this matter that one of the first to realize in an agony of spirit the terrible injustice and ruthless cruelty of the then new individualistic industrialism was also one of the best known of architectural critics, John Ruskin. In a lecture before the Royal Institute of British Architects, after an interesting discussion of architectural education, occurs this passage: "Pardon me that I speak despondingly. For my part, I feel the force of mechanism and the fury of avaricious commerce to be at present so irresistible that I have seceded from the study not only of architecture, but nearly of all art; and have given myself as I would in a besieged city, to seek the best modes of getting bread and water for the multitudes, there remaining no question, it seems to me, of other than such grave business for the time." This savage indictment seems as true today as when it was uttered eighty years ago.

Ruskin saw architecture one-sidedly; to his acute insight and powerful ethical sense, there was little place in life for the architect when poverty and misery were calling poignantly for relief on all sides. But to Ruskin architecture meant decoration and ornament, to him the architect was primarily a decorator, and it is this misconception which gives such a sad and discouraged tone to this passage. To the modern architect, who realizes that decoration is but one of the several elements of his great art, the call of poverty and misery and maladjustment is only an inspiration to a more careful exercise of his skill and a more absolute devotion to his profession.

And it is precisely here that the true professional attitude enters in. For it is the essence of a true profession that it always bears in mind the public good; though it may work for and be paid by the individual, it must never do the individual's bidding to the harm of society as a whole. In matters of building, then, the architect, if he is true to his profession, must needs think primarily in community terms; he stands, as it were, as a bulwark protecting social and community advantage against possible individual aggression. He sees that his buildings obey building and zoning regulations; he seeks in his design to create a building in harmony with its surroundings, a building that shall be a true addition to the beauty or the amenity of the community of which it is a part. And in so doing—that is, in following the dictates of his profession—he makes architecture an art of tremendous social importance, shedding true benefits not only on the building's owner but on all people who see or use each structure.

The first great benefit which the art of architecture confers on the commonwealth lies in the fact that true architecture is devoted to the sincere attempt to solve in the best possible practical way all the various problems set before it by every building that is to be designed. The implications of this are extremely far-reaching. Not only can the individual architect, by the careful design of each building, improve the conditions under which the users of the building live, or work, as the case may be, but, in addition, the gradually growing number of such carefully designed buildings raises the entire architectural standard in the nation—slowly, it is true, but irresistibly.

School architecture today reveals perfectly how architecture not only interprets social movements but also, by applying creative imagination to the needs they engender, assists their development. A century and more ago in the United States, under the leadership of Horace Mann, a revolutionary new educational idealism was born. Henry Barnard published a book on school architecture at that time, incorporating in it the requirements which the new vision made essential—well-designed individual seats and desks, good ventilation, ample lighting, recreational and gymnastic equipment, scientific laboratory materials. A host of early academies and public schools were built; many were excellent in design—efficient and attractive. Few of these remain, and those which do are largely forgotten today; for ever since that era educational ideals have gone on changing and developing, and the newer schools have always attempted to embody the most recent educational developments, so that older buildings, however good for their time, have rapidly become obsolete and been replaced or abandoned.

After the Civil War the unprecedented growth of cities, the floods of immigrants from Europe, and the general instability of conditions all affected school design. Larger and larger buildings were called for, and more and more of them were necessary. The thronging press of pupils made building programs years behind the needs even before the buildings they called for were erected. An era of crowding and confusion set in; school architecture, like all the other architecture of the time, descended to low levels; schoolhouses, built in haste to supply the growing demand, were often unbeautiful as well as unhealthy. Ill-ventilated rooms, dark corridors, and dangerous wooden stairs were the rule. Between 1870 and 1890 many schools were gloomy structures of brick, outside; within, they were heavy with coarse wooden trim, and children were herded together in rooms little fitted to receive them. The old adequate, even advanced, standards of the Horace Mann era were neglected, buried as they were under the mounting flood of pupils and the backwardness of city officials and boards of education. The problem seemed almost insoluble.

The coming of the twentieth century brought a revolution in school design. Public opinion was at last aroused; people in general demanded better things for their children. And architects were ready to respond to the need, for, even before the public had begun to realize the horrors of dreary and dangerous schools, architects here and there had devoted much thought to the problem, as occasional exceptionally excellent school buildings, designed by good architects, testify. And, once an aroused public opinion had created an opportunity for architects to put their knowledge to practical use, they not only seized upon it but, in the buildings that resulted, frequently went far beyond the standards which the people demanded and boards of education required. They created a new schoolhouse type —the vast, carefully planned, centralized, and efficient educational machine—and gave it exterior decency and interior pleasantness. Those huge schools, however, are not in accordance with the educational theories of today—they are too large, too impersonal—but the best of them are superb answers to the needs as they then existed. They were safe. Their classrooms were well lighted by long banks of windows. Their corridors and stairs were ample, efficient, direct. Their gymnasiums, their laboratories, their libraries, and their special rooms and special equipment for the sciences and for manual training became the models to which the rest of the world turned for inspiration. The school architect of that time, as of today, was never content with following the minimum demands of the law; he was always studying and restudying the problem, applying his expert knowledge and skill to the task of producing a building which not only should satisfy the public demand but also, by demonstrating as far as possible the high ideals for the building which had existed in his trained mind, should make the public demand more—greater safety, more space, more beauty. If his building did not far surpass the expected standards in efficiency, in healthfulness, in safety, and in beauty, the good architect felt that he had failed. As a result, standards of school excellence kept rising, and the many-windowed schools by C. B. J. Snyder in New York, by William B. Ittner in St. Louis and the Middle West, brought new beauty into cities and new vitality to education.

The last twenty years have witnessed another revolution in education through the work of John Dewey and others, and again the architects have been in the forefront of the campaign for better school buildings. City growth, meanwhile, has become slower; population increase the country over has declined. It has become possible for communities to catch their breath, so to speak, and to re-evaluate the whole problem of child education. Educators, moreover, are coming to realize anew that education must primarily be addressed to the individual child. They have become increasingly conscious of the importance of *doing* in the process of education—of the importance of making things, of play, self-expression, physical activity, and occasional change of environment. And they are realizing that the vast city school buildings which were the only possible answer to the problem of the too rapidly growing communities of the immediate past are ill fitted for the realization of these ideals. Something different is needed.

The best recent schools show how these new demands are being satisfied. Classrooms with movable furniture replace the mechanical rows of old fixed desks. Areas for work—carpentry, modeling, painting, and what not—open off or are part of each classroom. Cabinet and storage and bookshelf spaces are increased. Off many classrooms, especially those for the younger children, open inviting outdoor teaching or play areas. And the whole orientation of the design has changed; it has more and more turned to the child as the center. Things must be in child scale; colors must be gay and attractive to children; everything must be done to make school buildings not the gigantic and sometimes oppressive enclosed structures of the past but buildings a child will love and instinctively understand, for *schools are for children.*

The result, of course, is a structure quite different from that of a

PLATE XXIX

Les Terraces, Garches, France. Le Corbusier, architect

Zehlendorf Housing, Berlin. Bruno Taut, architect

PLATE XXX

Crow Island School, Winnetka, Illinois
Saarinen & Swanson and Perkins & Will, architects

Community Hall, Channel Heights, California
Richard Neutra, architect

PLATE XXXI

Housing at Channel Heights, California
Richard Neutra, architect; Lewis Eugene Wilson, consultant

Shopping Center, Linda Vista, California
Earl F. Giberson and Whitney R. Smith, architects

PLATE XXXII

Baldwin Hills Village, California
Lewis Wilson, Clarence Stein, and others, architects

few years ago—more spread out, more open, less monumental in the oppressive sense of that word. Fewer children will be in each class, fewer classrooms in each building. Many inviting, wide-spreading, one-storied schools in California show the type; from the demands of the new educational program architects have created new loveliness for the world. And, still more important, by creating these more delightful schools, architects have continually raised public taste and increased the standards of amenity which the public demands. Dudok built an extraordinary series of schools in a small Dutch residential city, Hilversum—schools distinguished by beauty and originality of conception, by exquisiteness of detail. They became world-famous among architects and the more advanced educators, and as a result the whole standard of school design was elevated the world over. English architects in some of their new village "colleges" have developed a new type of combined school and community center; their influence is growing. Because Saarinen & Swanson and Perkins & Will designed the Crow Island School in Winnetka (Plate XXX)—a school of charming plan and of quiet, winning aspect— many other communities in the Middle West are demanding, and getting, more human and more beautiful school buildings. And so it goes; the architect, in working devotedly for society, not only gives society what it demands but also helps society to demand what it should; his contribution to social progress is undeniable.

The same is true of another pressing public question—the problem of housing—which has risen perennially ever since industrialism first drew hundreds of thousands of people into towns unfit to receive them, and rapacious landlords seized upon the opportunity for ruthless exploitation which the influx offered them. Ever since that period, too, there have been housing reformers—men who have seen the horror, the sickness, the excessive mortality, the ruined lives, the delinquent children, the criminality which this crowding of people into ugly, ill-built warrens brought in its train, and who have sought for some means of ameliorating the condition. For nearly a century men have been protesting against and seeking to rid the world of slums, yet slums continue, and today veterans returning from the war can find no decent homes for themselves and their families.

This deplorable condition is a standing indictment of our culture, and it may be well to examine the position of architects and architecture in the whole discouraging picture. The most cursory examination will show, we believe, that little blame can be laid to them; that, on the contrary, architects have generally been in the vanguard in all matters pertaining to housing, and that it is architecture which is responsible for such improvements in the situation as have been attempted. Sir Raymond Unwin and Barry Parker made over the housing ideals of England; deeply influenced by Sir Ebenezer Howard's concept of the "Garden City"—the united, organic relationship of industrial, agricultural, and residential areas—they created housing with a new validity; they studied street compositions, the relationships of house to garden, the basic functional arrangements of buildings and the streets which led to them, as such matters had never been studied before, and their work has improved housing standards ever since. In Germany architects developed suburbs and industrial housing of a new amenity, and later German architects like Bruno Taut and Ernst May achieved housing groups (see Plate XXIX) which had a great influence on the development of contemporary architecture as well as on housing itself. In the United States the pioneer work in housing done by Grosvenor Atterbury in Forest Hills Gardens, by Henry Atterbury Smith in various "model tenements," by Richard H. Dana, Jr., and by Henry Wright, Clarence Stein, Electus Litchfield, and others at the time of the First World War has contributed to our knowledge of what housing should be. No, architecture cannot be blamed for our housing failures.

We are in the habit even now of thinking of our city slums as rather terrible places; but if we could picture them as they were thirty years ago we should realize what progress has been made in bettering the living conditions of the poor. It is true that architects are not responsible for all the improvements, but it is equally true that architecture has not lagged behind. And for many improvements architecture is directly responsible. The "open stair" tenement, one of the greatest steps forward in tenement design, in which all interior public corridors are abandoned; the careful arrangement of tenement units so as to give well-ventilated light courts that are real courts, airy and capacious and pleasant; and the gradual reclamation of the waste roofs—all these are changes which architects have initiated. These are real reforms, and it is only the tremendous shortage which makes it possible still to fill the terrible old "dumbbell" flats, with their dark and dreary rooms, their six-story air shafts two or three feet wide, and their indecent and dirty sanitary arrangements.

Yet for much improvement in the situation architecture is certainly responsible—the fact, for instance, that the general standards of house and apartment planning are definitely higher. It is architects who have studied the elimination of waste corridor space, so that larger court or garden areas may be possible; who have considered most deeply the questions of the relation of open space to space that is built upon, and the relation of buildings to wind and sunlight; who have sought so to place apartments in a group that every suite shall have cross ventilation and at least a modicum of sunlight. It is architects who are at the head of our present rebellion against the dingy horrors of "railroad" and "dumbbell" flats, and even of many of the so-called "new law" tenements that have sometimes replaced them; who are striving to develop for all people homes which shall be healthy, yes, but beautiful too. And it is architects who are at the forefront of those who work day in and day out to remove the leaden apathy by virtue of which alone our slums exist today.

In fact, the progress that has been made has been largely architectural. Our slums of the early nineteenth century were utterly terrible holes in which the poor had to live—holes the like of which one may conceive from the labyrinthine alleys of parts of Liverpool or Naples or eastern London; vast areas of unplanned hovels and unkempt courts, black, fearfully unhealthy, without adequate water, without any attempt at sanitation; reeking hotbeds of disease and vice and despair, into which were crowded all the unfortunate castaways of commercial individualism. Much of that misery, at least, was fast disappearing in the years before the First World War. Many cities in Europe accomplished an extraordinary amount of slum clearance. In England especially, great blocks of insanitary courts and alleys were condemned, wiped out, and replaced with better and less congested dwellings; between 1875 and 1908, London cleared 104 acres of slums, Birmingham 93, Leeds 75, Glasgow 88. This movement grew rapidly in the years just after the First World War, and architects had to furnish new housing not only for those displaced by slum clearance but for new populations in new centers as well.

Germany (in the pre-Hitler years), England, Holland, and Vienna (under its socialist administration) were leaders in this post–First World War movement. Russia was striving mightily to improve its housing. France and Italy were making great strides. Only America lagged. A trip around Amsterdam in Holland, to take but one example, was for an American like a visit to a new world. Can it be true? he asked himself, as he passed through one tree-and-flower-grown street after another and saw the neat and airy and sometimes gay apartment houses succeeding each other, block after block, and the wide-windowed, inviting schoolhouses at what seemed extravagantly close intervals. And these were not, as they seemed to the American, the houses of the well-to-do or even of the lower executives of Dutch business—these were working-class dwellings! And the same was true in one small town after another, not just the great centers; in the little fishing village of Scheveningen, for example, the wives of the fisher folk, still wearing their traditional gold-decorated caps, stepped down out of new and modern and convenient apartment houses into gardened streets.

Such progress in new residential buildings as was made in America at that time lay chiefly in the increasingly high standards required by most of our city building codes rather than in any large amount of construction or advanced design. In obtaining such city legislation the architects were influential far beyond their numerical strength. For the opinion of the architectural profession is powerful; organized as it is in architectural societies all over the country, it has no little influence on legislation. Every architectural society has committees which devote a great deal of time to legislative matters. These committees examine every law proposed which can have any bearing whatsoever on building; they are always discussing sanitation and fire prevention and building codes and, by means of public agitation and education, striving always to raise building standards in this country in every respect with regard to both safety and beauty.

If architecture has been successful in bettering the standards of residential structures in large cities, it has had an even greater effect on the appearance and the livability of suburbs and smaller manu-facturing towns. Here again Germany and England originally took the lead, so that the contrast between the carelessly planned and poorly built rows of the nineteenth century and the housing groups that were built twenty years ago is striking. There is nothing more depressing, for instance, than the average English suburb built be-tween 1860 and 1890—street after street exactly alike, lined with ugly houses; "rows," or "terraces," or "semi-detached villas," each group of dirty, blackened brick, without distinction, utterly unde-signed, and brooded over always by tiers of great factory stacks, gaunt and stark against a grey sky, stacks that belch endless torrents of black smoke which the wind smudges across the clouds and de-posits thickly over roofs and gardens and houses. Such a suburb is as dreary, as uninteresting, and as cursed with colorless anemia as the flat, stale life it produces. It is dull with a cruel and despairing hope-lessness. H. G. Wells and Arnold Bennett have revealed in many stories the profound effects of this hopeless ugliness. Such suburbs one may still see from the car windows as the train rushes through the ragged skirts of southern London, or through the busy black country of the Midlands; their like also occurs even in the United States, in many towns in our own New England or in Pennsylvania.

It is a far cry indeed from such deadening monotony and squalor to the best that the post–First World War years produced. The curving streets and the white houses by Ernst May in Römerstadt, outside of Frankfurt-am-Main, to cite but one example, had variety and charm; here the landscape was made the ally of the architecture. Around Berlin were dozens of suburbs where trees surrounded the flat-roofed houses and where one felt that life was lived and not merely endured. And outside of London there is still not only the rural (and perhaps, in the modern view, sentimental) loveliness of Parker and Unwin's Hampstead Garden Suburb, with its quiet lanes and little houses, but a whole series of excellent suburban groups built by the London County Council.

During the First World War there were symptoms of a similar development here in America, but it was only a flash in the pan. Even at its best, it was a movement largely superficial, founded on the unstable bases either of charity or of company paternalism, except in the groups, some of them excellent, built by the Federal government —groups, for instance, like much of the work by Clipston Sturgis in Bridgeport, Connecticut, or like Yorkship Village, by Electus Litchfield, near Camden, New Jersey. Significantly enough, these better groups remain today as permanent benefits to their communities, whereas many of those less good have disappeared or faded into undistinguished drabness. That was about all, for American opinion then was not prepared to look the most important truth of housing full in the face.

That truth is that in the American financial sense housing cannot pay. In the larger sense, decent housing for the multitude is a necessity which, literally, the masses cannot "afford." Their wages are not sufficient for rents large enough to cover inflated private land values, profits to builder and dealer, high interest rates, and all the other multitudinous expenses that private speculative development makes inevitable. Housing must be considered a public matter. We must be prepared to furnish it either by means of governmental agencies or with a governmental subsidy.

It took the great depression to force this lesson on us. Then at last, under the guise of furnishing employment to the building trades, the Federal government went to the root of the matter, and a series of laws were passed which set up a national housing authority with power to approve housing schemes presented by local housing authorities, and to enable the nation to subsidize the approved schemes so that they could actually be built and people of low income could actually live in them. Sociologists, economists, labor unions, and many others backed this legislation, but architects were also among its eager supporters, and it was to architects that fell the chief task of devising proper standards which the new housing was to follow, as well as of designing the actual projects that resulted. Their record in the controversies that surrounded the passage of the Housing Act and its administration is a proud one. When pressure was brought to bear on the Housing Authority for ever more stringent economies in design, it was architects who fought to preserve standards of decency in space, appearance, and amenities. Architects have worked constantly to obtain higher standards in this government housing, and to see that community halls and sufficient community facilities of all kinds were furnished. It was largely architects, in fact, who saw to it that these government housing groups did not become mere barracks, as many reactionary politicians wished and many real-estate interests hoped.

Not all the recent government housing has been beautiful; some of it is very bad indeed. Not all architects are great designers, and not all local housing authorities are immune to political and economic pressure. There have been ill-advised economies, mistakes in placing the groups, mistakes in design. Yet, taken by and large, the government housing program has accomplished much. The 170,000 dwellings it has erected have, to be sure, only scratched the surface of the country's dire need for homes, but they have set standards of light and air, garden and play space, and efficient unit planning which had not existed before. And for this result architects, both those who designed actual groups and those who acted as consultants and advisers to the housing authorities, deserve much of the credit.

When war industries sprang up like mushrooms in the early 1940's, vast amounts of housing for workers in the new locations became absolutely necessary. Both private enterprise and governmental action helped to furnish it. Much of it was slapdash, now-or-never work, and the standards of some of it were limited by the need for speed and by shortages of materials. Yet much of it was good—fresh and new and inventive—and for this architects were largely responsible. The best of it was excellent. not only furnishing adequate dwellings for workers and their families but also making the projects into true communities, where in community halls, in schools and playgrounds, and in efficient and attractive shopping centers lives could be enriched and in every important phase made fuller lives than the inhabitants of the new communities had known before, in surroundings infinitely pleasanter and more beautiful (see Plates XXX and XXXI). And again it is to architects that much of the credit for this must go. Through the efforts, the imagination, and the skill of the best housing architects, we are at last beginning to learn the requirements of a true community and some of the best ways those requirements can be met. In the field of housing the architect has generally lived up nobly to the heavy social responsibility that is his.

Of course the fulfilling of obvious practical needs is not the only social service that architecture performs. The dual idealism the architect should always possess, which makes him not only alert to practical requirements but avid of beauty as well, prevents him from ever being satisfied with the mere crudely necessary, however perfectly functional. The true architect, like every true artist, sees life in a manner too broad for that. He sees life as a matter of ideals as well as of bread and butter; he is always alert to the large place beauty must have in making any life rich and full. He realizes how a yearning for beauty when it is starved is twisted and perverted to find unhealthy expression in all sorts of vice and crime. He realizes concretely that a passionate need for beauty is innate in the very tissue of every life, and that it is a real need, coextensive with the need for health and life itself and definitely requiring satisfaction to produce a sane and happy commonwealth.

The tragedy of the slum lies almost as much in its ugliness as in its crowded and unhealthy condition. In fact, the two qualities are inseparably connected. The gaunt and terrible ugliness of the typical American manufacturing town sheds perpetually a subtle, baneful influence, all the more dangerous because so impalpable, on the life of that town, adding always to class hatreds, piling always inflammable fuel on the hot fires of envy and greed and rebellion—an influence, more potent than is usually realized, in arousing the angry heart of strife, in turning boys to drink and drugs or girls to a flashy promiscuity in the effort to fill empty lives with at least a little of excitement and of beauty. Could we but substitute for the raw blackness of a mining town, or the slipshod squalor of the ordinary factory center, some semblance of order and beauty, the results in increased orderliness and sanity in popular life would be amazing.

Experience has shown that this is no idle and baseless assertion; police-court statistics, case histories in sociological surveys, the findings of probation officers, and the studies of psychologists all bear witness to its truth. The emotional effect of beautiful buildings, however unconsciously felt, on the other hand is never lost, and a civic consciousness truly alert must feel and try to satisfy the need for beauty as strongly and conscientiously as it is cognizant of and seeks solutions for problems of public health. Ruskin—moralist that he was—saw the spiritual effect of beauty as supreme; we, perhaps, are given too much to a consideration of its merely physical side. At the conclusion of the lecture from which the quotation on page ooo was taken there occurs this beautiful passage, which all of us might do well to take to heart:

But there is, at least, this ground for courage, if not for hope. As the evil spirits of avarice and luxury are directly contrary to art, so, also, art is directly contrary to them; and according to its force, expulsive of them and medicinal against them. . . . In the fulfillment of such function, literally and practically, here among men, is the only real use or pride of noble architecture, and on its acceptance or surrender of that function it depends whether, in future, the cities of England melt into a ruin more confused and ghastly than ever storm wasted or wolf inhabited, or purge and exalt themselves into true habitations of men, whose walls shall be Safety, and whose gates shall be Praise.

If all this is true, it should be obvious that men's whole lives are deeply influenced in every way, for better or worse, by the communities in which they live. And it naturally follows that, in order to have the greatest possible richness in their lives, men need communities fitted to produce it. We can have communities—villages, towns, cities—of many different types; in order to plan them intelligently, we must know the kind of life we wish to encourage. Community planning, therefore, is as broad in its implications as human life itself.

First of all, communities must be *healthful*. They must have good water supplies, sanitation, sewage-disposal systems. They must be laid out with imagination and in intelligent relation to winds and sun. This is all elementary; as long ago as the time of Augustus, the architect Vitruvius listed approximately this same series of town requirements. Second, communities must be *workable*. This is a more difficult matter; it means that there must be adequate communication with the outside world, and carefully planned and convenient transportation within the community itself. It means that food supplies must be easily obtained and distributed, and this can be brought about only through intelligent study of the placing of wholesale and retail markets and food stores. It means that there must be a careful consideration of the ways by which the community is to support itself—its industries, its agriculture, its business of all kinds. And there follows necessarily the matter of the convenient relationship of residence to work. Third, communities must be *economically practical*. This is a still more thorny problem, for it brings up questions of land values, wages, taxes, payment for capital invested, rentals, and home ownership. A consideration of this phase will show at once the tremendous importance of true economy in planning— economy in the matter of waste time in community life (such as long travel to work, or long and difficult deliveries of goods), as well as economy through the elimination of wasteful expenditure. But who is to judge as between life values and money values in this study of economy? Who is to assay the relative worth, say, of parks or schools? These questions will demand answers of some kind; the answers they receive will be a candid and unconscious expression of our entire system—ethical, economic, and political.

Thus, already, in dealing with the merely factual sides of community planning, we are forced into a consideration of intangibles, of ideals, of ethical choices—and we have scarce begun. For a healthy, workable, and economically practical community might also be a devastatingly inhuman community. Some prisons, for instance, might be considered healthy, workable, and economically practical, yet they could hardly be called ideal environments for rich living. Any true community must also be a pleasant, comfortable, and, in the larger sense of the word, inspiring place to live in, a place where children can grow up naturally, where adults can work happily and rest easily and pleasantly. And what a host of problems these requirements arouse! House design and arrangement, green spaces for quiet relaxation, play areas for active play, schools and their placing. . . . In addition, there also comes up inevitably the problem of appearance, harmony, visual repose, variety without confusion; of views out and beyond; of fountains, perhaps, and lakes and streams and trees, and the harmony of green growing things with buildings. All these are amenities people desire and advantages which as far as possible a community should furnish.

These two great sides of community planning—the practical and the aesthetic—are inseparable. An efficiently studied street pattern will determine much of the visual effect a city makes; conversely, the preservation of desirable open spaces will affect the placing of many purely utilitarian features. Community planning is therefore necessarily an art, not a science; an art as architecture is an art, founded on the interplay of both practical and aesthetic considerations. This similarity between community planning and architecture is one of the reasons why architects have played such an important part in the community planning movement. But there is another reason, equally cogent—the simple fact that architects have never been completely satisfied with designing single buildings. Their every observation forces them to realize that the effect of a single structure can be made or marred by its surroundings, and that architectural perfection demands harmony of the building with its site, with the approaches to it, and with surrounding structures—a harmony which only the design of the entire neighborhood can give. If architecture is to have its fullest value, the community itself must become a work of art—and essentially of architectural art.

The concept of the city as a consciously designed work of art is not a new one; it has been in the background of all schemes of city beautification and rearrangement everywhere. The Egyptians built orderly towns, consciously arranged; the people of western Asia obviously sought order, system, and appearance in their walled towns, their city gates, their palace terraces. In the Far East, too, Angkor Wat was a palace temple at the center of a magnificently conceived city; farther north the Chinese laid out capitals with broad, straight streets, rectangular walls, and axially placed palaces and temples. Peking

(Peiping) is today one of the world's most beautiful cities because of its conscious and skillful design. Evidently the urge toward city planning is universal.

In the Western world, as well, conscious architectural planning of cities is inbred in our whole cultural tradition. The Greeks were great city planners. The Piraeus, Priene, Selinus—these all show a superb sense of site, proportion, discrimination in the placing of temples and agoras, preservation of views, contrasts of small and big. In Rome the emperors added forum to forum as the city grew, opened shopping centers (see Plate XV) and public porticoes around gardened courts, widened and straightened streets. Provincial Roman cities, like Timgad and Leptis Magna in Africa, rose according to studied plans, and Vitruvius, the Augustan architectural writer, devotes many pages to city planning.

Even during the Middle Ages, when Rome had fallen and a new culture was developing above the ruins, the city-planning urge still persisted; the culminating period of this culture, the thirteenth century, produced in *villes neuves* and *bastides* many towns where harmony was the rule, where order in street layout was strict, and where the placing of church and market was planned for beauty as well as for use. Fountains in little squares afforded frequent open spaces in the larger towns, and the *grande place*, the central, chief square, of many Gothic cities was a superb, informal, balanced composition of great buildings magnificently placed. Viterbo, Verona, Siena, Brunswick, Frankfurt, Erfurt, Bruges, Brussels—these all show (or did, before they were shattered by bombs) the widespread power of this concept of the city as a work of art.

Another great era of city planning arose in the seventeenth century, when local dukes and princes and kings all over Europe sought to express the wealth and the advanced culture of their dominions in the beauty and magnificence of their capital towns. Great coaches were coming into common use, bringing with them the necessity of wide roads and straight streets. Artillery of longer range made straight streets a military asset, and long avenues were admirable for the great reviews and parades in which these courts delighted. There was an intimate relation between the city planning of this period and the landscape architecture then current; the ideals of Le Nôtre—strong axial patterns, careful focusing on one or more points of climax, broad concepts of space, careful and "architectural" use of lawns and trees, and broad avenues with grass plots and trees overarching them—became important even in city planning. Karlsruhe and Versailles show the system in its most artificial aspects. The great improvements made in Paris, especially under Louis XIV, are more successful—superb compositions of buildings, greenery, direct and effective distant views. The boulevards began to replace old fortifications; the great Tuileries, Tuileries Garden, Place de la Concorde, and Champs Elysées development was evolved under the reigns of the three Louis, and many other similar developments of great beauty and essential usefulness were undertaken in Bordeaux, Nancy (perhaps the most beautiful of all), Copenhagen, and other cities in Europe. It was this Baroque development that went far in forming the popular ideal of what a city should be and governed most city-planning aims in the nineteenth century.

But the nineteenth century brought other thronging problems— enormous city growth, new concepts of sanitation, tremendously increased amounts of city traffic of all kinds, railroads, trams, factories, industrial centers. The old Renaissance and Baroque towns were manifestly unfitted to absorb these new elements, and radical replanning was necessary as a mere matter of city self-preservation. The work Haussmann did in Paris, under Napoleon III, is typical. Great avenues were pierced through the welter of little streets of the earlier city; boulevards were carried farther than they had been and connected; the whole new street pattern was conceived as a net of traffic arteries intersecting in minor centers scattered through the town. In the design of these arteries the old Baroque ideals reigned supreme—uniform street façades; trees and planting spaces; fountains, sculpture, or public buildings at axial climax points. The results, in Paris at least, were visually superb; other cities, too, imitated these improvements with more or less success. It is the resulting repose, dignity, and beauty, the feeling of definite *form* throughout the city, the harmonious contrast of green and building, which are among the chief reasons why certain cities of Europe have become, as it were, meccas for tourists, who, coming from towns amorphous or depressing, find a new exhilaration, a new inspiration in these planned, formed, well-defined cities.

In the United States, too, the concept of the city as a planned entity is not new. The typical New England village, with its town green or common surrounded by churches and public buildings and an orderly succession of dwellings approximately at equal distances one from another—this harmonious and lovely whole is the result not of accident but of the original layout of common, house lot, and ground reserved for public structures. The early plan of Philadelphia, though strictly rectangular, had open parked squares reserved at frequent intervals; the few that survive indicate something of what the original intent was. Savannah was built on a magnificent scheme of frequent commons connected by broad streets and avenues; the resulting parks and parked streets make it today one of the most beautiful of American cities, where green greets the eye at almost every other block even in the downtown business area.

Washington, of course, was planned, and the magnificent scheme of broad vista from the Capitol, cross vista from the White House, and radial avenues overlying a rectangular block pattern, which Major Pierre l'Enfant designed at the behest of George Washington, is still compelling and effective. And when new settlers from states farther east opened up Ohio and Michigan in the old Northwest Territory and carved out cities in the wilderness, they usually gave those towns forms that were definite, forms with architectural as well as practical meaning (see Figure 29). Public buildings and churches were effectively placed, space for town squares or parks was reserved, streets more than ample in width were devised to give dignified as well as efficient approach to the town center. In 1811, when the commissioners who planned Manhattan Island brought in their report, they apologized for reserving so little space for parks and squares on the ground that the unusually healthy location between two fair rivers made such public areas unnecessary. Adequate city planning, in which amenity and effect as well as practical efficiency are considered, is thus an integral part of the American tradition.

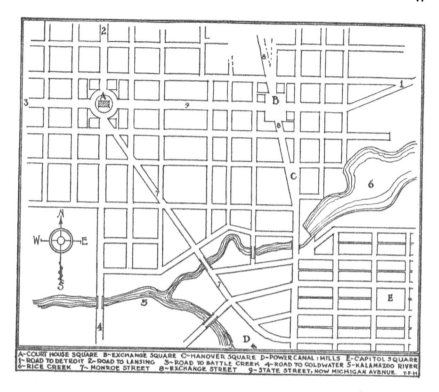

A~COURT HOUSE SQUARE B~EXCHANGE SQUARE C~HANOVER SQUARE D~POWER CANAL:MILLS E~CAPITOL SQUARE 1~ROAD TO DETROIT 2~ROAD TO LANSING 3~ROAD TO BATTLE CREEK 4~ROAD TO COLDWATER 5~KALAMAZOO RIVER 6~RICE CREEK 7~MONROE STREET 8~EXCHANGE STREET 9~STATE STREET, NOW MICHIGAN AVENUE. T·F·H

FIGURE 29. PLAN OF MARSHALL, MICHIGAN (REDRAWN WITH SLIGHT MODIFICATIONS FROM A SURVEY BY O. WILDER, CIRCA 1831)

At this period Marshall was being considered for the capital of Michigan, and a site for the proposed capitol (E) was set aside in the town plan. Both diagonal streets (7 and 8) have been blocked for part of their length in the century and more since this plan was made, and three-quarters of Exchange Square lost. Almost every change in the original town plan has been a change for the worse.

But this earlier tradition largely passed away in the drab and flashy years which followed the Civil War. In those bustling, booming days when American industrialism and commerce were growing with mushroom rapidity, and cities were springing up all over the country, little thought was given to town planning save as planning could aid in the selling of lots. The city fathers merely laid out a crisscross of streets, all at right angles to each other; the real-estate promoters got hold of as much as they could, and speculation and chaos were the inevitable results. Buildings went up here and there, with no correlation, and each landowner built exactly what he pleased, wherever he pleased. Fads and fashions boomed now one portion of the town, now another; residential areas became business areas; business areas faded and died away into emptiness; factories were built in places where they spoiled promising residential developments. Cutthroat speculation and competition followed no ideal, recognized no checks. The resultant chaotic inefficiency of such a city is amazing, and it is a characteristic all too universal in this country. Under any such anarchy real estate becomes a questionable investment, for real-estate values soar and die unaccountably. The scattering of business and manufacturing makes necessary a great deal of trucking that might easily be avoided. It necessitates an endless loss of time and money in the ordinary run of the day's work, and it produces a city in which it is both difficult and unpleasant to live.

Eventually, toward the beginning of the twentieth century, conditions had become unbearable. A renascence of decent city planning was inevitable, and in this early phase of the movement architects played a large, even a dominant, part. Great schemes were developed for the improvement of New York, Chicago, Cleveland, San Francisco; the principle of the city as a work of art again asserted itself. Yet the actual results of this early "city beautiful" move- ment were most disappointing: in New York, practically nothing; in San Francisco, nothing; in Chicago, on the other hand, many street improvements and a magnificent park system, though the large elements of the grand design for the city center were never even begun; in Cleveland, a civic center, nobly conceived, but carried out only in fragments, and its effect largely destroyed by newer "improvements," real-estate juggling, and railroad chicanery.

But one of the important results of this early twentieth-century American city-planning movement has been the creation and wide acceptance of the theory and practice of "zoning." The old, anarchic development of American cities had become a menace; unnecessarily large buildings were creating insuperable congestion, the character of neighborhoods was changing almost overnight, and there seemed to be no prospect of permanence in anything. Values rose and fell, localities and streets became fashionable or the reverse, districts grew crowded or were deserted, all with disturbing rapidity. In order to check the resultant waste in human happiness and wealth, it became necessary to establish standards for each part of the community—in other words, to zone it. In general, cities are zoned in three different categories—height, area, and use. In other words, the general character of any neighborhood in a city is prescribed by law, and the beneficial effects of the system are now realized almost everywhere.

The reasons for the general failure of the movement were many. For one thing, its ideals were too largely based on the concepts of grandiose baroque planning and the imposed patterns of Haussmann in Paris. The planners conceived of the city too largely in terms of axes, streets, effects, and traffic in the abstract, and not in terms of people and what people want to do. Cities so founded could never appeal to the whole population with sufficient strength to make the citizens exert their political power and force improvements; the real-estate interests, entrenched financial power, and political apathy remained largely supreme. It took the strains and suffering of the depression, and the necessity of creating new towns for war workers, to bring into being a new ideal in city planning and at last to awaken public officials to its importance.

The orientation of the city-planning movement today is essentially different from that of the early twentieth-century phase in two ways: first, it is based primarily on the city's inhabitants, on *persons*; and, second, it attempts to conceive of the community, new or old, as an *organism* that is growing, changing. It requires a knowledge of the physiology of this organism before it attempts a cure; hence its insistence on statistical surveys—studies of land values, building uses and conditions, movements of produce and of goods, traffic counts, existing facilities for recreation and education, and so on. It considers the position of railroads and main highways and tries to arrange for manufacturing districts and wholesale markets in connection with terminal schemes. If the city is on the ocean or a navigable river or lake, it attempts to develop port facilities in the most efficient possible way, coupling them up with railroad or warehouse or market, and at the same time arranging some means by which the population of the city may enjoy the peace and quietness and cool breezes which large bodies of water always produce. In a word, modern city planning is concerned with every single feature of city life—housing, water supply, food supply, drainage, railroads, port facilities, education, amusements, recreation, means of transit, streets, parks, and so on—so that there is not one of us but derives benefit from the city planner's work.

But, just as architecture can never forget that it is an art, so city planning can never lose sight of aesthetic values, and every question should be considered from a double viewpoint. The good city planner forgets neither his sewers nor his views and vistas, and he designs his parks as well as he does his docks, for only by the combining of the useful and the beautiful can the ideal city arise.

And it is here where one of the dangers of the modern city-planning movement lies, here where the architect can perform, and does perform, one of his most valuable functions. For, just as the older type of city planning paled into ineffectuality because of its obsession with superficial beautification, so the present movement is in danger of fading into limbo because it is draped too heavily with its own statistics. Sociologists, economists, taxation experts, and engineers delight in statistics, and just because of this new importance of factual studies many city-planning reports today are almost unreadable compilations of tables which tell us, if we are patient enough to plow through them, that the city being studied is inefficient, formless, and has slums and blighted areas—all of which we knew before. Such studies, in themselves, will not produce better cities; diagnosis is not a cure. And it is even more difficult to arouse the public by pages of tables than by pretty pictures. Upon this depressing study must be erected something *new*, something creative, which will make for a better and a more beautiful city. Out of this chaos, form must arise. Naturally the architect city planner finds here his great opportunity; it is he better than anyone else who can give form to the whole and preserve among the ideals of the planned city the great function which beauty must perform. For an ugly city, however "efficient," as we have already noted, is not a fit home for human beings.

Modern city planners naturally have developed utopian ideals to which they direct their efforts. Here, too, caution is necessary. Le Corbusier wishes a great, geometrically organized town, with concentrated areas for business, industry, and residence, connected by overhead speed highways over which automobiles can roar at sixty miles an hour. Frank Lloyd Wright conceives "Broadacre City" as his ideal, with every family on an acre or more of gardened ground, and with industries widely scattered; he sees the city *as such* as a menace to human individuality. Mies Van der Rohe designs a community of widely scattered, close-built suburbs, on a strictly geometric pattern of identical buildings. Many city planners, like Clarence Stein and Henry Churchill, conceive of a city as a group of neighborhoods, each with its shopping center, its schools, its community facilities, all separated from each other by parked strips or main highways, with a metropolitan center of commercial and higher education buildings conveniently related to all. Who of these is right? Which concept should we follow?

Perhaps we cannot choose between them. Perhaps all are right and all are wrong. Cities are for *people*; that is the great thing to remember. Trade and commerce, automobiles and airplanes, railroads and subways, streets and buildings, all exist for people, not the reverse. And people, one discovers, are infinitely various. Some like country life, some like cities. Many seem to like the warm constant contacts of crowds; others are appalled by them. Some like apartment living, some prefer individual houses; some have the "green thumb," and to others the idea of gardens suggests merely backache and sunburn. If cities are for people, should they not be for all types of people? In their eagerness to improve conditions, city planners must hesitate to impose too strict a living pattern on town dwellers; one of the great beauties of a true city is the variety of opportunity for different kinds of living which it offers. And the architect—who has had the experience of designing buildings for many individuals and is forced by the demands of his practice to know their infinite variety—is admirably fitted to keep alive this sense of creative human variety.

Yet, whichever type of city we desire or plan, there are certain things which can be demanded of it. Our ideas of these requirements have immensely clarified of recent years, and the design of wartime communities has given us new experience in what is desirable and necessary. If we list some of these objectives, few will deny their validity. If people as a whole could come to understand them and demand them, our cities would soon show a new flowering of safety and order and beauty. These objectives are:

1. Decent, attractive housing in pleasant, open surroundings, with plenty of sun and air, and with conveniently accessible outdoor sitting and play space.

2. Elementary schools within safe walking distance (safe for a child) from every dwelling.

3. Shopping areas for food and other daily needs within short walking distance from every dwelling. To save steps and trucking, shops for each neighborhood should be grouped, and in each group there should be provision for leaving children or baby carriages in safe, protected, and pleasant areas.

4. Community recreation and social facilities, also within easy walking distance from each dwelling. Wartime experience, as well as that of well-run housing groups, has proved the value of these community facilities.

5. Attractive play areas, conveniently placed, for young children, for older children, for adolescents, and for adults. Young children should not be forced to play hopscotch on street sidewalks, nor their parents to play *bocci* on asphalt traffic streets.

6. Park areas, for quiet walking or sitting, large enough to give a sense of natural space.

7. Work places not too far from dwelling areas, to avoid time waste and traffic jams in busses, subways, or streets.

8. Streets designed functionally for use and minimized in number. Through traffic streets, local traffic streets, residential streets, parkways, and free ways all have different uses and require different designs.

9. Relation of street and building such as to minimize street crossing in the average day's work or play; the use of large blocks, "super blocks," with interior walkways, is one of the means of accomplishing this.

10. All existing natural advantages—views, hills, waterfronts, and the like—to be preserved and taken advantage of.

11. A decent harmony in architectural design throughout. This has already been referred to on page 243.

12. Large shops, department stores, museums, universities, opera houses, and all such elements, which require the patronage or attendance of large numbers of people for support, to be centrally located, harmoniously designed, and convenient, with adequate parking areas.

13. Public buildings placed with care for utility and beauty.

14. Communications with the outside world carefully planned—railroads, airports, and through highways placed in safe and convenient positions, and adequate for the traffic they bear.

15. Elimination of automobile hazards as far as possible—hazards both to pedestrians and to automobile drivers and passengers. The present rate of automobile accidents and deaths is one of the most shocking and inexcusable features of modern life. Planners can help enormously in reducing it.

These objectives are not merely utopian, nor are they impossible to realize. Architects have again and again embodied them in actual communities. Radburn, New Jersey, by Clarence Stein and Henry Wright, was a pioneer in this development. Baldwin Hills Village, California, by Stein, Wilson, and others (Plate XXXII), is a beautiful group of livable houses because the architects have in it so thoroughly realized these objectives. Dozens of war-industry towns and scores of wartime housing groups show how architects have responded to the challenge of these new city-planning concepts. Vanport, Oregon, with its neighborhood schools and shopping centers and community halls; Vallejo, California, a mushroom growth, but nevertheless a true town, with interesting houses climbing its hills and with adequate and attractive schools; Coatesville, Pennsylvania, by Kahn and Stonoroff, with inexpensive houses that are nonetheless good to look at, pleasant to live in, and beautifully related; Channel Heights, California, by Neutra and others (Plate XXXI)— these are but a few of many such new communities in which the new town pattern developed by the needs of today is gradually emerging. Airy and open schools, community buildings gay with flowers (see Plate XXX) and welcoming with their wide openings and their great windows of clear glass and both sunny and shaded outdoor sitting areas, shopping centers with covered walkways connecting the shops and surrounding attractive quiet courts, streets designed for use and for safety—these all show architecture making its accustomed contributions to the life we live today (see Plate XXI).

Architecture, then, has been true to life, for architecture has reflected the socialization of consciousness, which is such an outstanding development of these days. And not only has architecture reflected this movement; it has also been of unique service to it in three different ways. Architecture is able to fulfill the practical needs of the people; architecture is able to give us ideals of better and finer cities than any we know; and architecture has been the creator of an infinite amount of concrete and palpable beauty to enrich the popular life. Engineering can build us factories of a kind, and schools and churches of a kind; sanitary science can keep us in bodily health; painting and sculpture and music can give us the poignant delight of beauty; but it is the art of architecture alone which takes the engineering and the sanitation, and all the rich beauty of constructed form, and is able to synthesize them into noble buildings and noble cities which are alike mechanically efficient and spiritually inspiring for all time.

EPILOGUE

YOU WILL recall that it has been stated several times in this book that architecture is an emotional art. It is always necessary to keep this in mind, for, since architecture excites principally the more formless and vaguer emotions, there is a strong temptation to forget the emotional appeal altogether and to regard this art as something purely intellectual. Any such attitude is to be avoided, because it will lead to an appreciation of architecture at best one-sided, and true appreciation is never like that. A true appreciation of architecture can come only to one who studies it with an eager sympathy, and with all sides of his nature alert and receptive. He must blind himself neither to the intellectual nor to the emotional aspect of the art: he should consider structure, planning, and abstract beauty, but at the same time he should preserve an attitude keenly alive to the emotional message which the art may bring. The value of such an attitude is more than personal, for it will react inevitably on the standard of popular taste, and thus eventually on the art of architecture itself. The greater the number of persons who adopt such a thoughtful, sensitive attitude, the sooner the day will come when architecture will be able to give to the world all the beauty, all the inspiration, which lies within its power.

SUGGESTED SUPPLEMENTARY READING

THE BIBLIOGRAPHY of architecture is vast. The list of books given below is merely an indication of its richness and has been limited to works which, to the best of the author's belief, might prove most helpful to the reader who wishes to study further in this fascinating but perplexing field. Many of the books listed themselves contain extended bibliographies, and all have been chosen for their special appeal of one kind or another to the general reader. Some, especially in the history section, may appear technical at first glance; but none are so specialized that they require a technical or professional training to understand them. For convenience this bibliography is divided into a number of sections according to the basic subjects covered.

I. BOOKS ON GENERAL AESTHETICS

Dewey, John. Art as Experience. New York, Minton, Balch & Co. [c1934].
A readable and persuasive presentation of an important trend in modern aesthetic thought, basically pragmatic.

Greene, Theodore Meyer. The Arts and the Art of Criticism. Princeton, Princeton University Press, 1940.
An encyclopedic work on the relation of form and content; well illustrated.

Listowell, Earl of (William Francis Hare). A Critical History of Modern Aesthetics. London, G. Allen & Unwin, Ltd. [1933].
A useful guide to the chief types of aesthetic systems.

Parker, DeWitt Henry. The Analysis of Art. New Haven, Yale University Press; London, H. Milford, Oxford University Press, 1926.
A definite, well-written essay in eclectic aesthetics.

II. BOOKS DEALING CHIEFLY WITH ARCHITECTURAL CRITICISM

Butler, Arthur Stanley George. The Substance of Architecture. New York, Lincoln MacVeagh, The Dial Press, 1927.
A clear discussion of architecture as a visual art; little on planning or structure.

Giedion, Sigfried. Space, Time and Architecture. Cambridge, Harvard
    University Press, 1941.
    An interesting attempt to analyze and evaluate the development of
    architecture from the Renaissance to today; superbly illustrated.
Ruskin, John. Seven Lamps of Architecture. Any good edition.
    The romantic attitude towards architectural criticism, written with the
    rhythmic power of which Ruskin was such a master; out of date, but
    still stimulating.
Schopenhauer, Arthur. The World as Will and Idea (the section on
    architecture in the discussion of aesthetics). Any good edition.
    The clear presentation of the application of a personal aesthetic theory
    to architecture; important for its consideration of structure as part
    of aesthetics.
Scott, Geoffrey. The Architecture of Humanism. Boston, Houghton Mif-
    flin Company, 1914.
    A pungent criticism of the romantic attitude toward architecture, and
    an attempt to regard architectural aesthetics realistically, with emphasis
    on the importance of "empathy."

                        III. ARCHITECTURAL HISTORIES

Fletcher, Sir Banister Flight Fletcher. A History of Architecture on the
    Comparative Method, 11th revised edition. New York, Charles Scrib-
    ner's Sons, 1943.
    A description of the major architectural expressions, analytically con-
    sidered as almost isolated creations; clearly illustrated; a useful com-
    pendium.
Hamlin, Talbot. Architecture through the Ages. Revised edition. New
    York, G. P. Putnam's Sons [1944].
    A history of architecture as an expression of human culture as it changes
    and develops; contains extended sections on the architecture of the
    nineteenth and early twentieth centuries; well illustrated.
Simpson, Frederick Moore. A History of Architectural Development.
    3 vols. London, New York, etc., Longmans, Green & Co., 1905–11.
    A systematic and beautifully written account of the development of
    the main stream of western architecture; especially valuable in its clear
    illustrations and in its treatment of the Renaissance in Italy, France,
    and England.

            IV. WORKS ON THE ARCHITECTURE OF THE UNITED STATES

Eberlein, Harold Donaldson. The Architecture of Colonial America.
    Boston, Little, Brown and Company, 1915.

A pioneer attempt to define and clarify the complex body of early American architecture usually called Colonial.

IIamlin, Talbot. The American Spirit in Architecture. Vol. XIII in the "Pageant of America." New Haven, Yale University Press, 1926.
A comprehensive pictorial survey; its later pages are no longer valid.
—— Greek Revival Architecture in America. London, New York, etc., Oxford University Press, 1944.
An account of some phases of American architecture between 1810 and 1860; well illustrated.

Hitchcock, Henry Russell. The Architecture of Henry Hobson Richardson and His Times. New York, The Museum of Modern Art, 1936.
A scholarly monograph, richly illustrated, on the life and work of one of America's most important nineteenth-century architects.

Kimball, Sidney Fiske. American Architecture. Indianapolis and New York, The Bobbs-Merrill Company [c1928].
An excellent, terse general survey of American architecture up to the boom of the twenties.
—— Domestic Architecture of the American Colonies and of the Early Republic. New York, Charles Scribner's Sons, 1922.
A scholarly history of the development of house design in the Colonial period and during the early decades of independence; carefully documented and well illustrated.

Morrison, Hugh. Louis Sullivan, Prophet of Modern Architecture. New York, The Museum of Modern Art and W. W. Norton & Co. [c1935].
An interesting account of the work and significance of one of the world's pioneer modern architects, Louis Sullivan of Chicago.

Mumford, Lewis. Sticks and Stones. New York, W. W. Norton & Co. [1933].
A series of thoughtful critical essays on American architecture.
—— Brown Decades. New York, Harcourt, Brace & Co. [c1931].
A re-evaluation of the real accomplishments of certain nineteenth-century American architects and artists; an attempt at discovering the true American tradition.

V. WORKS DEALING SPECIFICALLY WITH CONTEMPORARY ARCHITECTURE

Ford, James, and Katherine Morrow Ford. Design of Modern Interiors. New York, Architectural Book Publishing Co. [c1942].
—— The Modern House in America. New York, Architectural Book Publishing Co. [c1940].
Two stimulating and valuable pictorial surveys of recent American house design, outside and in, presenting work of many different types.

Gropius, Walter. The New Architecture and the Bauhaus. London, Faber and Faber [1935].
The ideals of the International Style as developed in a famous revolutionary school of architecture and the allied arts, the "Bauhaus."

Hitchcock, Henry Russell. Modern Architecture, Romanticism and Reintegration. New York, Payson and Clarke, Ltd., 1929.
A pioneer attempt at writing the history of the early development of the present architectural movement; thoughtful and well documented, but slightly over-simplified.

—— In the Nature of Materials; 1887–1941; the Buildings of Frank Lloyd Wright. New York, Duell, Sloan and Pearce, 1942.
An almost complete corpus of the work of Frank Lloyd Wright, shown in plan and photograph, with a short commentary.

Hitchcock, Henry Russell, and Philip Johnson. The International Style: Architecture since 1922. New York, W. W. Norton & Co. [c1932].
An essay describing the characteristics of the new architecture of the early thirties, with essays on individual architects; well illustrated.

Le Corbusier (Charles Édouard Jeanneret-Gris). Towards a New Architecture. New York, Payson and Clarke [1927].
One of the pioneer works supporting a new architecture for a new world, written with passionate conviction; perhaps the most influential architectural book of its time.

—— Précisions sur un état present de l'architecture et de l'urbanisme. Paris, G. Crés et cie [1930].
The clearest account of the ideals of its author; a full statement of his beliefs on architecture and city planning.

New York, Museum of Modern Art. Modern Architects. New York, The Museum of Modern Art and W. W. Norton & Co. [c1932].
A richly illustrated catalogue of an important exhibition, with descriptive notes.

—— Built in U.S.A., 1932–1944. New York, The Museum of Modern Art [1944].
Outstanding examples of American architecture from 1932 to 1945, with a penetrating essay; important as showing the growing freedom and variety of present-day architecture.

Wright, Frank Lloyd. Modern Architecture. Princeton, Princeton University Press, 1931.
A series of important lectures giving the essence of Wright's architectural philosophy.

—— An Autobiography. New York, Duell, Sloan and Pearce [1943].
An important document.

VI. BOOKS ON CITY PLANNING AND HOUSING

Adams, Thomas. Recent Advances in Town Planning. New York, The Macmillan Company, 1932.
A useful handbook of the general principles of city planning and some of their applications.

Bauer [Wurster], Catherine. Modern Housing. Boston and New York, Houghton Mifflin Company, 1934.
The best account of the origin and development of the modern housing movement, and an eloquent statement of its ideals and some of its achievements; interesting, exciting, and sound.

Churchill, Henry S. The City Is the People. New York, Reynal and Hitchcock [1945].
The best introduction to the problems of city planning today, and the most cogent statement of its vital importance to a healthy society.

Mumford, Lewis. Technics and Civilization. New York, Harcourt, Brace & Co. [1934], [1943].
A broad and intensely interesting survey of the impact of industrialism and changing technical methods on urban form and human ideals.

—— The Culture of Cities. New York, Harcourt, Brace & Co., 1944.
A historical survey of the relationship between city form and cultural ideals; eloquent and stimulating.

Saarinen, Eliel. The City, Its Growth, Its Decay, Its Future. New York, Reinhold Publishing Co. [1943].
An analysis of the influences—social and economic—which affect the planning of cities, and the necessity for broad social and economic concepts in order to bring form and order into the chaos of today.

Sert, José Luis. Can Our Cities Survive? Cambridge, Harvard University Press, 1942.
A compelling diagnosis of the ills of the present city, and some suggestions as to possible cures; largely based on the work of the Congrés International des Architects Modernes (CIAM).

Wright, Frank Lloyd. The Disappearing City. New York, W. F. Payson [c1932].
An eloquent and characteristic argument for the author's ideals of an agrarian culture, based on bringing people into an organized system where each family shall have at least an acre of land; the text illustrates his design for "Broadacre City."

INDEX

Abu Simbel, temple at, 180
Academie Royale d'Architecture, 87
Acanthus leaf, conventionalized, 172, 173
Acoustics, 53
Acropolis, Athens, capital from, *fig.*, 207
Adam decoration, 90, 176
Adams, Henry, 216
Aesthetics, theories of, 6 f.; *see also* Beauty
African huts, 106
Albany, N.Y., Protestant Cathedral, 130
Alberti, Leo Battista, 147
Alhambra, Granada, Spain, 127
Alpine countries, roofs, 106
"American style," 202; *see also* United States
Amiens Cathedral, 31, 62, 76, 77, 87; plan, 63; interior, 31, 34, 81, 164, *Plate XXIII*
Amsterdam, Holland, housing, streets, schools, 236
Amusement places, 17, 32, 34; theaters, 9, 17, 52, 53, 55
Angkor Wat, temple, 243
Animals as decoration, 148
Anthemion, 172
Apartment houses, 235 ff.; doorways, 114; *see also* Housing
Applied decoration, *see* Decoration
Appreciation of architecture, 3 ff., 35, 66, 99, 145, 146, 255; its growth, 3; kinds and sources of pleasure given, 4-9
Ara Pacis Augustae: panel from, 173, *Plate XXV*
Arch, arched and vaulted construction, 22, 23 f., 28, 31, 34, 134, 135; origin and development, 23, 113, 117; grouping of windows under, *fig.*, 119; in concrete and tile, 138 ff., *Plate XIX*; laminated, 140; stepped, 155; combination with column or pilaster, 187, 188
Architects, relation of engineers and, 8; creative twentieth-century pioneers, 14;

must be sociologist, engineer, artist, 36; importance of plan to, 37; of U.S. Capitol, 68; collaboration with sculptors and painters, 170, 186, 197; early exponents of modern style, 204; awareness of the social value of their profession, 226, 228; changing types of patronage, 227; professional attitude, 229; vanguard in the housing movement, 234, 236, 239; organization and power, 236; influence on legislation, 236, 238; role in community planning movement, 243
Architecture, appreciation of, 3-21, 35, 66, 99, 145, 146, 255; pleasure obtained from, 4 ff.; aesthetic doctrines, 4; use and structure, 8; results of separation from engineering, 8 f.; a science as well as an art, 9; integration of its three factors, 10; history of mankind written in, 13-15; also a protest against unsocial exploitation, 14; an emotional art, 15 ff., 255; analogous to music, 16; inspirational quality, 18; criticism (*q.v.*), 66, 71, 99, 145, 191, 222, 256; dominant qualities, 71; rules of composition, 72 ff.; musical analogies, 81 f.; organic, 96; component elements, 100 ff.; fundamental and important materials, 101 (*see also* Materials); composition and detail, 143; the "craftsman" movement and other revolts against eclecticism, 177; patterns of thought and taste, 191; as a key to history, 200; complete expression of life, 201; eclectic, 216 ff. (*see also* Eclecticism); international academic tradition, 218; ferment of new creativeness, and its results, 220 ff.; relation to the community, 225-54; social opportunity and social value, 226 ff.; Ruskin's view of, 229, 241; similar to community planning, 243
Architrave (frame) of door, 114, 164